AF695191

OECD Economic Surveys: Norway 2018

OECD
BETTER POLICIES FOR BETTER LIVES

This document, as well as any data and map included herein, are without prejudice to the status of or sovereignty over any territory, to the delimitation of international frontiers and boundaries and to the name of any territory, city or area.

Please cite this publication as:
OECD (2018), *OECD Economic Surveys: Norway 2018*, OECD Publishing, Paris.
http://dx.doi.org/10.1787/eco_surveys-nor-2018-en

ISBN 978-92-64-28640-5 (print)
ISBN 978-92-64-28637-5 (PDF)
ISBN 978-92-64-28644-3 (epub)

Series: OECD Economic Surveys
ISSN 0376-6438 (print)
ISSN 1609-7513 (online)

OECD Economic Surveys: Norway
ISSN 1995-3321 (print)
ISSN 1999-0383 (online)

The statistical data for Israel are supplied by and under the responsibility of the relevant Israeli authorities. The use of such data by the OECD is without prejudice to the status of the Golan Heights, East Jerusalem and Israeli settlements in the West Bank under the terms of international law.

Photo credits: Cover © Comstock/Comstock Images/Getty Images.

Corrigenda to OECD publications may be found on line at: *www.oecd.org/about/publishing/corrigenda.htm*.

© OECD 2018

You can copy, download or print OECD content for your own use, and you can include excerpts from OECD publications, databases and multimedia products in your own documents, presentations, blogs, websites and teaching materials, provided that suitable acknowledgment of the source and copyright owner is given. All requests for public or commercial use and translation rights should be submitted to *rights@oecd.org*. Requests for permission to photocopy portions of this material for public or commercial use shall be addressed directly to the Copyright Clearance Center (CCC) at *info@copyright.com* or the Centre français d'exploitation du droit de copie (CFC) at *contact@cfcopies.com*.

Table of contents

Basic statistics of Norway 8
Executive summary 9

Assessment and recommendations 13
Recent macroeconomic developments and near-term prospects 17
Price and financial stability: tweaks to monetary policy, ongoing macro-prudential moves 21
Adjusting the fiscal rule, ensuring efficient tax and public spending 27
Easing the transition toward dynamic non-oil businesses 35
Retaining high labour-force participation and raising skills are key for Norway's future 42
Tackling environmental issues 46
Policy Recommendations 48
Bibliography 48

Annex. **Progress in structural reform** 51

Thematic chapters

Chapter 1. **Maintaining a successful business sector in a changing world** 57
Key features of Norway's business sector 58
Challenges and opportunities for Norway's business sector 61
Specific policy areas for Norway 67
Scaling back and rebalancing taxation 68
Promoting flexible markets and competition 70
Improving resource reallocation through firm dynamics 74
Targeted support for innovation 77
Facilitating new forms of business 85
Maintaining strong and flexible labour supply 89
Education to help business and households thrive under globalisation 93
Policy recommendations 96
Recommendations on maintaining a successful business sector in a changing world . . . 96
Bibliography 97

Chapter 2. **How to improve transport-infrastructure investment** 99
Geography and socio-political priorities strongly influence Norway's transport investment 101
Funding and responsibility for transport infrastructure 104

Transport-infrastructure investment is driven by multi-annual National Transport Plans 106
Project appraisal and selection processes....... 109
Challenges in the project appraisal and selection processes....... 112
Project implementation, delivery and ex post assessment 116
Summing up the strengths and weaknesses 117
Policy recommendations 118
Recommendations on how to improve transport-infrastructure investment in Norway 118
Bibliography....... 118

Boxes

1. Predicting downturn in Norway using the OECD's resilience database....... 22
2. The relationship between Norway's wealth fund and fiscal balances....... 27
3. Norway's petroleum sector: Its role in the economy 36
4. Recommendations from the Green Tax Commission – a selective summary ... 48
1.1. Norway's productivity growth over the longer term....... 64
1.2. Production cost issues in oil and gas 67
1.3. Recent amendments to Norway's competition legislation 73
1.4. Key elements of insolvency 77
1.5. A selective summary of recommendations from the OECD Innovation Review (2017) 81
2.1. The role of the Norwegian Public Roads Administration....... 106
2.2. OECD Framework for the Governance of Infrastructure....... 106
2.3. The new National Transport Plan 108
2.4. Infrastructure planning and financing in the city of Oslo....... 109
2.5. Norway's "Circular R-109" guidelines for cost-benefit analysis 110

Tables

1. Macroeconomic indicators and projections....... 20
2. Possible extreme shocks to the Norwegian economy....... 21
3. Implementation of past recommendations on monetary and financial stability .. 27
4. Implementation of past recommendations on fiscal policy, public spending and taxation 35
5. Implementation of past recommendations on improving business conditions .. 41
6. Implementation of past recommendations on human capital, jobs and welfare....... 45
7. Implementation of past recommendations on tackling environmental challenges....... 48
1.1. Possible scenarios for Norway's petroleum sector 67
1.2. Key elements in Norway's innovation support 80
1.3. Block-grant funding for higher education following the reforms of 2017..... 85
1.4. Selected tax details relevant for the sharing economy 87
1.5. Norway's sickness and disability system: Key features and recent initiatives .. 91
2.1. Population and transport-network densities in selected countries....... 102
2.2. Norway's transport network: selected figures....... 102

2.3. Benefit-cost summary for major road corridor projects initiated in the period 2014-17 (NOK million) 113
2.4. Strengths and weaknesses in transport-infrastructure investment 117

Figures

1. Norway's GDP per capita remains impressive, though growth has slowed.... 14
2. Norway continues to deliver good scores in well-being.... 15
3. Productivity slowdown, unit labour costs and oil-price fluctuation present challenges.... 16
4. Recent macroeconomic developments.... 18
5. Supportive monetary and fiscal policy in recent years 19
6. Recent data suggest there is some risk of a downturn.... 22
7. House prices, household debt and new house sales 24
8. Capital requirements on Norwegian Banks.... 25
9. The latest house-price data suggest the market may be turning.... 25
10. Developments in the value of the fund and in structural non-oil deficits 29
11. General-government expenditure and revenue 30
12. Norway has long had a substantial level of public investment.... 32
13. The corporate tax rate is now middle-ranking, personal-income tax remains high.... 34
14. Norwegian business operates in a high-cost environment.... 36
15. Norway's export-market profile.... 37
16. Regulatory indices on product markets and services trade point to room for improvement 38
17. The OECD's insolvency indicators suggest room for improvement in Norway 39
18. Norway's R&D spending is middle ranking 39
19. Norway's employment rates remain high 42
20. Norway's education and skills performance 44
21. Environment indicators 47
1.1. The composition of Norway's economic activity 9
1.2. Much of Norway's inclusiveness derives from high employment rates and small gaps in earnings.... 60
1.3. Norway scores reasonably in environment-social-governance (ESG) indicators 61
1.4. Norway's labour costs remain high in international comparison 62
1.5. Norway's unit labour cost (ULC) indices remain high despite recent falls 63
1.6. Productivity growth has slowed.... 64
1.7. Combined oil and gas production has already declined 66
1.8. Mainland oil and gas are projected to decline steadily over the long term 66
1.9. Norway's corporate tax rate has been lowered 69
1.10. Norway performs reasonably in top-level indicators of the business environment.... 71
1.11. Sub-components of the OECD PMR indicator flag Norway's state stakes in business 72
1.12. The OECD's Services Trade Restrictiveness Index also flags issues in Norway 72

1.13. Norway's insolvency system is low cost and has a high recovery rate 75
1.14. A new OECD indicator suggests weaknesses in insolvency restructuring and efficiency 76
1.15. Domestic R&D activity in Norway is middle ranking 79
1.16. Government expenditure on R&D is comparatively high 80
1.17. Norway's R&D tax break is slanted to supporting SMEs........ 83
1.18. Norway scores reasonably in collaborative research 84
1.19. Recipiency of Disability Benefit is declining among older cohorts but rising in young age groups........ 90
1.20. Norway has been a leader in getting women on company boards........ 92
1.21. Paid parental leave is comparatively long 92
1.22. Many vocational-stream students do not complete courses........ 95
2.1. Norway makes sizeable investment in transport infrastructure 100
2.2. Low transport-network densities partly reflect low population density...... 101
2.3. A comparatively large number of airports 103
2.4. Mediocre scores in the World Economic Forum transport indicators 104
2.5. Norway's Quality Assurance regime for major public investment projects ... 112
2.6. Investment efficiency of projects selected in Norway's National Transport Plan 2014-23 114

This Survey is published on the responsibility of the Economic and Development Review Committee of the OECD, which is charged with the examination of the economic situation of member countries.

The economic situation and policies of Norway were reviewed by the Committee on 2 November 2017. The draft was revised in the light of the discussions and given final approval as the agreed report of the whole Committee on 14 November 2017.

The Secretariat's draft report was prepared for the Committee by Philip Hemmings under the supervision of Patrick Lenain, and the general supervision of Alvaro Pereira. The Survey benefitted from contributions by Jagoda Egeland, Juan Garin, Camilla Vamalle and Nick Vanston, along with comments from OECD staff.

Statistical research assistance was provided by Damien Azzopardi and administrative support by Brigitte Beyeler, Stephanie Henry and Dacil Kurzweg.

The previous Survey of Norway was issued in January 2016.

Follow OECD Publications on:

http://twitter.com/OECD_Pubs

http://www.facebook.com/OECDPublications

http://www.linkedin.com/groups/OECD-Publications-4645871

http://www.youtube.com/oecdilibrary

http://www.oecd.org/oecddirect/

This book has...

StatLinks
A service that delivers Excel® files from the printed page!

Look for the *StatLinks* at the bottom of the tables or graphs in this book. To download the matching Excel® spreadsheet, just type the link into your Internet browser, starting with the *http://dx.doi.org* prefix, or click on the link from the e-book edition.

BASIC STATISTICS OF NORWAY

(Data refer to 2016 or latest available. Numbers in parentheses refer to the OECD average)*

LAND, PEOPLE AND ELECTORAL CYCLE

Population (million)	5.2		Population density per km²	14.3	(37.5)
Under 15 (%)	17.8	(18.0)	Life expectancy (years)	82.4	(80.7)
Over 65 (%)	16.6	(16.5)	Men	80.5	(78.1)
Foreign-born (%)	13.9		Women	84.2	(83.3)
Latest 5-year average growth (%)	1.1	(0.7)	Latest general election	September 2017	

ECONOMY

Gross domestic product (GDP)			Value added shares (%)		
In current prices (billion USD)	371.1		Primary sector	2.4	(2.5)
In current prices (billion NOK)	3,117.0		Industry including construction	32.0	(26.6)
Latest 5-year average real growth (%)	1.8	(1.9)	Services	65.6	(70.4)
Per capita (000 USD PPP)	59.3	(42.0)			

GENERAL GOVERNMENT
Per cent of GDP

Expenditure	50.8	(41.5)	Gross financial debt	42.8	(108.4)
Revenue	54.8	(38.6)	Net financial debt	-289.4	(69.9)

EXTERNAL ACCOUNTS

Exchange rate NOK per USD	8.40		Main exports (% of total merchandise exports)		
PPP exchange rate (USA = 1)	10.03		Mineral fuels, lubricants and related materials	53.0	
In per cent of GDP			Food and live animals	12.6	
Exports of goods and services	34.1	(28.1)	Machinery and transport equipment	12.1	
Imports of goods and services	33.3	(27.7)	Main imports (% of total merchandise imports)		
Current account balance	3.87	(0.22)	Machinery and transport equipment	40.3	
Net international investment position	197.6		Miscellaneous manufactured articles	16.4	
			Manufactured goods	14.1	

LABOUR MARKET, SKILLS AND INNOVATION

Employment rate for 15-64 year-olds (%)	74.3	(66.9)	Unemployment rate, Labour Force Survey (age 15 and over) (%)	4.9	(6.5)
Men	75.7	(74.7)	Youth (age 15-24, %)	11.0	(12.9)
Women	72.8	(59.3)	Long-term unemployed (1 year and over, %)	0.5	(2.0)
Participation rate for 15-64 year-olds (%)	78.2	(71.7)	Tertiary educational attainment 25-64 year-olds (%)	43.0	(35.7)
Average hours worked per year	1 424	(1 763)	Gross domestic expenditure on R&D (% of GDP)	1.9	(2.4)

ENVIRONMENT

Total primary energy supply per capita (toe)	5.4	(4.1)	CO_2 emissions from fuel combustion per capita (tonnes)	6.9	(9.3)
Renewables (%)	49.2	(9.7)	Water abstractions per capita (m^3)	643	(812)
Fine particulate matter concentration ($PM_{2.5}$, $\mu g/m^3$)	9.1	(15.2)	Municipal waste per capita (kilogrammes)	446	(520)

SOCIETY

Income inequality (Gini coefficient)	0.26	(0.31)	Education outcomes (PISA score, 2015)		
Relative poverty rate (%)	8.1	(11.5)	Reading	513	(493)
Median disposable household income (000 USD PPP)	25.2	(22.9)	Mathematics	502	(490)
Public and private spending (% of GDP)			Science	498	(493)
Health care, current expenditure	10.5	(9.1)	Share of women in parliament (%)	39.6	(28.7)
Pensions	7.9	(9.1)	Net official development assistance (% of GNI)	1.11	(0.39)
Education (primary, secondary, post sec. non tertiary)	4.5	(3.6)			

Better life index: *www.oecdbetterlifeindex.org*

* Where the OECD aggregate is not provided in the source database, a simple OECD average of latest available data is calculated where data exist for at least 29 member countries.

Source: Calculations based on data extracted from the databases of the following organisations: OECD, International Energy Agency, World Bank, International Monetary Fund and Inter-Parliamentary Union.

© OECD 2018

Executive summary

- *Norway should prepare for a possible housing market correction*
- *The revised fiscal rule will better preserve oil wealth across generations*
- *A dynamic businesses sector will support inclusive growth*

Norway should prepare for a possible housing market correction

Mainland GDP growth and house prices

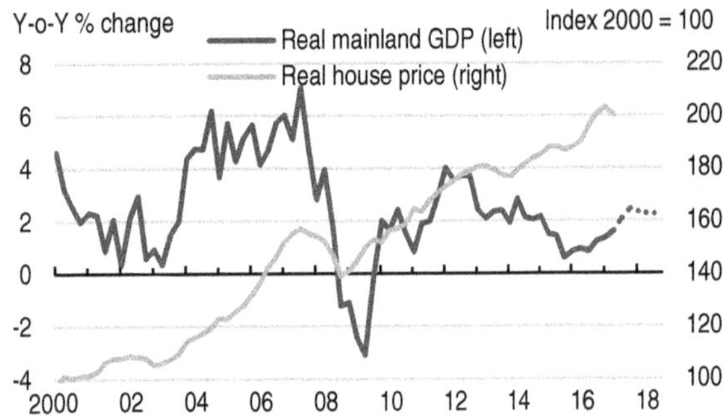

Source: OECD Economic Outlook 102 database.

StatLink http://dx.doi.org/10.1787/888933638448

The Norwegian economy continues to perform well, despite low oil prices, a testimony to policies that insulate the country from volatile petroleum markets. Output growth is recovering, well-being remains high in many dimensions, and Norway stands as one of the OECD's most inclusive countries in terms of income equality, labour participation and gender gaps. Accommodative monetary policy continues to support demand but has fuelled worryingly strong house-price increases and credit growth. House prices now appear overvalued and seem to have peaked. A rapid price correction could have severe effects on households' balance sheets, banks' financial health, and could be critical to Norway's economic outlook.

The revised fiscal rule will better preserve oil wealth across generations

Structural non-oil deficits

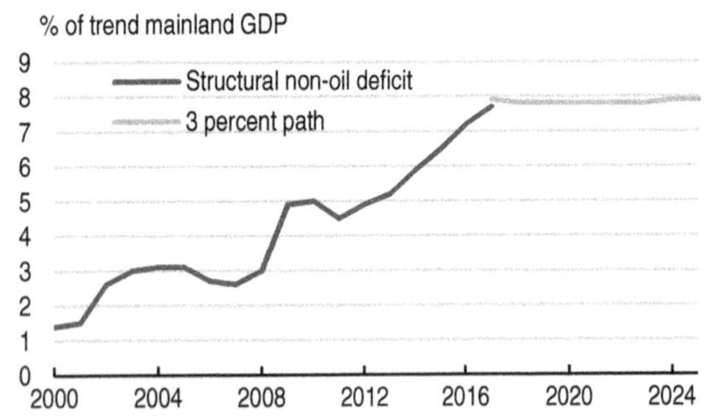

Source: Ministry of finance.

StatLink http://dx.doi.org/10.1787/888933638467

Returns on Norway's wealth fund finance substantial non-oil fiscal deficits. Reflecting lower returns on assets globally, Norway's fiscal rule has been made more prudent. Budgets will now aim at structural non-oil deficits equivalent to 3% of the value of the wealth fund, rather than 4%. This implies a change from an expansionary to neutral fiscal stance. Shift to neutrality should be achieved through efforts at improving public spending efficiency, where scope prevails, which would make space for reducing high tax rates. This *Survey* focuses on improving value for money from transport-infrastructure investment. Governance of the sovereign wealth fund is also being adapted to its vast size.

A dynamic businesses sector will support inclusive growth

Trend labour productivity

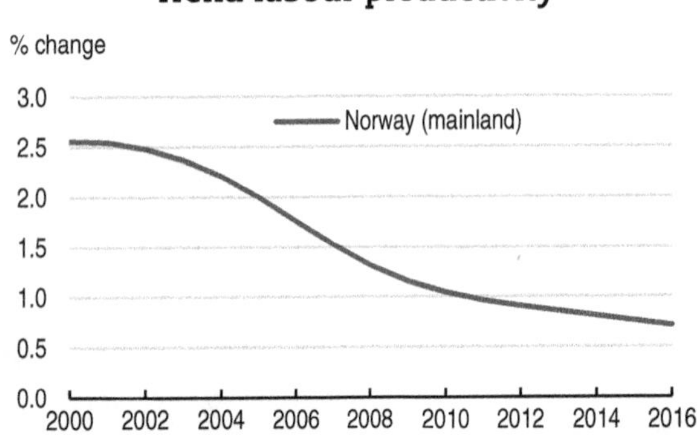

Source: OECD analytical database.

StatLink http://dx.doi.org/10.1787/888933638486

Sustaining Norway's inclusive society will require successful economic diversification away from oil-related activities. Removing obstacles that impede the reallocation of business activities and drag down productivity growth is therefore crucial. While generally there is a friendly environment to do business, progress could nonetheless be made toward tax reform, stronger competition, more efficient insolvency procedures and better sectoral regulation. The reallocation of skills calls for further reform of vocational education to embrace the opportunities offered by digitalisation and globalisation. Also, labour market participation among older cohorts needs to strengthen.

MAIN FINDINGS	KEY RECOMMENDATIONS
Normalising the monetary stance, preparing for housing price correction	
Monetary policy has supported growth after the oil price fall. The housing market appears to have turned around. Finally, house prices have begun to fall but substantial concern about debt levels remains.	Normalise the monetary stance as forecast, with rate increases starting in late 2018. Be prepared to make a wide-ranging response in case of a hard landing in the housing and debt markets. This should include, as necessary, delay to monetary policy normalization and targeted fiscal policy.
Ensuring fair access to resource wealth across generations, increasing value for money in public spending	
Change from a "4%" to a "3%" fiscal rule better assures the wealth fund remains intact for future generations given upcoming population ageing and the likelihood of lower wealth-fund returns.	Focus on restraint in government spending and public-service efficiency to ensure the switch from a sustained period of expansionary fiscal stance to neutrality. Intensify regular spending reviews to enhance efficiency. For transport-infrastructure investment, strengthen the influence of cost-benefit analysis in project selection and improve checks against cost inflation after projects are selected.
Facilitating diversification to non-oil sectors, seizing opportunities from globalisation and digitalisation	
Norway's high tax levels make it tough for businesses to compete in the global economy and distortions in the tax system misdirect saving and investment.	Complete the programme of income-tax rate cuts, and consider further reductions. Reduce the tax distortions in housing. Either carefully phase out mortgage-interest relief or increase property taxes on housing as a proxy for implicit rental income while paying attention to symmetries in the tax system. Consider further wealth tax reduction given its substantial impact on the returns to saving in the current low-return environment, while paying attention to inequalities.
Norway's high labour costs need to be offset by an excellent business environment in other respects to help business thrive.	Continue strengthening competition policy; in particular eliminate sectoral exemptions in agriculture. Reduce state stakes in business further, especially in well-functioning markets. Strengthen routes to recovery in the insolvency regime for businesses in difficulty. Replace the taxi-licencing system with less restrictive regulation to address availability and consumer-protection.
Preserving high levels of inclusiveness through improvements to skills and labour participation	
Many upper-secondary students in the vocational stream fail to complete courses, which increases the risk of low-paid and unstable employment for the longer term and compromises the supply of vocational skills for employers.	Raise awareness among employers about the availability of incentives to offer apprenticeship places. Strengthen incentives for employers to offer apprenticeship places by lowering costs, either through lowering apprentice wages or through providing additional subsidies.
Labour supply remains compromised because the sickness and disability system does not adequately encourage and facilitate those with work capacity to re-enter the labour force.	Press on with reform to sick leave and disability benefit including through an employer-financed phase of sick leave and tighter medical assessment.
Environmental sustainability	
Environmental taxation is well developed and the Green Tax Commission proposes further improvement.	Make environmental taxation more uniform across sectors and activities when tackling specific issues, notably climate change.

© OECD 2018

Assessment and recommendations

- *Recent macroeconomic developments and near-term prospects*
- *Price and financial stability: tweaks to monetary policy, ongoing macro-prudential moves*
- *Adjusting the fiscal rule, ensuring efficient tax and public spending*
- *Easing the transition toward dynamic non-oil businesses*
- *Retaining high labour-force participation and raising skills are key for Norway's future*
- *Tackling environmental issues*

Business dynamism and sound management of natural resources wealth has helped propel Norway among the highest levels of GDP per capita in the world (Figure 1). Combined with its "Nordic model" ensuring inclusiveness and low inequality, Norway exhibits impressive levels of well-being in many dimensions (Figure 2, Panels A and C). Its society has an egalitarian approach to income distribution and has prioritised reducing gender discrimination, resulting in levels of inequality that remain well below the OECD average (Figure 2, Panels B and D). Comprehensive provision of education, healthcare and family support has been a key driver. Maintaining these high standards of well-being, seizing opportunities from automation and globalisation and overcoming challenges from long-term decline in oil and gas production, requires ensuring that policies remain at the forefront of good practice.

Figure 1. **Norway's GDP per capita remains impressive, though growth has slowed**

Constant USD prices, 2010 PPP

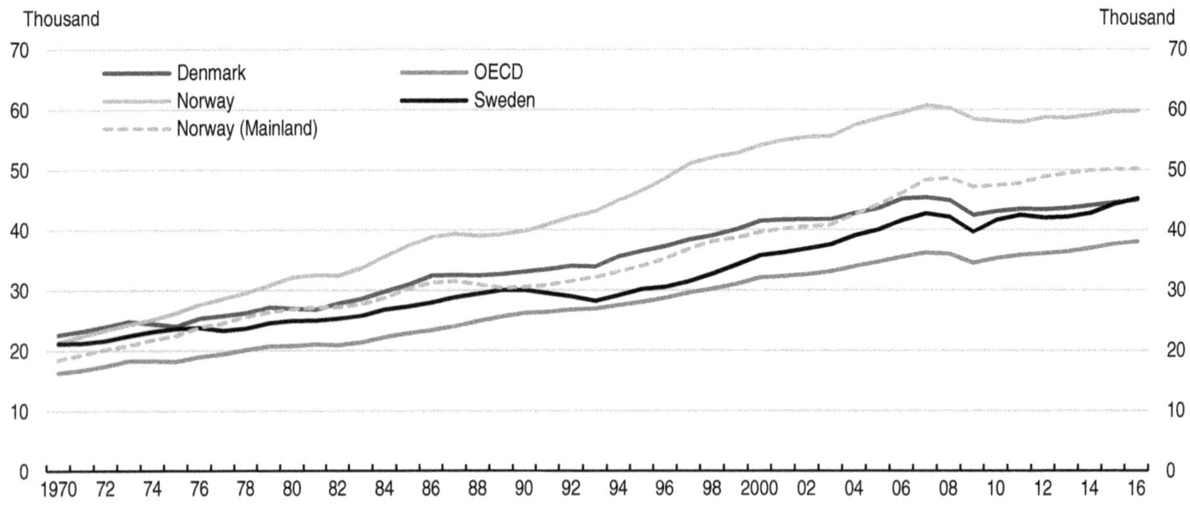

Source: *OECD National Accounts Database, and OECD Analytical Database.*

StatLink http://dx.doi.org/10.1787/888933638505

For Norway's society to remain inclusive as its petroleum resources decline and its population ages, the business sector will have to diversify to non-oil sectors and continue to exploit opportunities from globalisation and technological change. The policy environment is business-friendly in general, with sound framework conditions and macroeconomic management. In particular, the floating exchange rate has proved a critical mechanism in adjustment to shocks, such as the large oil-price drop in 2014 (Figure 3, Panel C). Also, the partial protection from "Dutch disease" provided by foreign-asset purchases for Norway's main wealth fund supports diversification of the economy. However, policy cannot afford to stand still. The house-price correction that is currently underway in a context of high household debt potentially poses near-term policy challenges.

Figure 2. **Norway continues to deliver good scores in well-being**

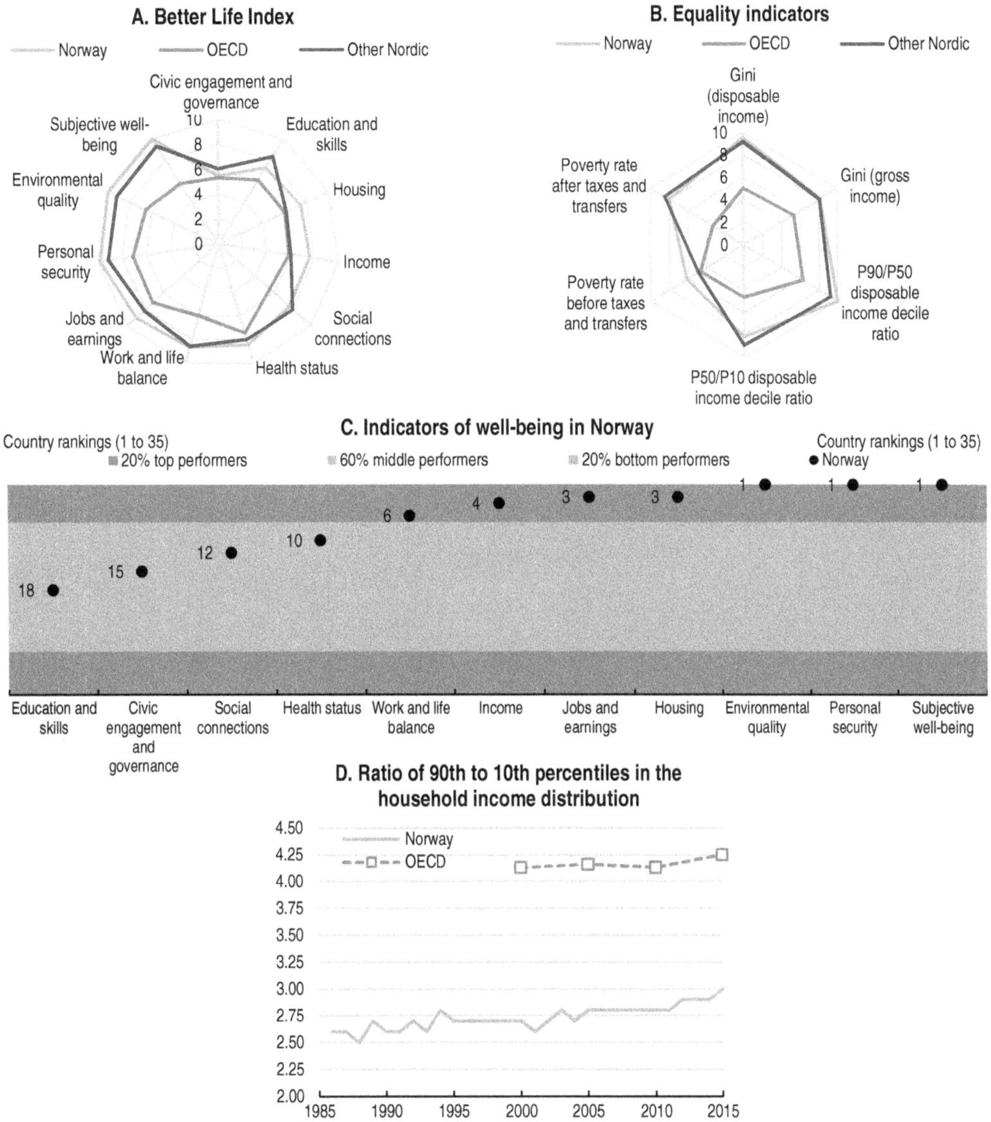

Note: "Other Nordic" group comprises Denmark, Finland and Sweden. Panel A and B, indicators are rescaled from 0 (worst) to 10 (best).
Source: *OECD Better Life Index 2016*; *OECD Income and Distribution Database*; and Statistic Norway.

StatLink http://dx.doi.org/10.1787/888933638524

Also, Norway, similar to many other economies, has experienced a step-down in productivity growth over recent years (Figure 3, Panel A) and a corresponding slowdown in GDP-per-capita growth (Figure 1). In addition, unit labour costs remain comparatively high, despite currency depreciation since 2014 (Figure 3, Panel B). Policy needs to help business seize opportunities from globalisation and facilitate diversification away from oil-related activities; this is the theme of Chapter 1 of this *Survey*. The dynamism of Norwegian businesses would be helped if the public sector became more efficient; delivering public services, welfare support and public investment at a lower cost. This would create room for lowering taxes, including those taxes that most strongly influence business costs and returns. The large role of publicly-financed services and investments in the economy means that returns to efficiency gains are substantial; releasing resources for new and better quality services, or reduced taxation for households and business. However, oil-and-gas

Figure 3. **Productivity slowdown, unit labour costs and oil-price fluctuation present challenges**

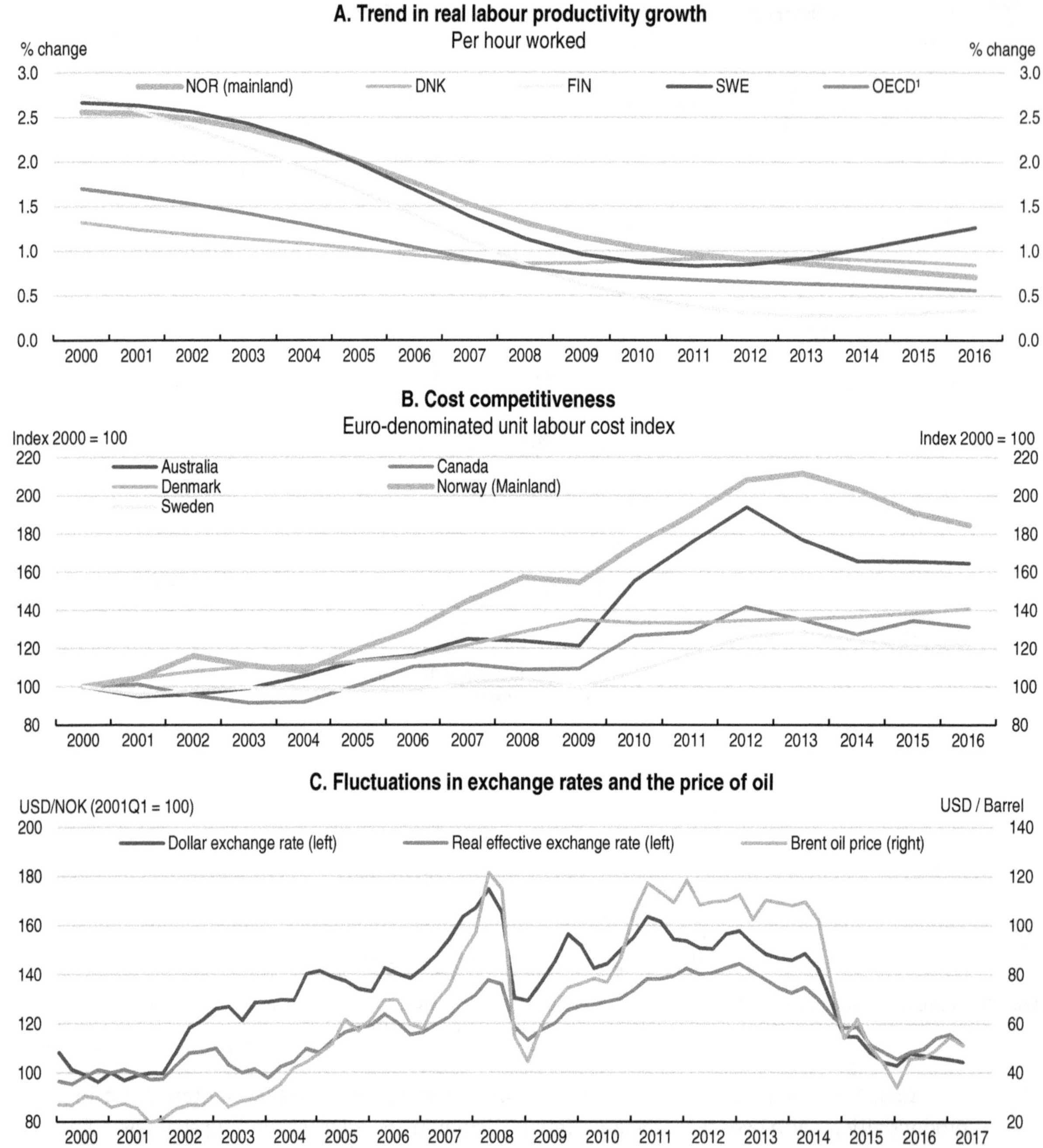

1. Per worker.

Source: *OECD Analytical Database*, and *OECD Economic Outlook Database*.

StatLink http://dx.doi.org/10.1787/888933638543

wealth has traditionally diminished motivation for seeking such gains. There is a tendency to use high-cost options in policies and inertia in reform. Chapter 2 of this *Survey* focuses on transport-infrastructure investment. Such investment can widen economic opportunities for business and increase welfare for households; expanding product and labour markets, reducing journey and delivery times, facilitating trade and widening social interaction. Realising these returns requires that transport-infrastructure investment is well chosen and implemented efficiently.

Against this backdrop, the main messages of this *Survey* are:

- It is crucial that policy facilitates transition away from oil-related activities and seizes opportunities from digitalisation and globalisation, through providing macroeconomic and financial stability along with improvements to structural-policy settings.
- Make public services more efficient, so as to reduce the injection of oil-money into the economy and to ensure an equitable participation in oil-wealth returns across future generations.
- Ensure transport infrastructure investment is well targeted and efficiently executed to maximise the returns to businesses and households in economic opportunity and welfare.

Recent macroeconomic developments and near-term prospects

Recovery from the oil-price collapse of 2014 and, more generally, weak demand appears well underway. Mainland real GDP growth has been increasing in year-on-year terms since early 2016 and the unemployment rate is falling (Figure 4, Panels A and B). Downward adjustment in the petroleum sector's investment has tailed off (Panel C), and the currency depreciation triggered by the oil-price fall (Figure 3, Panel C) softened the blow to the sector's income in local currency (Norwegian Krone). Currency depreciation also supported demand for non-oil exports and helped make Norwegian business more competitive. Consumer-price inflation, temporarily boosted by currency depreciation, is once again below the policy target of 2½ per cent (Figure 4, Panel E). However, long-run trends and expectations looking forward suggest consumer-price inflation is well anchored (Panel F).

Yet, there have been set-backs to recovery and housing-market concerns remain. 2016 saw sharp contraction in exports from oil-service companies, suggesting that reduced activity levels and cost cutting in the global oil industry continues. This contributed to softer mainland export growth along with falling aquaculture exports due to supply problems arising from disease in the fish stocks (Figure 4, Panel D). The housing market may be turning following a prolonged period of strong price and credit growth. If this is indeed the case, then the key question is now whether market is coming in for a soft or a hard landing and the consequent ramifications for the financial-sector stability, household and business balance sheets and consumption and investment demand (see below).

Macroeconomic policies have been providing significant support. Monetary policy has remained highly supportive. The policy rate has been 0.5% since March 2016 and Norges Bank is signalling continuation of a low-interest environment through its interest-rate projections (Figure 5). The latest forecasts have indicated an earlier start to rate normalisation, signalling confidence in the output-growth recovery. In addition, there has been active fiscal impulse, as seen through increases in the non-oil structural deficit (Figure 5). Furthermore, fiscal support has come from counter-cyclical processes that arise without active measures ("automatic stabilisers"), such as increased government spending from greater numbers receiving unemployment benefit and tax declines from falls in company profits (Figure 5).

Looking ahead, the OECD's central projection envisages continued recovery, with mainland output growth over 2% in 2018 and 2019 (Table 1). The recovery will include a switch from a negative to a small positive contribution from petroleum-sector investment. Household consumption growth is expected to remain strong, helped by employment growth and a further decrease in the rate of unemployment. Consumer-price inflation will

Figure 4. **Recent macroeconomic developments**

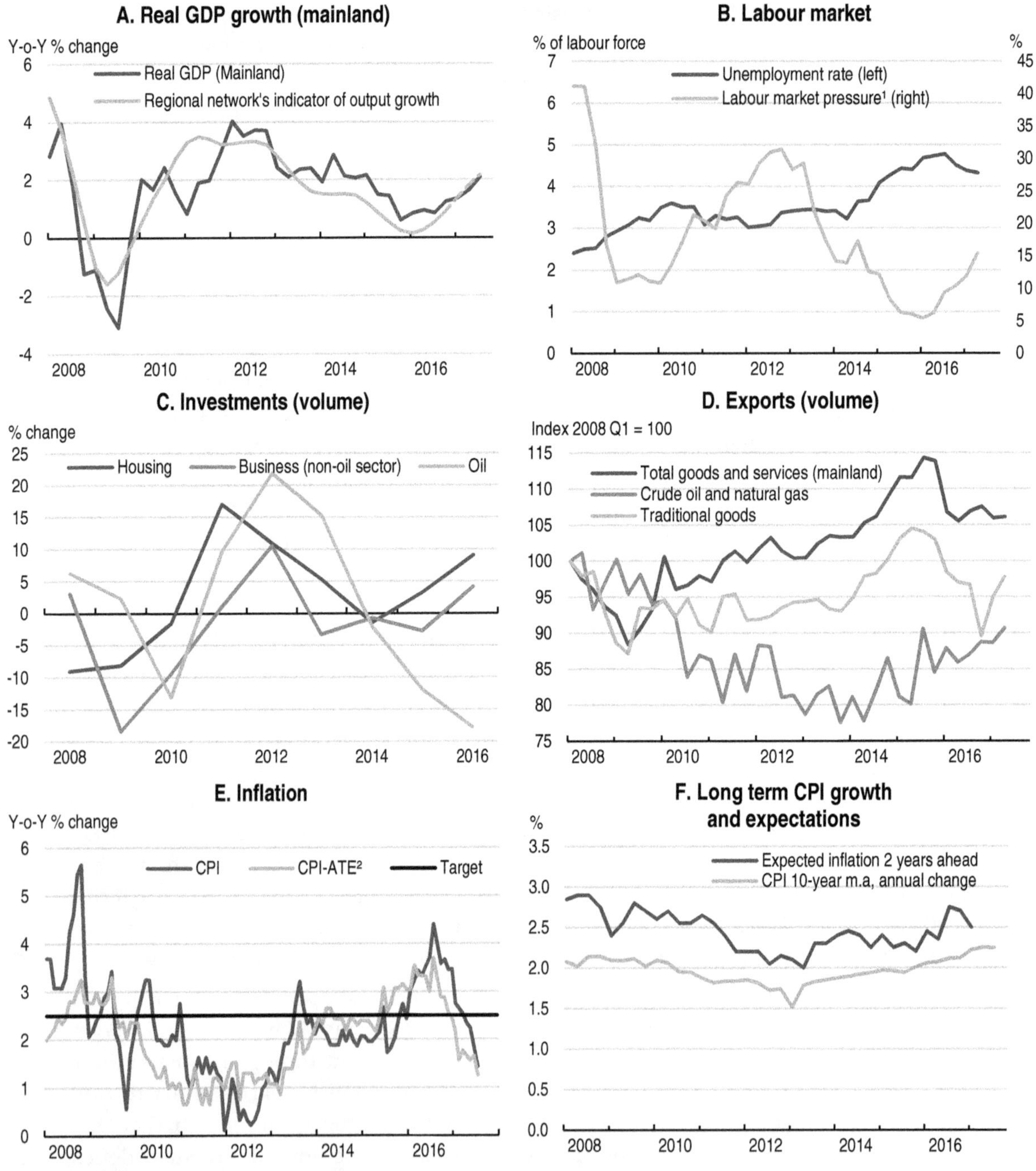

1. Share of contacts reporting that output is constrained by labour supply.
2. CPI-ATE is CPI adjusted for tax changes and excluding energy products.

Source: Statistics Norway, Central Bank of Norway; *OECD Analytical Database*; and *OECD Economic Outlook Database*.

StatLink http://dx.doi.org/10.1787/888933638562

fall somewhat in the near term but gradually increase thereafter as spare capacity diminishes. Nevertheless, inflation will continue well anchored, allowing monetary policy to stay highly supportive over the projection horizon. Active fiscal support through increase in the non-oil structural deficit is due to tail off in light of adjustment of the fiscal rule (see below).

Figure 5. **Supportive monetary and fiscal policy in recent years**

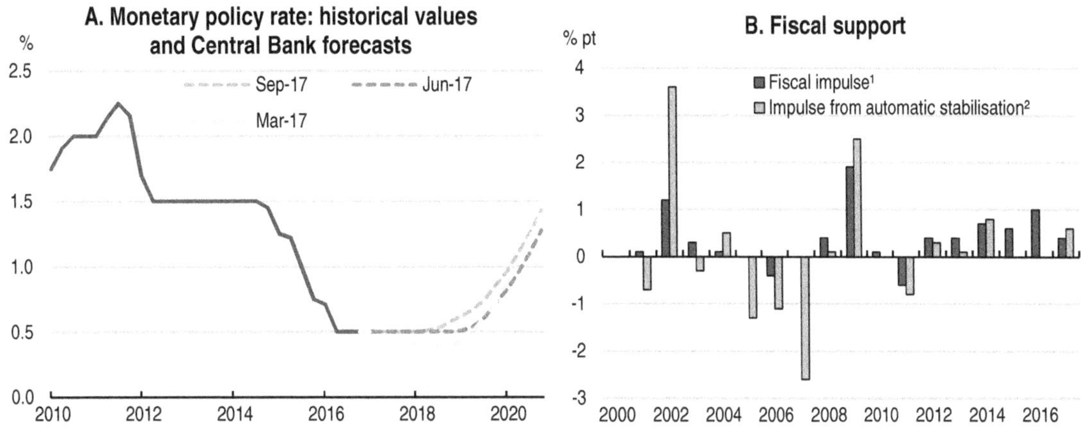

1. Annual change in the structural non-oil deficit.
2. Annual change in non-oil deficit (as % of trend mainland GDP) minus change in structural non-oil deficit (as % of trend mainland GDP).
Source: Central Bank of Norway; and Ministry of Finance.

StatLink http://dx.doi.org/10.1787/888933638581

Norway's key sources of risk (i.e. variation while staying broadly within the central macroeconomic scenario described above) are also its sources of vulnerability (i.e. tail-risk macroeconomic scenarios):

- *The housing market and household debt.* The consequences of tensions and pressures that have already arisen from house-price and credit growth, along with their future direction, remain both a risk and a vulnerability (discussed further below).
- *The global oil price.* Small movements from the current price level will not prompt substantial departure from the central growth scenario described in Table 1. This said, oil-price influences can shift quickly and neither a very large price increase, nor a very substantial fall from current prices should be discounted entirely, resulting in substantial departure from the central macroeconomic scenario (Table 2).
- *The global stock market.* In addition to the usual channels through which global stock markets affect the economy, variation in global-stock market valuation and dividends directly influence fiscal policy because this generates variation in the "allowable" government deficit under the fiscal rule.
- *External demand.* Norway's deep ties with the rest of Europe mean developments in demand in the region are a source of risk and tail-risk scenarios could develop from dramatic rise in protectionism for instance (Table 2).

Risks worth noting, but which are unlikely to destabilise the economy, include uncertainty about the pace of domestic-demand recovery from the "low-growth" malaise. Though consumer confidence has picked up, this has yet to be echoed in household consumption. Employment and wage growth have also yet to pick up substantially, and this is reflected in low household income growth.

Probability-of-recession estimates (Box 1) suggest there is some risk of downturn in the near term and appears to be linked to domestic credit and external factors (Box 1). Norway has substantial macroeconomic policy firepower to support the economy. Monetary policy can stay supportive and Norway's advantageous fiscal position thanks to petroleum-sector revenue and the wealth fund means substantial firepower is available for fiscal support from automatic stabilisation and policy-driven measures.

Table 1. **Macroeconomic indicators and projections**

Annual percentage change (unless otherwise indicated), volume (2015 prices)

	2014 Current prices (billion NOK)	2015	2016	2017	2018	2019
GDP volume (A)	**3 147**	**2.0**	**1.1**	**2.1**	**1.8**	**1.9**
Potential GDP		1.8	1.7	1.7	1.7	1.6
Output gap (% of potential GDP)		-0.8	-1.5	-1.4	-0.9	-0.4
GDP volume, mainland (B)	**2 540**	**1.4**	**1.0**	**1.9**	**2.3**	**2.1**
Petroleum-production contribution to GDP volume growth (A minus B)		**0.6**	**0.1**	**0.2**	**-0.5**	**-0.2**
GDP volume components						
Private consumption	**1 288**	2.6	1.5	2.5	2.6	2.3
Government consumption	**692**	2.4	2.1	1.9	2.0	2.0
Gross fixed capital formation	**749**	-4.0	-0.2	3.9	2.8	2.4
Housing	**156**	3.2	9.0	9.9	3.1	1.1
Business[1]	**449**	-7.9	-6.0	1.7	2.2	3.2
Non-oil sector	**223**	-2.8	4.1	6.0	4.2	2.9
Oil sector[2]	**231**	-11.9	-17.8	1.1	2.2	3.9
Government	**144**	0.2	5.9	2.2	3.7	2.0
Final domestic demand	**2 730**	0.7	1.2	2.7	2.5	2.3
Stockbuilding (percentage-point contribution to GDP volume growth)	**134**	0.0	1.4	-0.8	-0.4	0.0
Total domestic demand	**2 863**	0.7	2.7	1.7	1.9	2.2
Exports of goods and services	**1 220**	4.7	-1.8	2.2	1.2	1.8
of which crude oil and natural gas	**551**	2.1	4.3	..	..	..
Imports of goods and services	**937**	1.6	2.3	1.1	1.4	2.6
Net exports (percentage-point contribution to GDP volume growth)	**283**	1.3	-1.4	0.4	0.0	-0.2
Labour-market and households						
Employment		0.5	-0.1	0.3	1.2	1.5
Unemployment rate, %		4.3	4.7	4.3	4.0	3.7
Household saving ratio, net (% of disposable household income)		10.3	7.0	6.6	6.2	5.7
Deflators, prices						
GDP deflator		-2.8	-1.1	3.0	0.5	2.1
Consumer price index		2.2	3.5	1.9	1.6	1.9
Core consumer prices		2.6	3.3	1.7	1.4	2.0
Trade and current account balances						
Trade balance (% of GDP)		7.1	3.8	..	..	..
Current account balance (% of GDP)		8.0	3.9	4.5	4.6	4.6
Money market rates and bond yields						
Three-month money market rate, average, %		1.3	1.1	0.9	0.8	0.9
Ten-year government bond yield, average, %		1.6	1.3	1.6	1.8	1.9
General-government fiscal indicators (OECD)						
General government financial balance (% of GDP)[3]		6.1	4.0	5.4	5.8	6.0
General government net debt (% of GDP)		-284.9	-289.4	-280.7	-280.1	-275.2
Central-government fiscal indicators (Ministry of Finance)[4]						
Structural non-oil balance[5, 6]		-6.6	-7.2	-7.7	-7.7	..
Non-oil balance[5]		-7.1	-7.6	-8.1	-8.5	..
Government Pension Fund Global (% of GDP)		239.8	241.3	..	..	..
Structural non-oil balance (as a % GPFG)		-2.6	-2.7	-2.9	-2.9	..
Memorandum items						
Non-mainland GDP (petroleum and shipping)	**607**	4.5	1.0	4.1	1.0	-1.7

1. Also includes shipping sector.
2. Following the approach taken by the Norwegian authorities, oil-sector investment is included in mainland GDP as most of the investment activity takes place on the mainland.
3. Norway's general-government account notably incorporates offshore-sector tax revenues and income from the Government Pension Fund Global.
4. Figures published in the government's latest budget proposals.
5. The central-government non-oil balances notably exclude offshore-sector tax revenues and income from the Government Pension Fund Global. These balances are percentage of trend mainland GDP.
6. The "Structural Non-oil Balance" is the focus of government budgeting. "Structural" refers to adjustment for the business cycle made by the Ministry of Finance.

Source: OECD Economic Outlook 102 Database; Statistics Norway; Norwegian Ministry of Finance.

Table 2. **Possible extreme shocks to the Norwegian economy**

Shock	Possible impact
Large house-price correction and household debt deleveraging	Large house-price falls ("hard landing") could see a rapid household deleveraging, collapse in household consumption growth and firm activity accompanied by threats to bank stability from mortgage defaults
Large and sustained upward or downward shift in the oil prices from the current level	Very-low-price scenario. Collapse of oil and gas related activities, including investment in domestic production and export of oil-related goods and services. Large mainland job losses and falls in income and output, particularly in certain regions Very-high-price scenario. Increased wealth and incomes but a deepening of the challenges in managing oil wealth; exchange-rate appreciation choking non-oil exports, weak public-spending discipline
Global stock market collapse (or substantial further surge)	A global stock market collapse would likely lower the value of the wealth fund, however the leeway in the fiscal rule would allow for countervailing stimulation. Negative impact from stock-market collapse would likely come from weaker oil prices as well as other channels A substantial and sustained surge in the global stock market would allow, *inter alia*, room for larger deficits, providing opportunity to reduce taxation (or expand public services)
External demand shocks	Increased political and economic uncertainty globally has widened the range of possible extreme scenarios. A breakdown in trade from protectionism or a sharp downturn in China's economic activity, could for instance, destabilise Norway's economic recovery Conversely, positive shock, for instance from a larger-than-expected surge in European growth, could put Norway on an accelerated growth path

Price and financial stability: tweaks to monetary policy, ongoing macroprudential moves

As for many economies, monetary policy in recent years has been chiefly geared to support demand in light of weak output and price growth. Also, Norway is among the countries with growing concern about the sustainability of the strong house-price and credit growth that the low-interest environment has contributed to.

Some alterations and updating of the inflation-targeting regime

Broadly speaking, Norway's inflation-targeting regime continues to work well. Since its establishment in 2001, inflation has remained well anchored (exemplified in Figure 4, Panels E and F, for an in-depth assessment see Norges Bank 2017a). The regime has also proved adept at taking into account other economic considerations, most notably the prolonged low policy rates elsewhere, especially those in the Eurozone and the United States and, in recent years, the downturn in domestic economic activity following the oil-price drop of 2014. The policy rate, 0.5% as of December 2017, is appropriately supportive and should stay at this level for some time ahead. Eventually policy should tighten as growth picks up further. Norges Bank's interest-rate projection indicates policy-rate increase will begin towards the end of 2018 (Figure 5, Panel A).

Positive adjustment to the inflation-targeting regime has been made. Norges Bank announced in May 2017 various procedural changes to increase transparency, and the frequency of communication and decision making. There are to be eight monetary policy meetings per year instead of six and the minutes of the meetings are to be published (the in-depth *Monetary Policy Report with Financial Stability Assessment* will remain quarterly). Though there were no glaring problems to resolve, the moves bring practice more in line with inflation-targeting systems elsewhere.

A commission has proposed a new central bank act and substantial changes to Norge's Bank's role that would see a more separated and specialised structure – currently, much responsibility, management and decision making resides with the eight-member Executive Board. The commission favours a reform that would see management of the wealth fund

Box 1. Predicting downturn in Norway using the OECD's resilience database

Statistical methods can be used to develop leading indicators of past downturns and recessions using the OECD's database of vulnerability indicators (Hermansen and Röhn 2015; Röhn et al., 2015). The database comprises over 70 indicators across six categories of vulnerability (five domestic, one international).

For Norway the analysis is based on predicting periods of downturn identified by Norges Bank. These comprise, ignoring small gaps, essentially four downturn episodes. Principal components analysis was used to develop a single-number leading indicator. This indicator was then used to estimate the downturn probability at different time horizons (Figure 6).

Figure 6. **Recent data suggest there is some risk of a downturn**

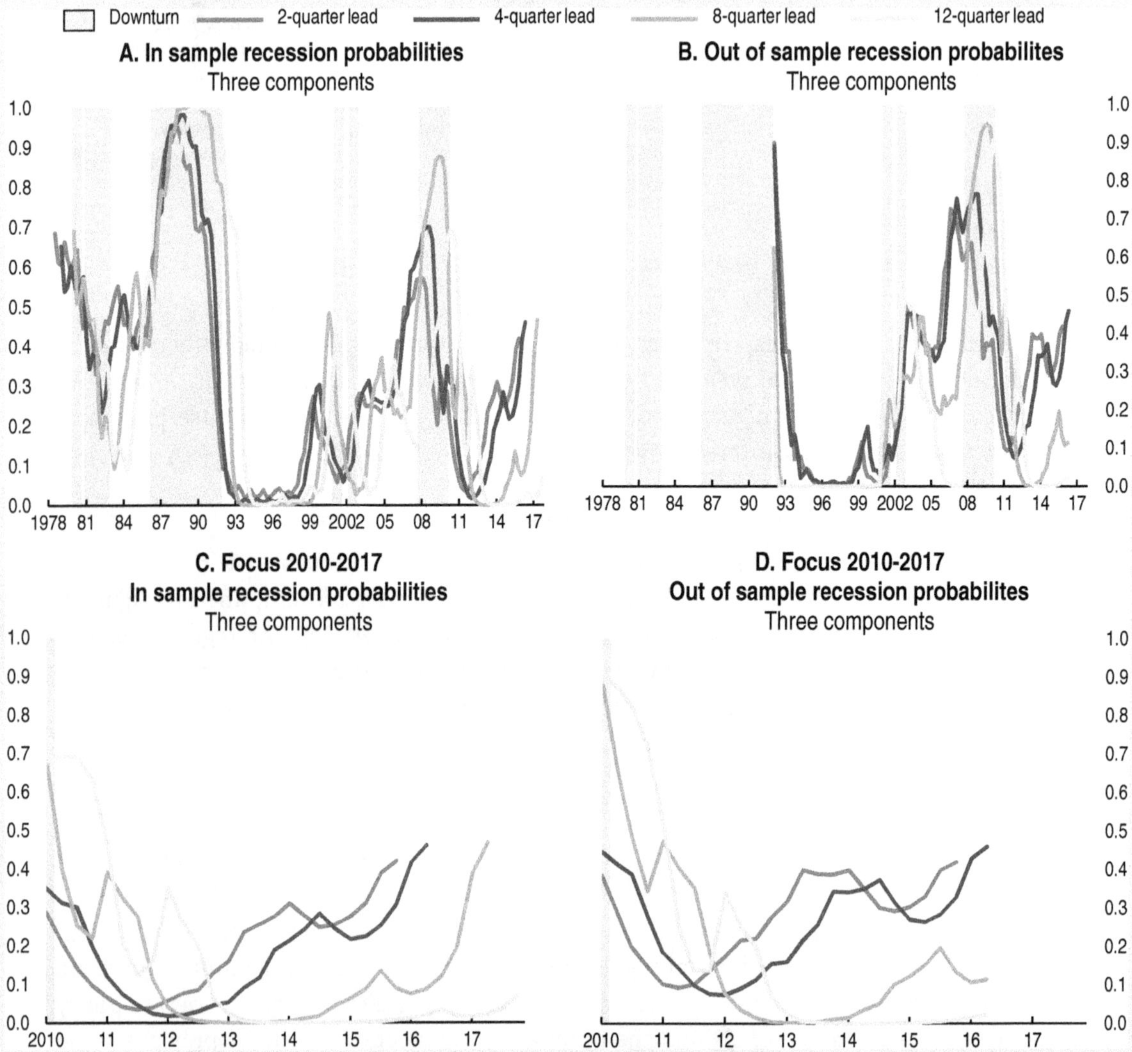

Note: The above panel shows estimates of the downturn probabilities at horizons of 2, 4, 8 and 12 quarters. The "in-sample" results use the entire data set to generate the indicators, the "out of sample" results generate indicators only from an initial period data (specifically, 1978 to 1992) and then project the recession probabilities. The red line in Panel C, for instance suggests that the 8-quarter horizon recession probability increased from about 0.1 at the beginning of 2016 to around 0.45 by the beginning of 2017.
Source: OECD calculations using *OECD Vulnerability Database*.

StatLink http://dx.doi.org/10.1787/888933638600

Box 1. **Predicting downturn in Norway using the OECD's resilience database** *(cont.)*

As similar exercises for other countries have found, the indicators developed from the resilience database are not hugely accurate. In Figure 6, the indicators are performing well if they peak around the beginning of a downturn. On this basis, some lag-lengths provided some warning of the latest two downturns. Yet none of the variables warned of the prolonged downturn that began in the mid-1980s.

Bearing in mind the limited accuracy, the growth in the short-lag variables in the most recent data suggests there is a non-negligible risk of downturn. Examination of the principle components analysis indicates that recent increased risk of downturn is due to variables reflecting domestic credit conditions and external risk factors.

passed to a newly formed management body, separate from the Bank (discussed further below) and a separate committee for monetary policy and financial stability. As regards the overall objectives to the bank it advocates adding a separate financial stability goal, in addition to price stability and adding an explicit duty to contribute to high and stable output and employment. In parallel, the Ministry of Finance has announced an overhaul of the monetary policy remit. Clarification of a central bank's role in supporting employment and output is relatively uncontroversial, a possible addition of an explicit financial stability objective, less so. However in the Norwegian context it would bring welcome transparency to an existing responsibility, given that financial stability already features in discussions and clearly has some weight in decisions, especially given housing-market developments. Such a move could be reflected in having separate committees for monetary policy and financial stability.

House prices and household debt remain a central concern

House prices have roughly doubled in real terms since 2000, with strong increases continuing in recent years (Figure 7, Panels A and B). In addition, Norway's rent-to-income ratio is high, which is also indicative of housing market pressure (Panel C). Furthermore, household debt is elevated; it is equivalent to 220% of disposable income, one of the highest levels in the OECD (Panel D). Once principal repayments are included, the household debt-servicing ratio is nearly 14%, a high level historically (Panel E). According to Norges Bank's financial stability assessment, this ratio would increase to nearly 18% if mortgage interest rates rose by 5 percentage points (Panel E). As in other countries with strong growth in house prices and associated borrowing, the prolonged low-interest-rate environment has been a primary driver. In Norway most mortgages are variable rate, thus amplifying the response to low interest rates. Localised demand pressure from continuing population shift to urban areas has also been playing a role. Supply response to the booming housing market in the form of new housing has been sizeable, especially in Eastern Norway (which includes Oslo) (Panel F).

Recognising the risks from elevated debt levels, the Norwegian authorities have been using macroprudential tools and strengthening capital requirements. Macroprudential measures implemented in January 2017 included a new requirement on mortgage lenders to limit a borrower's debt to five times gross annual income plus stricter repayment requirements. In addition, banking-sector capital requirements have increased substantially in recent years (Figure 8). These have partly come from Norway's counter-cyclical capital buffer which was introduced in 2015 as part of the phasing in of Basel III capital

Figure 7. **House prices, household debt and new house sales**

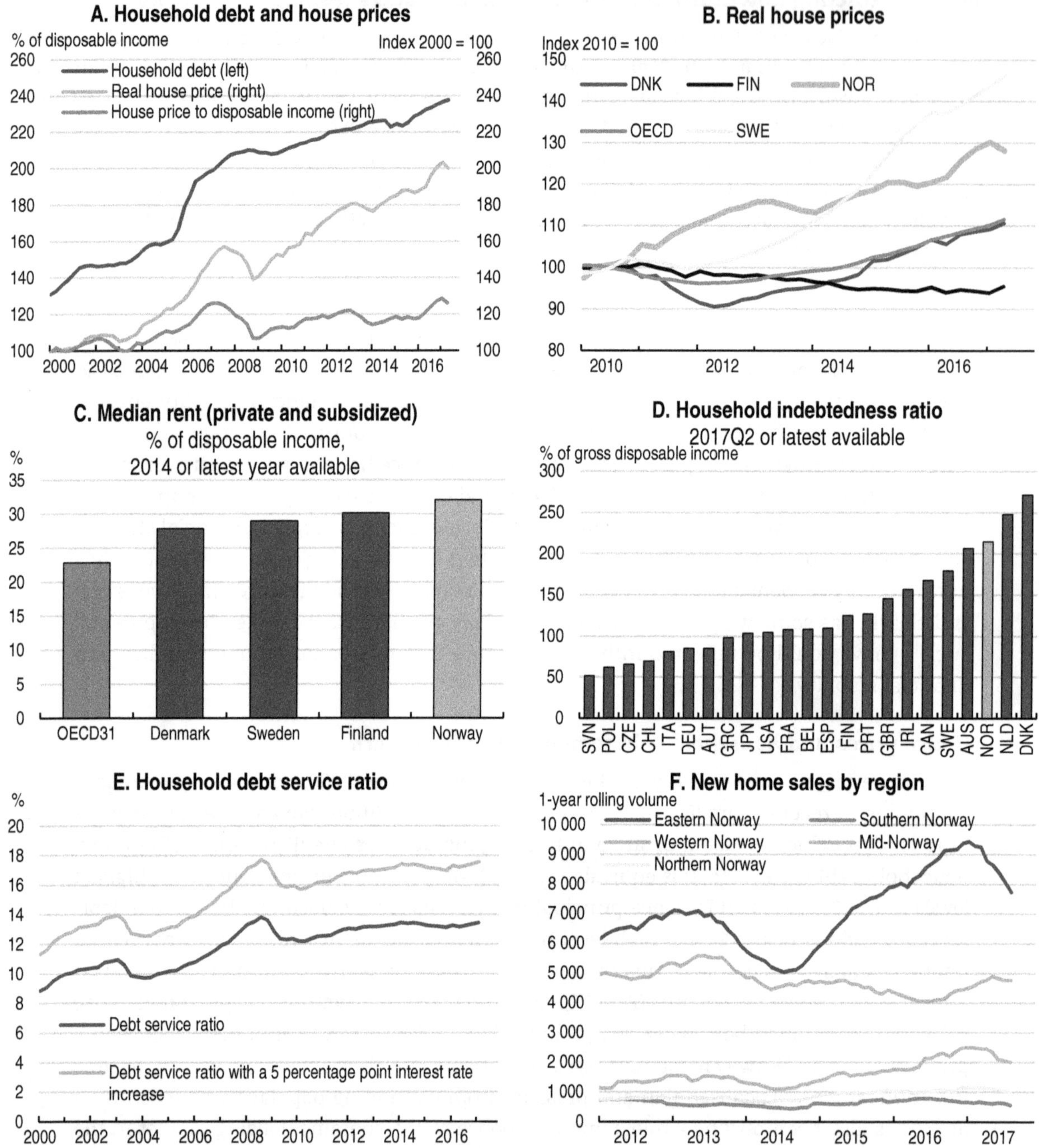

Source: Statistics Norway; Central Bank of Norway; *OECD Analytical Database*; OECD dashboard of household statistics and *OECD Affordable Housing Database*.

StatLink http://dx.doi.org/10.1787/888933638619

requirements. In addition, leverage-ratio requirements on banks were introduced in December 2016. Also, tighter capital requirements for insurance companies have been introduced via implementation of the Solvency II framework in 2016 (Finanstilsynet, 2016).

It appears that the market-cooling measures, in combination with the surge in housing supply, have borne fruit as house prices have been falling in recent months. This may mark the beginning of a sustained market correction. Several price falls have been recorded in the country-wide seasonally adjusted house-price index in recent months and quarterly data confirm falling prices in the Oslo area (Figure 9). New home sales have fallen off in Eastern Norway, also pointing to a softening of the market (Figure 7, Panel F).

Figure 8. **Capital requirements on Norwegian Banks**

Common Equity Tier 1 requirements in the new regulatory framework[1]

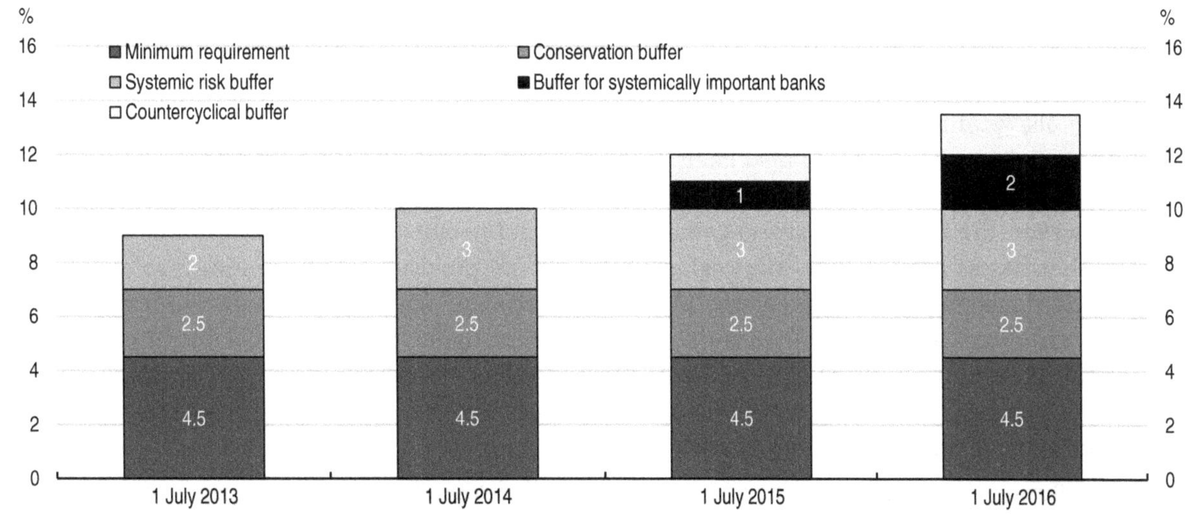

1. Ratio of Common Equity Tier 1 capital to risk-weighted assets.

Source: Central Bank of Norway.

StatLink http://dx.doi.org/10.1787/888933638638

Figure 9. **The latest house-price data suggest the market may be turning**

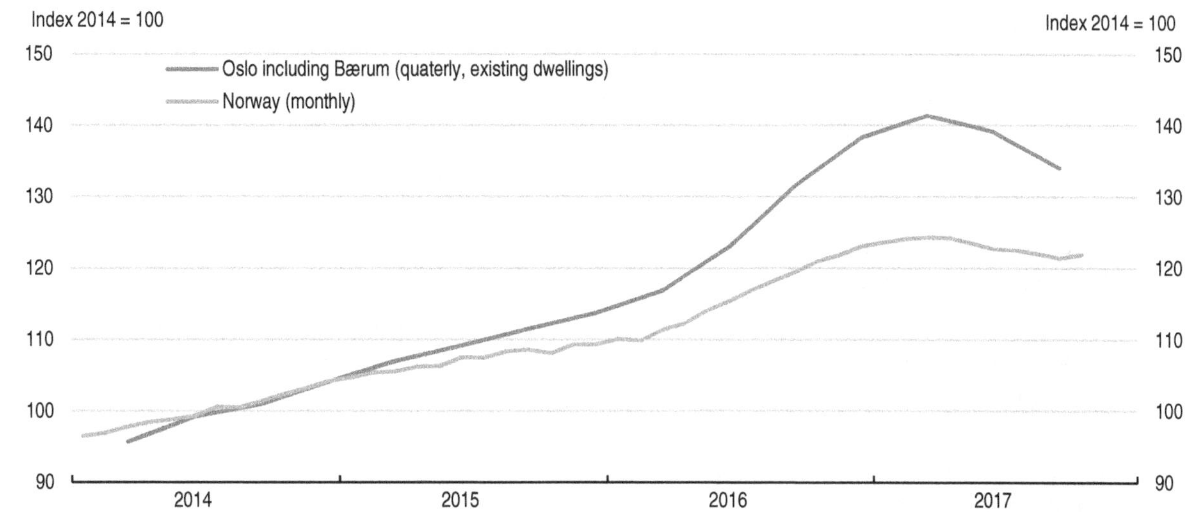

Note: The above series are seasonally adjusted.

Source: Statistic Norway; and Real Estate Norway (Eiendom Norge).

StatLink http://dx.doi.org/10.1787/888933638657

If the recent house price developments represent the start of a sustained correction, then the critical issue is whether the market is heading for a soft landing (smooth adjustment to a new equilibrium) or a hard landing (erratic adjustment, possibly with prices dropping below equilibrium before stabilising). An IMF house-price regression exercise suggests Norway's house prices were overvalued by around 15% at end 2016, which suggests a soft landing is possible. However, there are uncertainties in such regression results, and an average price correction can contain substantial adjustment in some market segments. Also, past OECD work has found soft landings are rare (Rae and van den Noord, 2006). In sum, there are no grounds for complacency.

In the Norwegian context, the chief economic impact from weakening house prices is most likely to come via dampened household consumption demand, due to negative wealth effects, precautionary saving responses and reduced expenditures related to the purchase and sale of housing (such as spending on renovation and interior decoration). This could, *inter alia*, lead to losses on loans to businesses thus putting stress on the financial sector. Financial-sector stress will also likely increase from mortgage borrowers encountering financial difficulty in the event of reduced income (for instance through redundancy). However, the risk of this stress causing a financial-sector breakdown is seen by the authorities as limited given Norwegian banks' capital provisions, the significant role of foreign banks in providing mortgages, plus the "full recourse" nature of mortgages in Norway (i.e. mortgages are backed by collateral and banks have rights to collect assets and pursue legal action in the event of non-payment). Banking-sector stress tests conducted by Norges Bank (Norges Bank, 2017b), which incorporate large house-price corrections, suggest a low probability of financial-sector meltdown.

Strong vigilance on housing and credit market developments needs to be retained and the authorities should be prepared to make a wide-ranging policy response. This should include, as necessary, delay to monetary policy normalization. Automatic fiscal stabilisation in the event of a macroeconomic downturn from the house-price correction could be augmented by welfare measures to provide extra support to low-income households most affected. Also, there may be need to support the banking sector, though as discussed above, the chance of this being required appears low.

Whether the housing market is heading for a soft landing or otherwise, efforts for structural improvement in the market should continue so as to reduce risk of overheating in the future. Ongoing efforts to facilitate supply through lighter planning regulation and procedure should continue (these efforts probably have already helped the supply response seen in recent years, Figure 7, Panel F). In addition, Norway's substantial tax advantages for home ownership continue to unhelpfully fuel the demand for housing, policy progress on this front would be welcome (see below).

In addition, further work in the regulation of foreign-bank branches operating in Norway would be welcome. The branches face the same regulation in some domains, such as the mortgage-lending requirements discussed above. However, in other domains the foreign-bank branches are governed by the banking regulation of their parent. Reciprocal agreements between Norway and key foreign-bank domicile countries (notably Denmark and Sweden) have eased problems generated by such regulatory differences but the issue remains. Furthermore, it has gained importance following the conversion of Nordea Bank Norge from a subsidiary to a branch of the parent bank. Following this move, foreign-bank branches occupy more than one third of Norway's market in corporate lending.

Table 3. **Implementation of past recommendations on monetary and financial stability**

Recommendations	Action taken since the previous *Survey* (January 2016)
Should house-price growth remain uncomfortably high, consider additional macroprudential measures while closely monitoring and reviewing their effectiveness. Specifically consider: • Further guideline loan-to-value ratios, reducing access to interest-only loans • Working with foreign regulators to close down any remaining loopholes ("regulatory arbitrage") that give foreign-owned branches and subsidiaries advantages in mortgage lending.	Tightening of macroprudential regulation continues. The latest measures became effective January 2017 and comprised: • Introduction of a limit on a borrower's total debt to five times annual gross income • A smaller allowance for loans that do not conform to macroprudential rules in the Oslo area (only 8% of lenders loans will be allowed to not adhere to macroprudential rules, instead of 10%) • Reduction in the loan-to-value ratio for home equity credit lines (the vehicle for interest-only loans) from 70% to 60%. A loan-to-value ratio of 85% continues to apply to mortgage loans, except for second homes in the Oslo area where the ratio has been reduced to 60%. Banking sector capital requirements. Phase in of new capital and buffer requirements for credit institutions and investment firms (based on Basel III standards and the CRR/CRD IV framework) was completed in July 2016. Insurance sector. The Solvency II framework was implemented January 2016, in parallel with the EU. This will imply significantly higher solvency requirements for Norwegian insurers
Facilitate more responsive housing supply. In particular, reduce incentives of local authorities to withhold land for development, other than those related to clear externalities that cannot be compensated with revenue raised from sales.	No major reform.

Adjusting the fiscal rule, ensuring efficient tax and public spending

The shift to a "3% rule" in fiscal policy: a sound move

Norway's fiscal rule states that the cyclically adjusted non-oil deficit (the "structural deficit"), should, over time, be equal to the expected real return on the wealth fund (the Government Pension Fund Global, GPFG, see Box 2). The rule implies an intergenerationally fair use of oil wealth because spending the real returns implies leaving the real value of the Fund intact for future generations. The fiscal rule puts emphasis on evening out economic fluctuations. Under the rule, actual deficits fluctuate around the structural deficit ("automatic stabilisation") and the structural deficit itself is allowed to move around the expected return over the business cycle (reflected in the "over time" wording of the rule, see above). This leeway for discretion in the setting of annual deficits enables fiscal policy to avoid unwarranted procyclicality due to fluctuation in the value of the fund. However, in recent years the scenario envisaged under the rule has not quite played out in practice largely because of rapid rise in the return on the fund (discussed further below).

Box 2. **The relationship between Norway's wealth fund and fiscal balances**

Norway's revenues from offshore petroleum production have enabled it to both accumulate a substantial wealth fund (the Government Pension Fund Global, GPFG, aka, the 'wealth fund') while also financing fiscal deficits in the mainland economy. The net cash flow from the petroleum sector (that is revenue from the state's direct financial interest plus tax revenues) is part of the wealth fund's income along with net financial transactions related to the petroleum sector and returns on the fund's assets. Under the fiscal framework, withdrawal from the fund covers the non-oil budget deficit. The fund is invested entirely in foreign assets abroad and this offsets pressure for currency appreciation from petroleum exports (Dutch Disease). There is therefore a trade-off between fund accumulation and running mainland deficits and this is governed by the fiscal rule (see main text).

In February 2017 the government announced that fiscal budgeting would be based on a 3% expected return, instead of the 4% that had applied since the fiscal rule was introduced in 2001. The parliament unanimously concurred. This reduction in the expected return has been a good move for two reasons:

- *The new rule more strongly assures intergenerational equity.* Calculations by a government commission (the Mork Commission, see NOU, 2016) and Norges Bank (Norges Bank, 2016) suggest future real returns will average closer to 3% compared with the 4% real return that was previously the basis of the fiscal rule. The prospect of continued low returns on bonds is a prime reason. Adoption of the 3% rule therefore means stronger adherence to the principle that (over time) deficits do not imply erosion (or build up) of the country's wealth-fund assets.
- *The target deficits implied by the "4% rule" had become too large.* Rapid growth in the fund in recent years, largely due to depreciation of the kroner, meant the target deficits grew rapidly (Figure 10, Panels A and B). According to the 4% rule this argued for substantial near-term fiscal expansion, but carrying through with this would have meant excessive fiscal stimulation. Furthermore, calculations of the 4% path suggested that target deficits would start falling in the future, so any rapid fiscal expansion up to the target level could then face an untimely and tough consolidation. These arguments helped restraint fiscal expansion to a level more appropriate with the cyclical position of the economy. There was some discussion (for instance, in the previous *Survey*) about the adoption of a supplementary rule to help guide fiscal policy over the medium term. The 3% rule has obviated the need for such measures. As shown in Figure 10, Panel C, it has usefully brought the target deficit much closer to current deficit levels, thus resolving tension (at least temporarily) between the fiscal rule and cyclical concerns.

Now that the actual and the target deficits are more aligned, the fiscal rule should operate more as intended, with the structural deficit fluctuating around the target value and reflecting the appropriate fiscal impulse for the cyclical position of the economy. The "over time" framing of the rule provides for a flexible and discretionary approach. This approach will probably work well, but if it proves inadequate then more precision on the fluctuations could be considered.

Importantly for government budgeting, the change to the 3% rule implies a switch to a neutral fiscal stance, or possibly even a contractionary one in the coming years. Between 2012 and 2016 the non-oil structural deficit increased, on average, by 0.6 percentage points of mainland GDP each year (Figure 5). Keeping the deficit in line with the 3% rule and given that business-cycle upswing is underway suggests an end to such fiscal expansion. Furthermore, given the inadvisability of containing deficits through tax hikes, especially in the Norwegian context, keeping to the 3% path will require an unfamiliar degree of belt-tightening in public spending, in particular reducing room for new spending initiatives (discussed further below).

The wealth fund has itself been the subject of some policy attention. The proportion of shares in the fund benchmark is to be increased from 62.5 to 70% (with a corresponding fall in the share of fixed-income assets). In addition, as discussed above, a commission examining the central bank's role and responsibilities favours a reform in which management of the fund would be transferred from Norges Bank to a new entity headed by a government-appointed board. This could potentially enhance the depth of expertise and specialisation in fund management. Clearly, the success of such a reorganisation depends whether governance

Figure 10. **Developments in the value of the fund and in structural non-oil deficits**

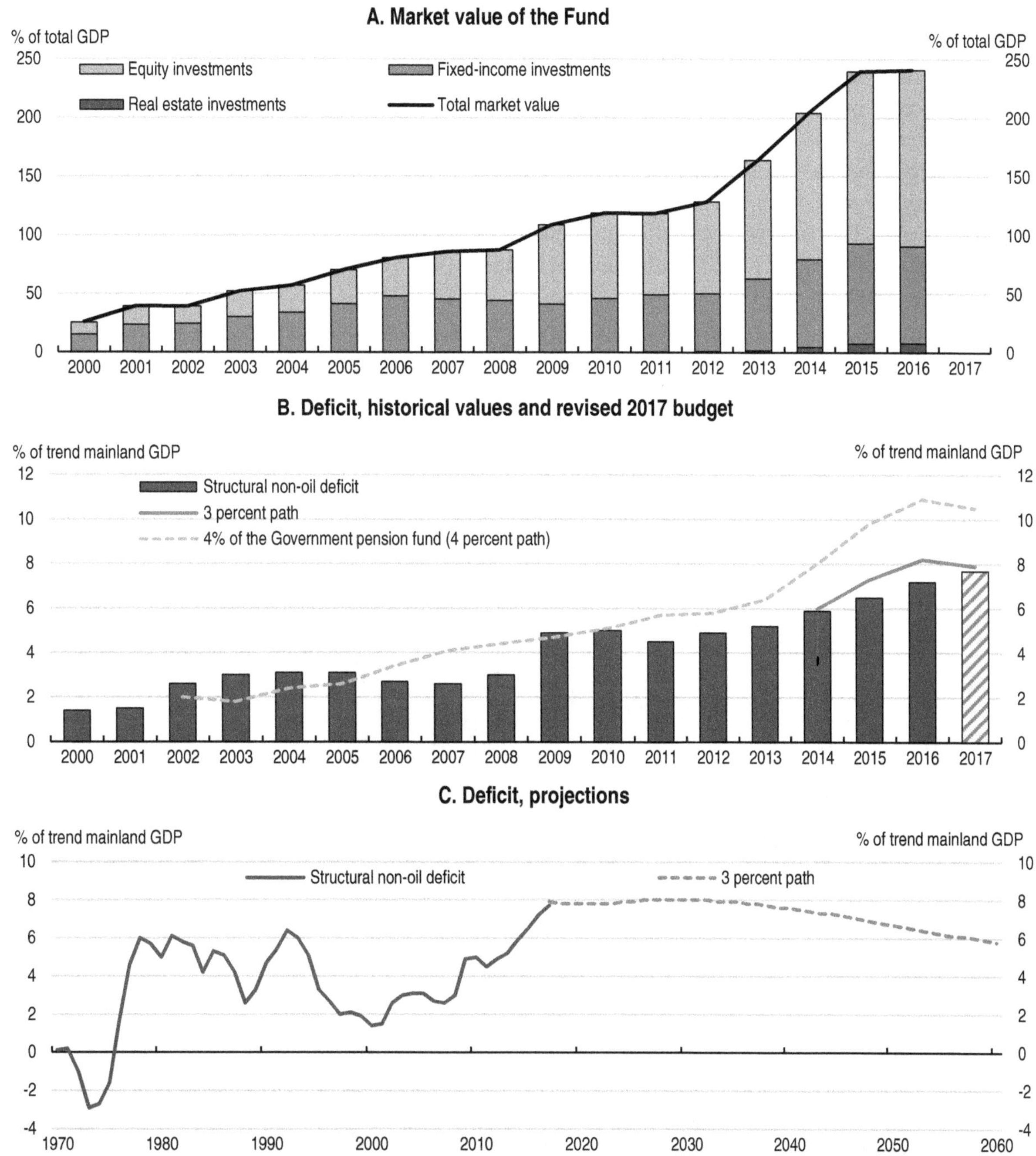

Source: Ministry of finance, 2017 revised budget; and Norges Bank Investment Management (NBIM).

StatLink http://dx.doi.org/10.1787/888933638676

risks are correctly identified and dealt with appropriately. The commission rightly identifies that removing the fund management from the bank potentially exposes it to greater pressure to shift away from the practices and principles of the fund. Because of this, the commission recommends that the role and objectives of the fund are embodied in legislation. Overall, there is much merit in the creation of a separate body to manage the wealth fund. Nonetheless, such a move needs to be approached with caution given the challenges of identifying unintended consequences from new governance structures.

Avenues for more effective public spending remain substantial

Comprehensive public services and investment are integral to Norway's socio-economic model. Public expenditure is equivalent to just under 60% of mainland GDP and fiscal revenues, even net of property income are also high in international comparison (Figure 11). Outcomes in public services are generally of good quality, comparing reasonably with other countries. However, efficiency continues to be a challenge. Despite countervailing mechanisms to ensure value for money in public spending and to control drawdown of resource wealth, more expensive options tend to be chosen and reform to existing systems is often slow. Past *Surveys* have, for instance, identified shortfalls in policy efficiency in sickness and disability benefit (OECD, 2010), higher education (OECD, 2016) and in agricultural support (OECD, 2016).

With the tighter budgeting implied by the 3% fiscal rule (see discussion above) budget constraints are set to harden, especially if a firm line is maintained on avoiding tax increases (or, indeed, continuing tax cuts). The challenge will be to ensure gains in public-spending

Figure 11. **General-government expenditure and revenue**

2016 or latest year available

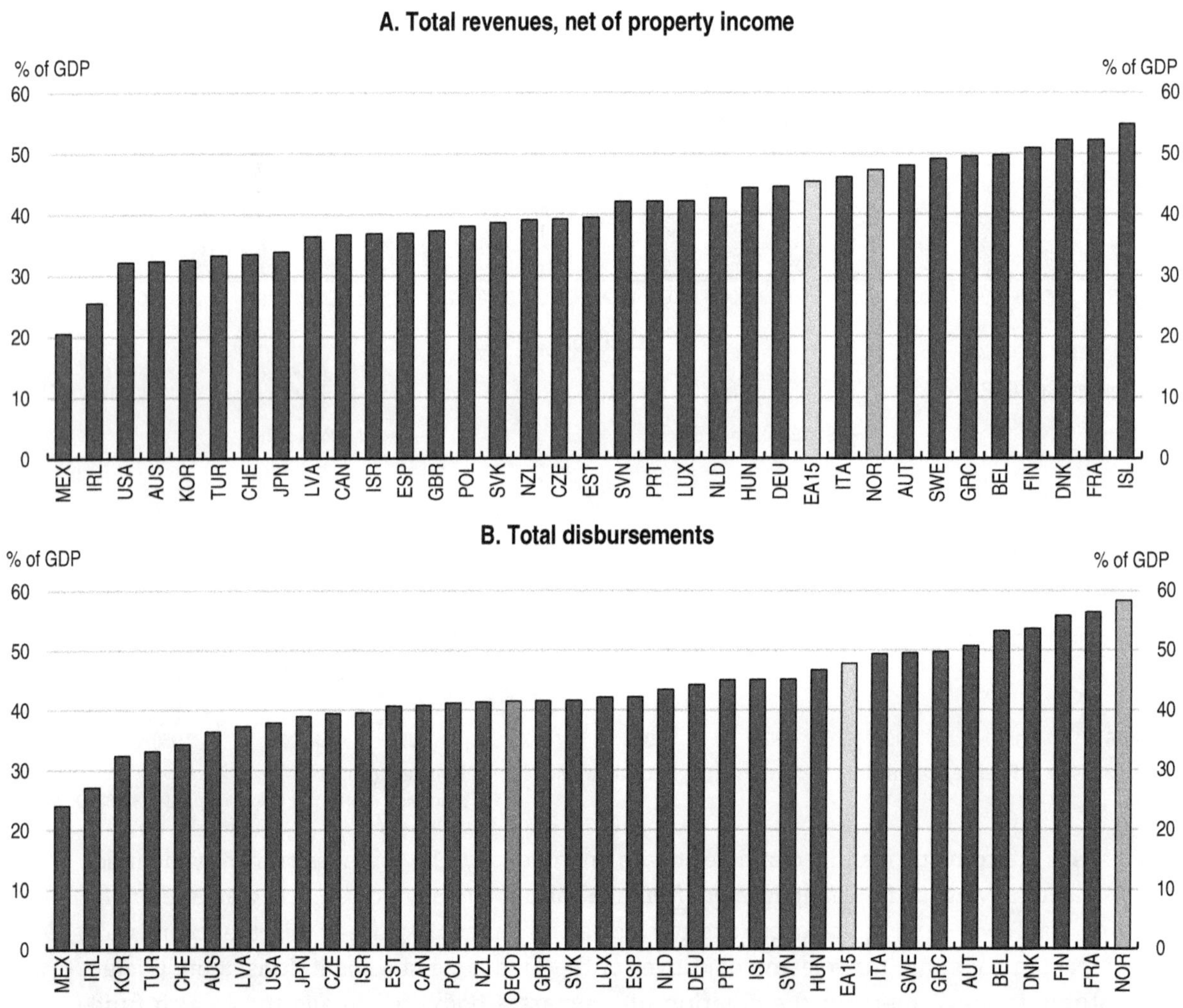

Note: Norway Total mainland receipts minus mainland property income, as % of mainland GDP; Total disbursements as % of mainland GDP.
Source: *OECD Analytical Database.*

StatLink http://dx.doi.org/10.1787/888933638695

efficiency so that room for new spending initiatives is preserved. Norway's "efficiency dividend" mechanism, operating since 2015, is well suited to addressing this issue. The dividends are part of a wider programme to encourage productivity gains in central government. The "dividend" is generated by lowering budget allocations for current expenditure to ministries and agencies by a small percentage, the principle being that there is headroom for public-service efficiency gains and that the reduced allocation prompts management to exploit them. In government budget proposals the dividend has always been set at 0.5% but in every year so far, this figure been increased following parliamentary budget negotiations. For instance, the dividend was set at 0.8% in the finalised budget for 2017. The proceeds of the dividends are pooled and used to fund new policy reforms or high-priority spending or tax measures. The mechanism should be maintained in the coming years to help create space for policy initiatives.

Other initiatives to improve budgeting and public-spending efficiency include the establishment of an advisory service for government agencies engaged in ICT projects (the Digitalisation Council, established in 2016), and a new body that scrutinises new laws and regulations with a view to minimising the impact on business (the Better Regulation Council). Establishment of these bodies reflects a multi-agency approach to budget discipline and scrutiny, and one reason why in a recent (re) assessment the authorities have concluded against establishing an independent public-efficiency unit (this has long been discussed in Norway).

Introduction of a medium-term expenditure framework could prove a useful addition to the budgeting system, helping spending stay on track under the 3% rule. This has long been suggested by OECD *Surveys* and there has been extensive consideration of such frameworks in a government-initiated commission that reported in 2015 (the Børmer Commission, NOU, 2015a). The commission recommended more comprehensive multi-annual budget projections and steps in this direction were included in the 2017 budget documentation. The commission, however, did not find merit for stronger multi-year guidance. It argued multi-annual appropriations to individual ministries and government agencies would not be helpful in the Norwegian context. It also argued that aggregate multi-annual expenditure ceilings, which have been the recommendation of past *Surveys*, would not be beneficial. While the commission's analysis has much merit, introduction of a medium-term expenditure framework should not be discounted completely as a policy option. The case for ceilings may well emerge, for instance if the risk of government resorting to tax-raising measures to achieve deficit goals increases.

Greater use should be made of regular spending reviews as a means of identifying and motivating opportunities for efficiency gain in public services. One approach would be to introduce a permanent fiscal council, along the lines seen in a number of other countries. Given Norway's fiscal experience of recent years, and outlook under the adjusted fiscal rule, a council with a strong focus on *ex post* evaluation on the expenditure side of the budget could be particularly useful. Alternatively, if the existing structure of institutional oversight (for instance, that provided by the Auditor General) is considered sufficiently comprehensive then greater use of ad hoc reviews of public spending could be pursued.

Inefficiencies in transport-infrastructure investment

Transport infrastructure is often costly with investment and returns spanning many years. Norway has long been investing heavily in this area and more so in recent years. The challenges in investing in transport in Norway include long distances, mountainous terrain and sparsely populated areas. In addition the long land border with Sweden involves cooperation on transport issues. Civilian public-sector investment has averaged 4.5% of GDP since the mid-1990s, one of the highest levels of investment in the OECD (Figure 12). Ensuring good selection of projects and cost-effective implementation is important. Transport-infrastructure investment accounts for a substantial proportion of public investment and Chapter 2 of this *Survey* takes an in-depth look the processes whereby infrastructure projects are selected and implemented.

Figure 12. **Norway has long had a substantial level of public investment**

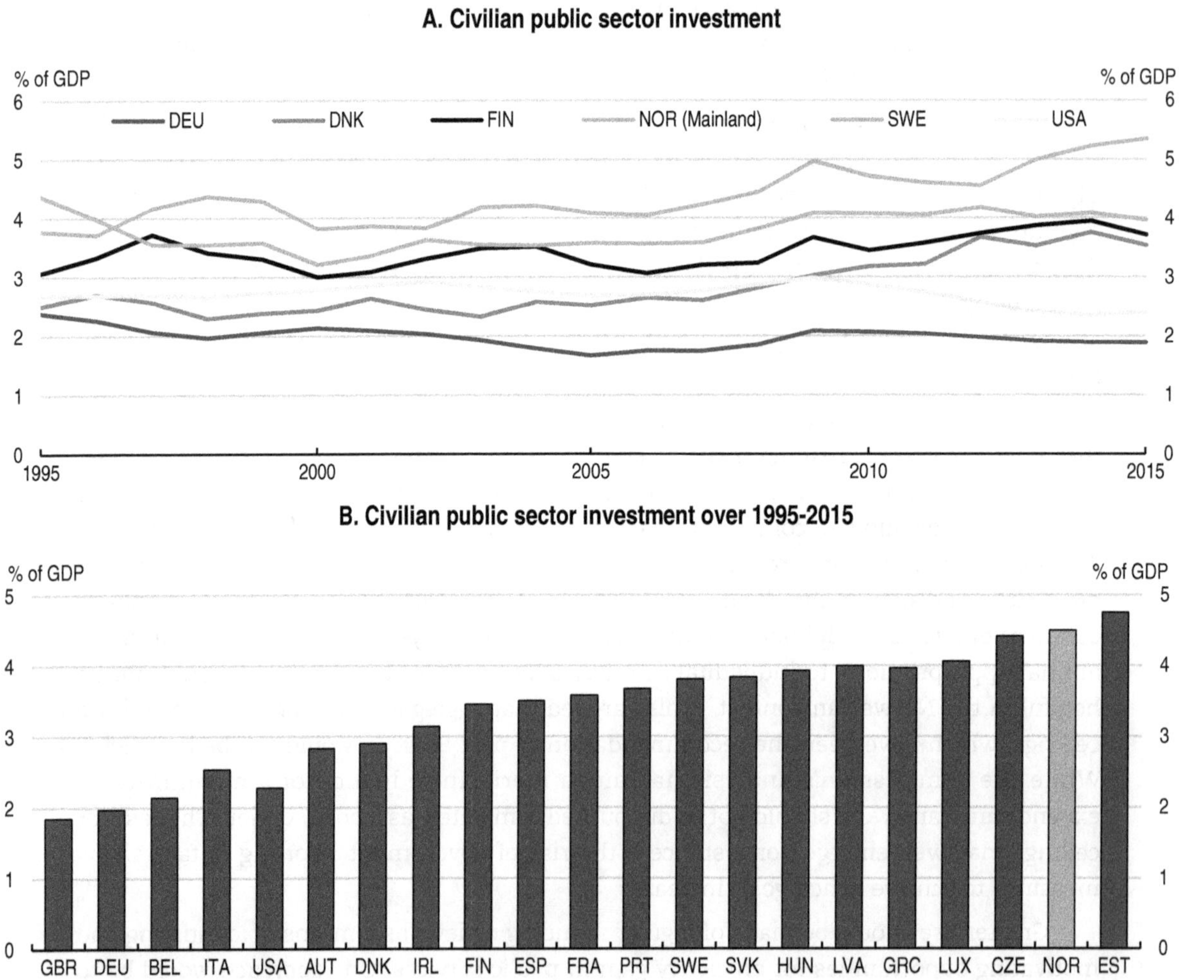

Source: OECD National Accounts Database.

StatLink http://dx.doi.org/10.1787/888933638714

There is room to improve the planning and decision making process, most importantly for large-scale projects. Governance has been improved with the recent establishment of two new management companies for road and rail infrastructure, which brings greater independence to infrastructure management. Yet challenges remain, in particular it is widely held that transport infrastructure projects could be better selected and cost less.

To date, major transport infrastructure projects have been launched via four-year rolling "National Transport Plans". The latest plan is different; it has a 12-year planning period split into two 6-year phases. This may imply the plan will be rolled over after 6 years; however this has yet to be decided on. Each transport plan contains a shortlist of projects. The process of compiling these shortlists begins with a "long list" with projects put forward by regional authorities as well as central government and the transport agencies. The transport agencies then deliver a planning proposal to the Ministry of Transport and Communications. Before projects are suggested for inclusion in the National Transport Plan by the transport agencies they pass through an appraisal process that assesses different solutions to the infrastructure problem being addressed. The resulting choice is then checked by an external quality assessment process. These assessments are then made available to the politicians responsible for selecting projects for the shortlists. There are two key issues:

- As project proposals are planned they often end up "gold plated", i.e. the proposals often switch to more expensive construction options, or additional features are added. This does not become apparent until projects pass through the internal cost-benefit analysis and quality assessment. Cheaper options are then seldom chosen in the final selection process.
- The projects shortlisted for the National Transport Plan have traditionally not always been the most highly ranked in the economic assessments and quality assessment. Politics often dominates the selection and the scope of spending gets expanded by projects with weak cost benefit results. This may be amplified by timing. By tradition, the planning cycle has been timed so that the shortlist is always drawn up in political negotiation within the government coalition of the day towards the end of its term of office, therefore in the run-up to an election (government terms are fixed at four-year intervals).

There is welcome recognition of these problems among many policymakers and a desire to fix them. One positive step already taken is the intention to have six year phases. This implies that the final shortlist may be drawn up half way through a government's term of office, which ought to depoliticise project selection, at least to some extent. However, the next rolling of the plan is not yet decided. The latest transport plan also endeavours to raise the profile of economic analysis. Chapter 2 recommends further steps follow the following themes:

- Strengthening of top-down influence in the planning process, such as in metropolitan areas to strengthen co-ordination across municipalities.
- Continue refining CBA techniques and coverage with a view to strengthening accuracy, credibility and scope, especially as regards economic benefits that are difficult to monetise.
- Strengthen the role of economic-efficiency considerations in project selection. Chapter 2, for instance, suggests taking further steps to deal with cost increases during the planning phase. For instance, in Denmark explicit buffers are included in the initial cost estimate.
- Reduce implementation delays and broaden *ex post* assessment. Chapter 2's recommendations include making greater use of "state-determined" planning in which central-government formulates integrated land use and transport plans for major national projects. It also recommends establishing an independent body to conduct *ex post* evaluations that complement the self-evaluations conducted by the transport agencies.

Scaling back and rebalancing taxation

In Norway general-government revenues (excluding petroleum-related) are equivalent to 45% of mainland GDP, which is among the highest shares in the OECD area (Figure 11). Commitment to comprehensive public services means comparatively high tax rates are unavoidable. Nevertheless, tax reform is feasible, especially if public-spending efficiency gains can be realised. As described in Chapter 1, recent reform has concentrated on shifting the tax mix away from direct income taxes towards indirect taxes. Income-tax reduction centres on reducing the rate of "ordinary tax", which is applied to most forms of income (including corporate income). The most prominent impact has been on corporate-income taxation (for employees there has been partial offset through increases in the progressive tax that applies to wage earnings). The rate of corporate tax is now middle ranking in OECD comparison, meanwhile income tax on households remains high (Figure 13).

Figure 13. **The corporate tax rate is now middle-ranking, personal-income tax remains high**

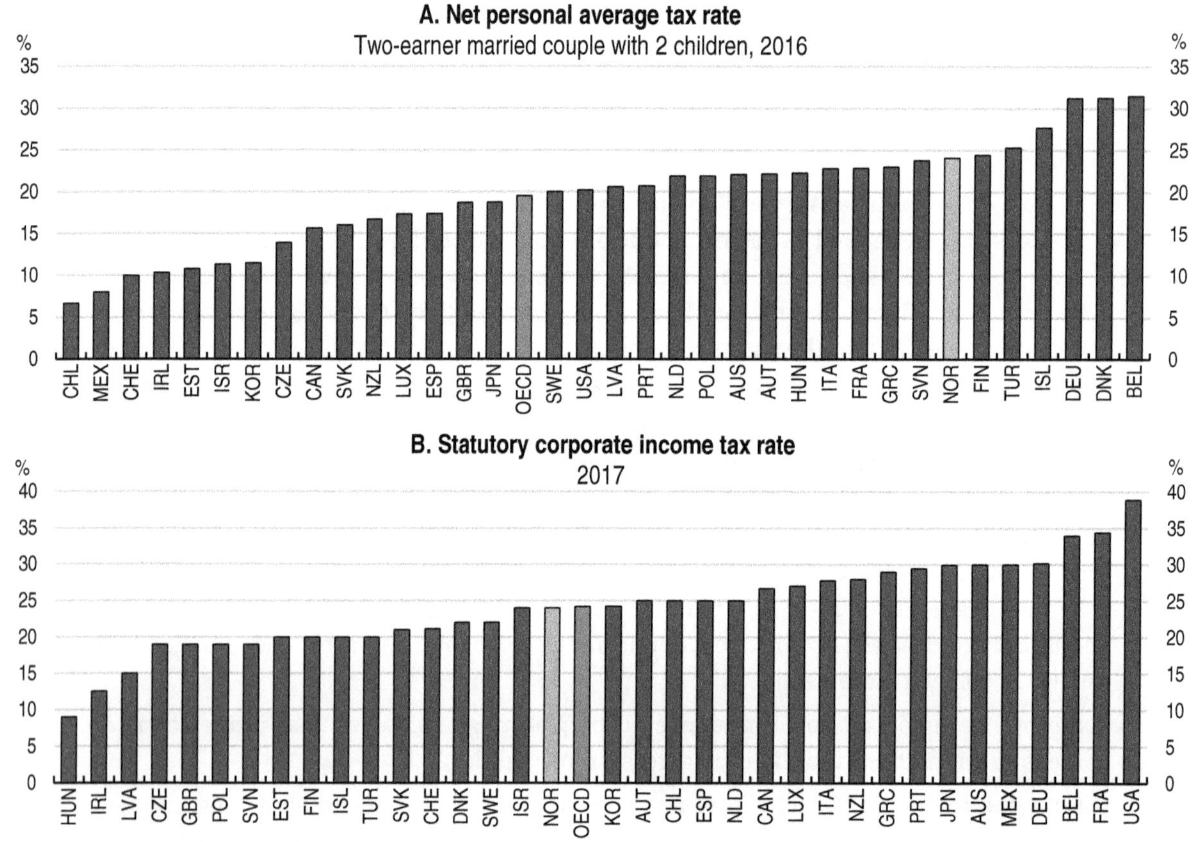

Source: OECD Tax Revenue Statistics.

StatLink http://dx.doi.org/10.1787/888933638733

Chapter 1 also underscores the benefits for further progress towards uniformity in VAT and supports the financial-activity tax that aims to substitute for the absence of VAT on financial services. The Chapter also recommends further reductions in the rates of wealth tax on non-housing assets; especially in an environment of low returns on assets, taxes on wealth can dissuade savings. Equality issues are important, and many countries use inheritance taxes to facilitate the redistribution of wealth across generations, but the effect is diminished by estate planning strategies. As explained in previous *Surveys*, an optimal approach to housing taxation involves a tax on imputed rental income, after deducting related expenses, such as interest payments. This was the approach used in Norway in the past, but the taxation of imputed rental income has been withdrawn. The Chapter draws attention to this generous tax treatment of housing.

Table 4. **Implementation of past recommendations on fiscal policy, public spending and taxation**

Recommendations	Action taken since the previous *Survey* (January 2016)
Review the "4% rule" Keep the deficit well below the fiscal rule to avoid unwanted fiscal expansion by providing guidance that sets a speed-limit on increases in the structural non-oil deficit.	The estimated real rate of return has been reduced from 4% of the value of the wealth fund to 3%. The lower rate will be first applied to the 2018 budget. The reduction in the drawdown rate obviates the need for additional guidance as recommended .
Increase public-spending efficiency, including through: • A stronger multi-annual approach to expenditure planning in the central-government budgeting • Ensuring impact analysis and cost-benefit analysis play a central role in decision making, notably in transport investment • Using more private-sector provision in public services, including in education and health care where outsourcing remains underutilised • Encouraging mergers among small municipalities.	Following recommendations of the 2015 commission on multi-year budgeting, the 2017 Budget more clearly communicates the multi-year revenue and expenditure outlook. "Efficiency dividends" continue to feature in budgeting. Establishment of the Digitalisation Council in 2016, an advisory service for government agencies engaged in ICT projects. Establishment of the Better Regulation Council, a body that scrutinises new laws and regulations with a view to minimising the impact on business. Following a central-government campaign, mergers are underway that will reduce the number of municipalities from 428 to 354 and the number of regions from 19 to 11.
Reduce taxation as a share of GDP and reduce tax distortions, including through: • Better alignment of taxation across asset classes in wealth tax and capital-gains tax, especially as regards housing assets • Further reduction in net wealth tax • Less generous tax treatment of housing. In personal-income tax, either incorporate imputed rental income or abolish mortgage interest deductibility.	Reductions in the "ordinary income" tax continue. This tax, which covers most forms of income, has been reduced further in 2017 to 24%. In VAT the 8% concessional rate was raised to 10% in 2016, narrowing the gap with other rate categories (which are 15% (food stuffs) and 25% (standard rate). Some further progress in alignment of taxation across asset classes. As of 2017: • The valuation for net wealth tax purposes of second homes is 90% and for businesses it is 80% (associated debt is valued accordingly) • There is a new valuation discount of 10% for shares and operating assets (to be increased to 20 % in 2018 (again, associated debt is valued accordingly). No major progress in reforming tax treatment of housing in personal income tax, though reduction in the tax rate on ordinary income reduces the tax value of the mortgage interest deduction.

Easing the transition toward dynamic non-oil businesses

Norway's socio-economic model requires a business sector capable of exploiting opportunities in globalised markets and supply chains while operating in a high-wage, high-tax environment (Figure 11 and Figure 14). As discussed in Chapter 1, globalisation and technological change have been re-shaping Norway in similar ways to many other advanced economies. In Norway, globalisation-related processes have so far not generated substantial socio-economic deprivation, partly thanks to comprehensive welfare support. Also, economic recovery from the oil-price drop in 2014 demonstrated Norway's capacity to absorb shocks. However, this should not give rise to complacency given the ongoing evolution of globalisation, and the prospect of declining in oil-related activities over the longer term (see Box 3). Decline in oil and gas exports are most likely to be steady but will nonetheless mark a profound change in resource allocation and in trade given these currently account for half of export earnings (Figure 15). Furthermore, Norway's high-cost environment underscores the importance of ensuring non-cost dimensions of the business environment are in very good shape. This would facilitate a reallocation of resources to high-productivity sectors that are at the top end of global supply chains. Chapter 1 of this *Survey* looks at a range of policy issues.

Box 3. **Norway's petroleum sector: Its role in the economy**

Norway's petroleum sector ("petroleum" covering both oil and natural gas) comprises offshore production facilities, and exploration activities plus a wide range of supply services, which account for most of the employment in the sector. Growth in petroleum investment and employment was particularly steep from the mid-1970s to mid-1980s and from 2005 to 2013, prior to the 2014 global-oil price fall. The supply sector is not necessarily linked to Norway's offshore fields, for instance providing services to non-Norwegian North Sea fields or oil and gas production elsewhere in the world. Also, the supply companies often provide goods and services outside the petroleum sector, which complicates estimation of the scope of petroleum-related activity. Direct employment in petroleum production only accounts for about 1% of employment but, according to Statistics Norway, 6.7% of total employment was directly or indirectly associated with the petroleum sector in 2016. Norway's south-east coast is particularly dependent on petroleum-related employment.

As underscored in the main text, the petroleum sector makes a large sizeable contribution to fiscal revenues. Net extraction revenues from production largely accrue to the state due to resource taxation and state ownership in production (the government has a 67% stake in the oil company, Statoil). In addition, corporate-tax revenues are generated by the petroleum supply industry.

The breadth of petroleum-related activity complicates assessment of future developments. Based on current output and estimates of developments in reserves, production in Norwegian fields will run out around 2060. However, new large finds are possible. Also the sector is not solely dependent Norwegian offshore production, and includes decommissioning activity, which tends to run countercyclically to developments in production and exploration.

Figure 14. **Norwegian business operates in a high-cost environment**

Hourly labour costs, 2016

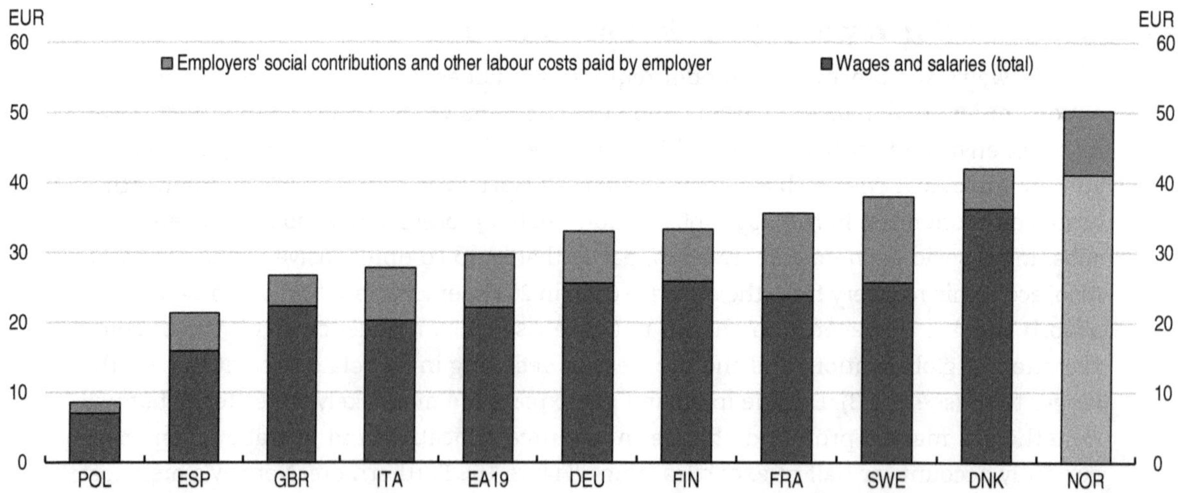

Note: Industry, construction and services (except public administration, defence, compulsory social security).
Source: Eurostat.

StatLink http://dx.doi.org/10.1787/888933638752

Figure 15. **Norway's export-market profile**

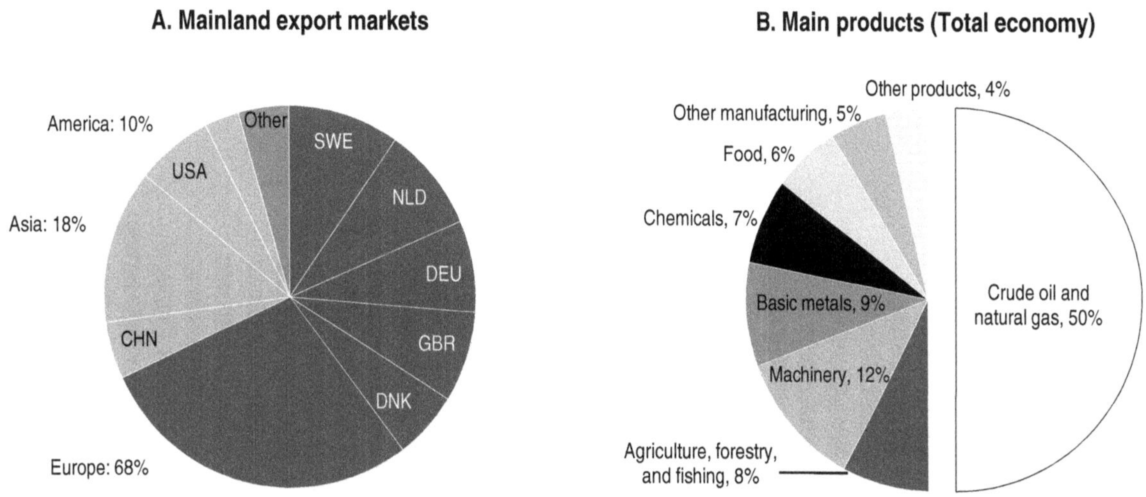

Source: Statistics Norway.

StatLink http://dx.doi.org/10.1787/888933638771

Framework conditions: avenues for improvement remain

Competitive markets can be a powerful driver of efficient resource allocation and productivity growth. Welcome attention is being paid to improving competition legislation. In particular the process for assessing business mergers has shifted away from a "total welfare" approach because it was allowing too many deals that risk limiting competition. Nevertheless, issues in the competition legislation remain. Sectoral exemptions (e.g. in agriculture) should be re-examined and the structure and conduct of supermarket chains within in the grocery supply chain has become hotly debated.

As Chapter 1 points out, state ownership of business enterprise in Norway has diminished, but is still extensive and this is reflected in Norway's scores in the OECD's Product Market Regulation Indicator and the Services Trade Restrictiveness Indicator (Figure 16). Around 11% of employees are employed in companies with partial or complete state ownership (Norwegian Ministry of Trade, Industry and Fisheries, 2016). State-ownership administration is many respects exemplary. For instance, governance guidelines generally follow accepted good practice. Also, some progress has been made in increasing the independence of the regulators of state-owned companies, though more could be done. Still, many of the state stakes are in companies operating in competitive and efficient markets where the rationale for retaining stake ownership indefinitely is weaker. It is encouraging that partial or complete sell offs continue. Chapter 1 also draws attention to other issues, in particular Norway's requirements that at least half of the board members and the manager (CEO) in corporations must be residents of Norway or the European Economic Area (EEA).

Healthy firm dynamics are also key to resource allocation and productivity growth. In Norway the processes associated with establishing and operating business in Norway are in reasonable shape. Nevertheless, new OECD data capturing the efficiency of insolvency processes indicates room for improvement (Figure 17). Time to discharge (i.e. the number of years a bankrupt person must wait until they are discharged from pre-bankruptcy indebtedness) is relatively long. Also, there are shortfalls in tools for prevention and restructuring. Some of these issues have been covered in a government-commissioned

Figure 16. **Regulatory indices on product markets and services trade point to room for improvement**

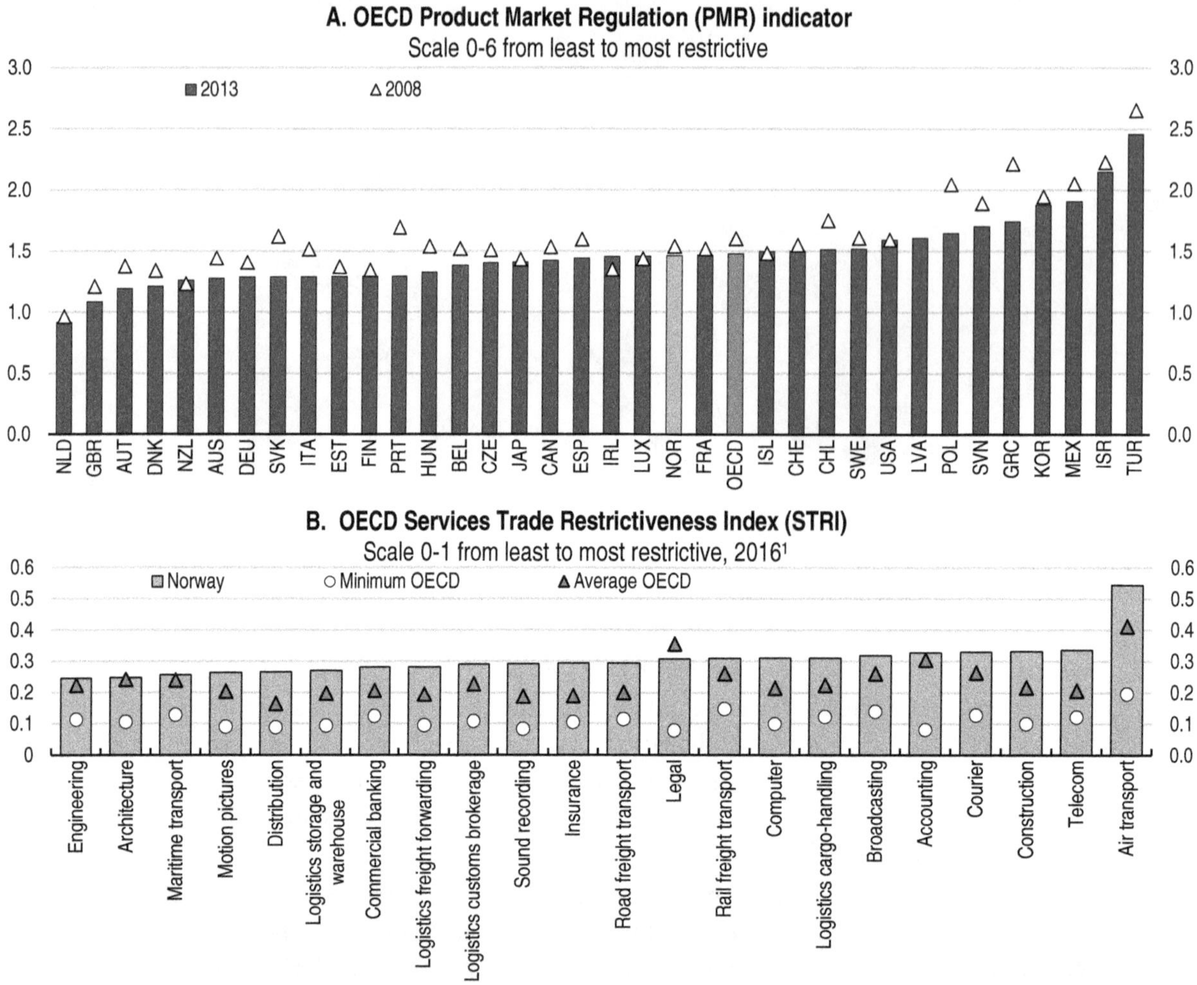

1. The index includes regulatory transparency, barriers to competition, and other discriminatory measures, restrictions on movement of people and restrictions on foreign entry. The STRI methodology takes into account different market and trade cost structures across sectors to ensure that they reflect the relative restrictiveness of each sector. Nevertheless, the indices may not be perfectly comparable across sectors. The indicators are for 2016 or the most recent year available.

Source: *OECD Product Market Regulation Database*; and OECD Services Trade Restrictiveness Index (STRI).

StatLink http://dx.doi.org/10.1787/888933638790

report that proposes changes to debt negotiation provisions ("reconstruction" provisions) in bankruptcy law. However, the government has yet to follow up on the commission's findings and work on other fronts is needed.

Targeted support for innovation

As a small open economy, much of Norway's productivity-enhancing innovation is "imported" in the form of tangible new products, machinery and equipment, or intangibles, such as software or innovation in processes. Nevertheless domestic R&D activity, and the policies to support it, has an important role to play. Norway's R&D expenditure is around 2% of GDP, much of it in the petroleum-related sector (Figure 18) while in all three of its Nordic peers, Denmark, Finland and Sweden, spending is closer to 3% of GDP. The OECD recently conducted an *Innovation Review* of Norway, which assesses the menu of support programmes

Figure 17. **The OECD's insolvency indicators suggest room for improvement in Norway**

Insolvency composite indicator, scale 0 (most effective) to 1 (least effective), 2016

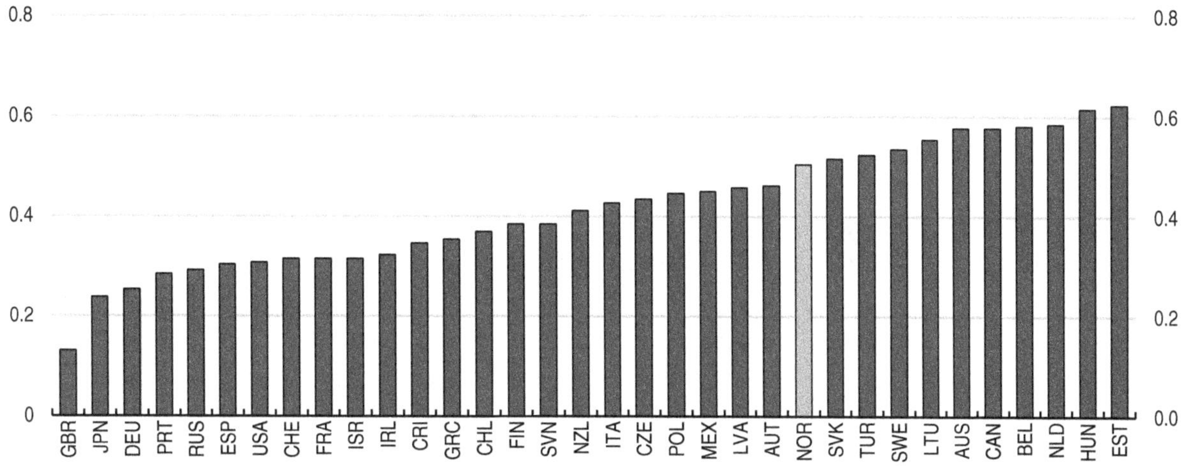

Note: The insolvency composite indicator is an unweighted average of 5 dimensions: treatment of failed entrepreneurs, prevention and streamlining, restructuring tools, and other factors.
Source: McGowan et al. (2017).

StatLink http://dx.doi.org/10.1787/888933638809

Figure 18. **Norway's R&D spending is middle ranking**

Gross domestic expenditure on R&D (GERD), 2015

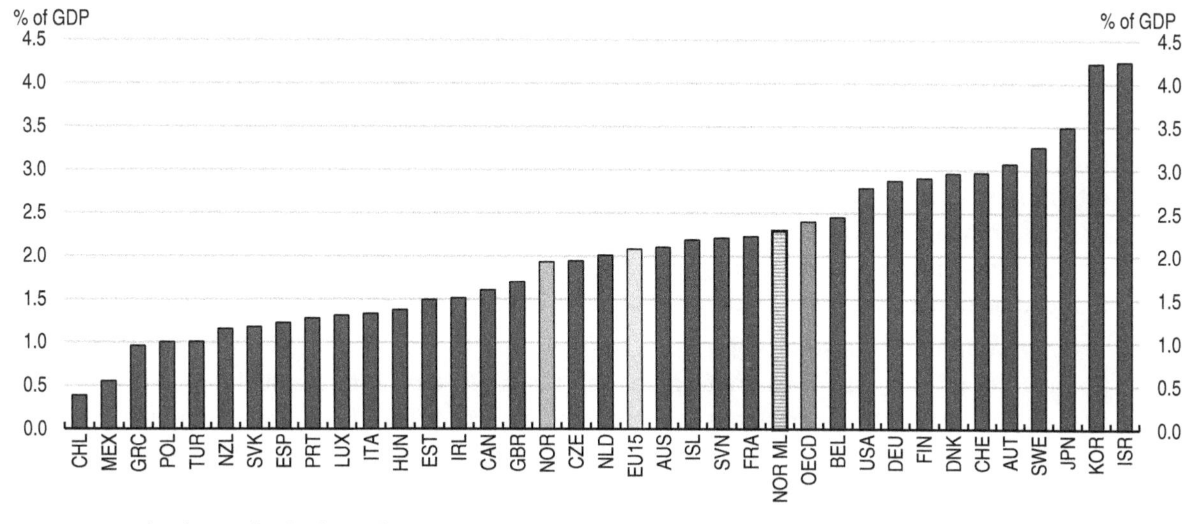

Source: *OECD Main Science and Technology Indicators Database.*

StatLink http://dx.doi.org/10.1787/888933638828

and contains extensive coverage on innovation conducted by public-research institutes and the higher education sector.

A tax-break programme (SkatteFUNN) forms the backbone of Norway's support for business innovation. The programme has strengthens, in particular it is refundable, which can help innovative enterprises at an early stage of development in particular. As elsewhere, measurement issues make the scale of impact on R&D activity uncertain. A new government-initiated impact evaluation is due to be published in 2018.

Considerable attention and fiscal resources are devoted to innovative firms. Currently, access to finance is high on the current policy agenda. Steps already taken include proposals for tax-deductability of investment in young start-up companies. Also, there are intentions to propose measures that will make share-option compensation of employees more attractive. Furthermore, a committee on access to capital is due to report in 2018, and will identify potential weak points. The policy attention to access to capital certainly has potential for useful impact, though as is the case for innovation support more widely, uncertainties in the effectiveness of measures implies that assessment processes are important for ensuring the development of a good menu of policies. More generally, it is a timely moment for a review of the full menu of innovation support measures. Public funding and the number of schemes have been expanding rapidly in recent years; a review of schemes' efficiency, and issues such as overlap between schemes, could substantially improve policy overall.

Research capacities of universities and research institutes are an important draw for business investment and scale effects from collaborative research networks can generate high-productivity growth clusters. Mergers underway in the higher education sector (which comprises universities and more vocationally oriented "university colleges") represent a substantial move towards scaling up and consolidating Norway's academic research capacities. There now only 21 higher-education providers compared with 33 previously. Structural change within the merged institutions, in particular the amalgamation of faculties, is progressing at varying speeds and the full impact of the reform will take some time to emerge. More mergers would be welcome in Norway's comparatively large research-institute sector too. Reforms to funding are being used re-shaped research incentives in both the higher-education and research-institute sectors, but more could be done. In higher education, a roll out of performance agreements is underway that will also see further alteration of research incentives.

Market disruption: taxi-market reform has proved particularly challenging

In Norway, new business models based on internet platforms in personal transport (e.g. Uber) and short-term accommodation (e.g. AirBnB) have received the most policy attention to date. Policy needs to embrace disruption, though not unconditionally. New business models for providing goods and services often improve household welfare in terms of consumption, but can bring downsides for consumers and employees, and can be founded on undesirable exploitation of loopholes in regulation or taxation.

A government-sponsored committee has assessed the "sharing economy", including taxi-market reform, which has not progressed far in Norway. Services such as Uber are available in parts of the country but in most cases paid rides are illegal due to compulsory licencing for taxi services. Uber ceased its ride-sharing service UberPop in Norway as of 30 October 2017, pointing to restrictive Norwegian taxi regulation as discriminatory and curbing its business model. The number of taxi licences is set by county governments, generating supply-demand mismatch. The taxi-licencing system has not moved with the times in other respects. For instance, driver regulations in some localities still include geographical-knowledge requirements. Replacement of the current taxi-licencing system with less restrictive regulation to address availability and consumer protection would be welcome.

New forms of accommodation have been less contentious. Short-term rentals via internet platforms, such as Airbnb, occupy a small but growing segment of the market. As of 2015, Airbnb accounted for nearly 2% of the total number of overnight stays (NOU, 2017). According to the "sharing economy" committee, rentals do not face significant issues of legitimacy and Norway's legislation already includes provisions to protect neighbours from noise or inconvenience. However, parliament has requested amendments in housing legislation concerning short-time rentals. Negative impact on the affordability of ordinary rents has yet to emerge as a major issue and may never do so because of the predominance of owner-occupiers. Policy should help ensure a balanced development in short-term rents. Policy can ensure good information on the rules and regulations.

As elsewhere, the wave of internet-platform businesses has generated some tax issues. Income of private home rentals is tax-exempt if less than half the property (by rental value) is hired out. In the 2018 finance bill, the government proposes to remove the exemption on short-time rentals (less than 30 days). Also, benefits from income-tax exemptions and uncertainties in the definitional boundary between private and commercial operation for tax purposes have come to the fore. The tax authorities are considering a disclosure duty for data-holders who enable or facilitate rentals or paid services via digital platforms. Private-accommodation rental is not subject to VAT. More generally, the prevalence of small-scale operators in disruption raises the question of VAT thresholds, which in Norway are relatively low. The tax authorities have creditably improved information for the increasing numbers of individuals in "sharing economy" activities.

Table 5. **Implementation of past recommendations on improving business conditions**

Recommendations	Action taken since the previous *Survey* (January 2016)
Improve framework conditions for business activity	
Address innovation and technology issues, including through: • Continued use of a competitive-bid approach for research grants and promoting framework conditions for clusters • Promotion of entrepreneurial skills such as project planning and STEM skills • Encouraging Technology Transfer Offices in universities • Strengthening the objectivity of evaluations of business-support programmes (notably innovation and R&D schemes).	The 2015 Budget proposed increasing support via the core programme, SkatteFUNN. The government has launched an evaluation of policy promoting university-business linkages, including assessment of whether technology transfer offices require more powers.
Improve transport services.	Road: A new company charged with planning, construction, operation and maintenance segments of the national road network has been established. Consolidation of road-toll companies continues. More extensive use of public-private partnerships is planned. Rail. A new infrastructure management company has been established.
Ensure strong market competition	
Adjust competition legislation and enforcement, including through: • Review of the "total welfare" criterion of competition policy • Increasing the regulatory power of competition authorities.	Assessment of mergers has shifted away from the "total welfare" approach towards a "consumer" approach.
Regarding state stakes in business: • Reduce the scope and size of stakes • Improve state-owned activities governance.	The state holding in one of Norway's largest real-estate companies, Entra ASA, was reduced from around 50% to 33% in 2016.
Strengthen competition in network industries (especially postal and rail services).	Postal services. A new Act came into force in 2016 that ends Norges Posten's monopoly on letters below 50 grams, and lightens the incumbent's universal service requirements. Parliamentary approval to reduce the state stake in Telenor has been granted. Rail services. A new infrastructure management company has been established.
Reduce barriers to entry in the retail sector.	No major reform recently.
Reduce state aid and subsidies	
Reduce support for agriculture and fishing sectors, including through: • Reduced import tariffs and direct subsidies to farmers • Removal of legislative biases that favour agriculture • Encouraging diversification of economic activity in rural areas by improving general framework conditions.	Agriculture: • Measures have been taken to encourage larger scale production, including higher ceilings on production quotas • Also, the removal of protective clauses in legislation so as to free-up price setting and permit corporate ownership is in the pipeline. • Parliamentary agreed to some limited reforms in April 2017. These include commitment for some simplification in policy and regulation, and rule changes on milk quotas • The parliament has voted to phase out export subsidies for agricultural products by 2020.

Retaining high labour-force participation and raising skills are key for Norway's future

A strong focus on employment in policy, and by society, is a central pillar of Norway's socio- economic model. High rates of employment ensure a strong supply of labour for business but are also core to Norway's low rates of poverty and inequality. Most notably, Norway's employment rate among women, a little below 75%, is nearly 15 percentage points above the OECD average and just a few percentage points below that of men (Figure 19). Combining family life and work for both men and women is facilitated by subsidised child care, working time flexibility and paid parental leave. Also Norway has been a leader in promoting women's career progression. For instance it was among the first countries to introduce women-on-boards rules (see 2016 *Survey*).

Figure 19. **Norway's employment rates remain high**

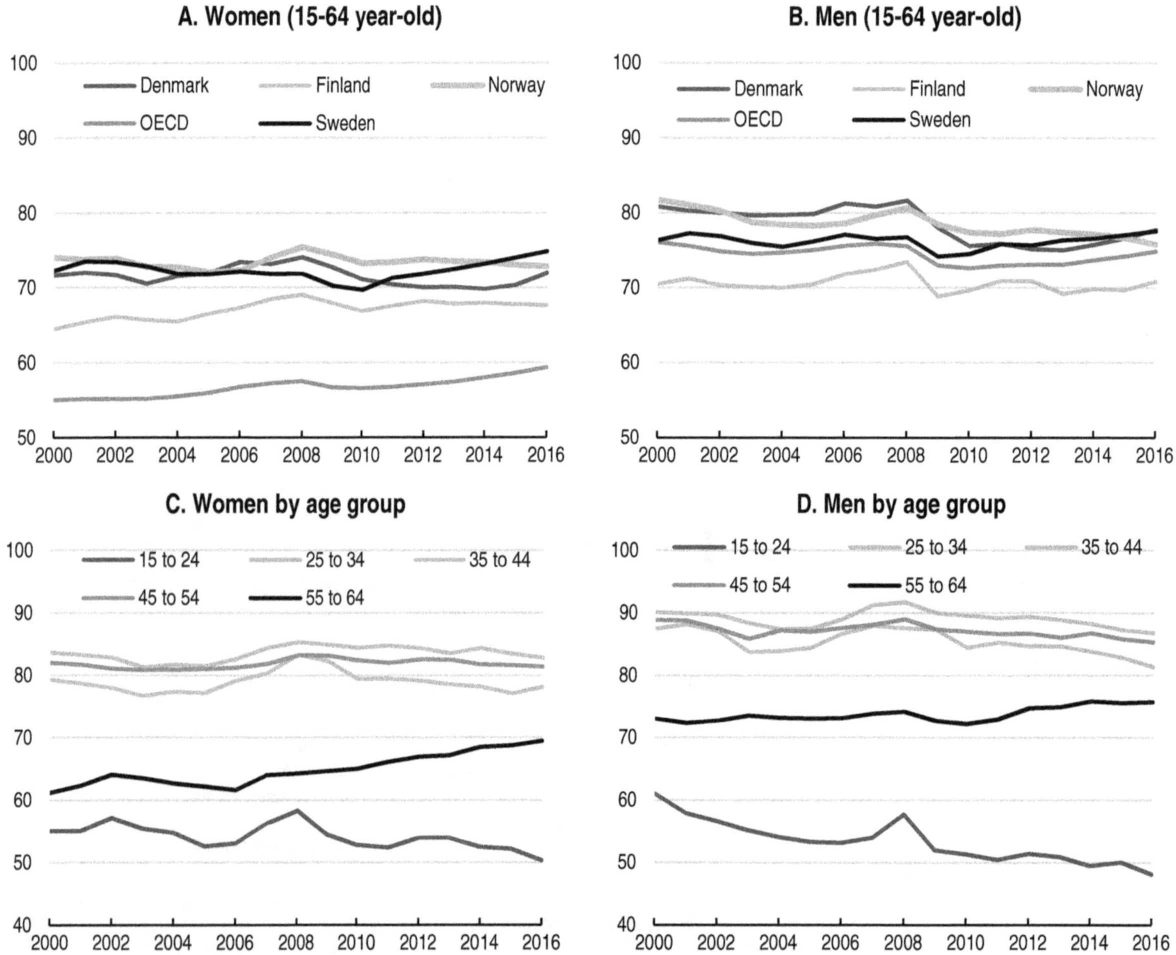

Source: OECD Labour Force Statistics.

StatLink http://dx.doi.org/10.1787/888933638847

Early retirement via sickness and disability system is not yet fully resolved

Norway's sickness and disability support system has, like those in a number of countries, become a channel for early retirement and remains a core issue for labour-market reform. As described in Chapter 1, individuals typically transition from sick leave to a rehabilitation-type benefit (the Work Assessment Allowance) and then to the national-insurance funded Disability Benefit. The share of persons receiving the Allowance has declined and also the Disability Benefit rates among older cohorts has dropped. Nevertheless, recipiency remains high, for instance nearly 30% of 50 to 67 year-olds receive Disability Benefit payments. Also, there has been an increase in the share of Disability Benefits among young and middle-aged cohorts.

Recent measures include piloting of a new medical assessment in sick leave, and from 1 January 2018 several changes in the Work Assessment Allowance will be implemented. Among others, the main rule regarding the maximum possible period of receiving the Allowance will be shortened from four to three years. Also people receiving the Allowance will be followed up more closely with an aim to increase the transition back to work. Future reform should consider prolonging the employer-financed phase of sick leave, reducing the generosity of payment and tightening medical assessment procedures, especially through more "third party" medical assessment. In addition, the long-standing series of agreements between the government, employers and unions, (the Inclusive Working Life Agreements) should be more ambitious (in particular as regards public-sector employees) as their impact on reducing sickness leave to date has not been obvious.

Declining employment rates among young and middle-age groups should be kept on watch

The rising numbers of Disability Benefit recipients among young and middle-aged cohorts almost certainly has some connection with the shallow decline in employment to population ratios and labour-force participation rates in these age groups (Figures 19). These declines have attracted attention, for instance a report for Norway's tripartite inclusive workplace ("IA") agreement discusses them at length (Inkluderende Arbeidsliv, 2017) and recent IMF assessment discusses them also (IMF 2017). Several factors are at play, some of little policy concern. The developments are probably, in part, cyclical, reflecting slowing growth in economic activity of recent years, such that resurgence in growth will bring partial reversal. Also the trends may partially reflect continuing shift in household arrangements, for instance as men extend child-caring roles. Among young cohorts, some of the employment-rate decline reflects extension of time spent in education. Yet there may also be worrying processes at work. Falling employment rates in young cohorts may partly reflect failure of education to keep pace with changing workforce demands. Prolonged time out of work can make re-integration harder as skills and work habits atrophy and as individuals grow accustomed to alternative ways of providing for themselves and their families. Some immigrant communities are particularly vulnerable to these problems due to weak education outcomes and concentration of employment in cyclically-sensitive and low-skill sectors (Includerende Arbeidsliv, 2017), thus widening economic and social divides (though, in general, Norway's immigrant communities are comparatively well integrated according to indicators in the OECDs *Indicators of Immigrant Integration*, OECD, 2015).

Vocational education is core to raising the supply of skills and preventing low-income

International tests of learning and skills tend typically show Norway as middle-ranking compared with other developed economies. There appears to be sustained progress in PISA's reading component (Figure 20) and the scores for mathematics and science increased between the 2012 and 2015. Nevertheless, Norway's scores remain around average. The middle-ranking performance is confirmed in the PIAAC tests of adult skills (Figure 20). As

Figure 20. **Norway's education and skills performance**

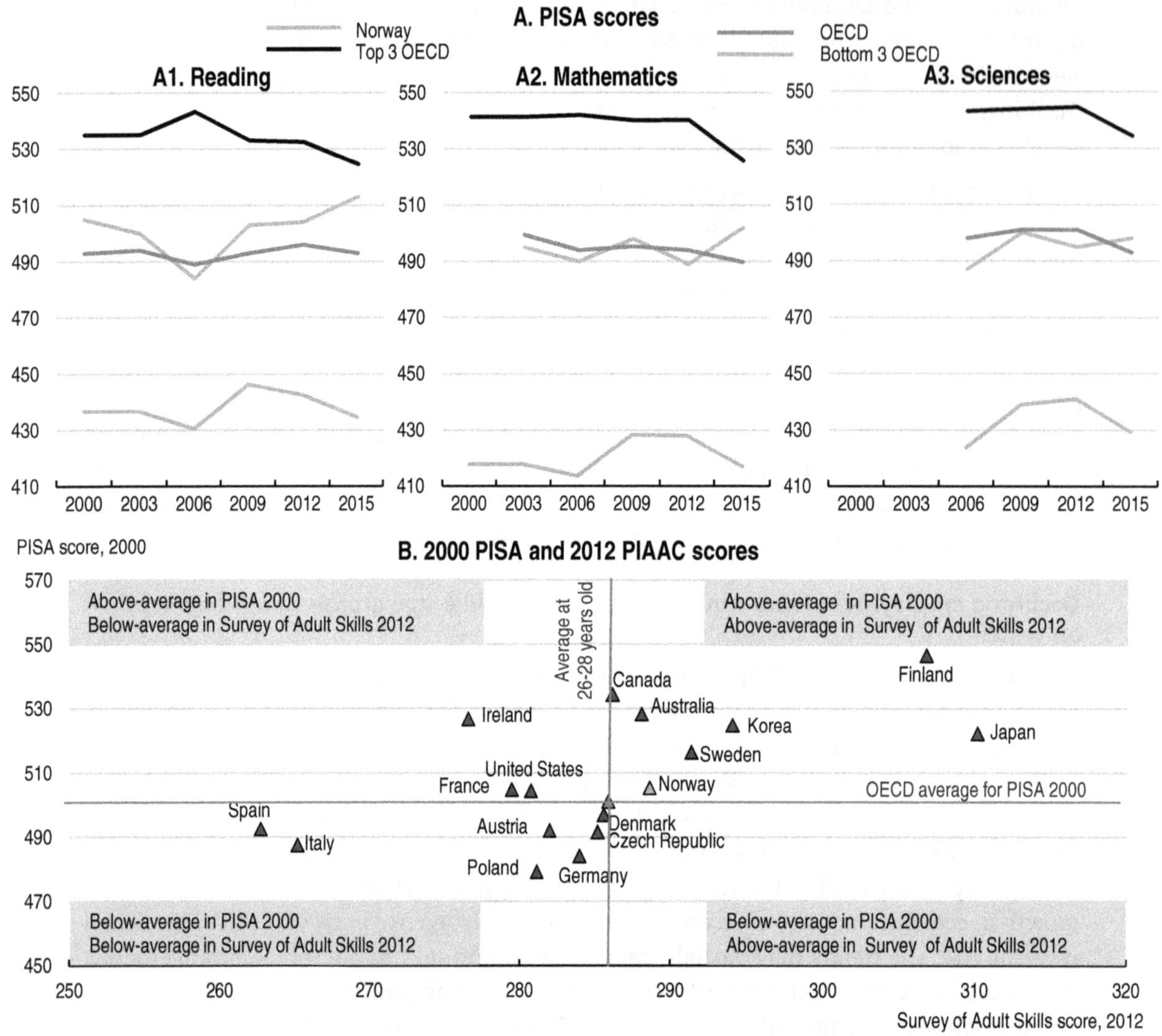

Source: OECD, *PISA 2000-2015 Databases*; and *Survey of Adult Skills* (PIAAC) (2012).

StatLink http://dx.doi.org/10.1787/888933638866

underscored in previous *Surveys*, Norway's rankings are particularly concerning given that public spending on education is comparatively high and given the importance of skills in sustaining Norway's high-income economy.

Globalisation further reinforces the importance of encouraging and facilitating skill-based education. The markets for jobs requiring little or no post-compulsory education are shrinking and are increasingly in areas where there is a strong supply of workers with comparatively low reservation wages (in Norway's case often via labour migration connected to membership of the European Economic Area). The continuous policy effort required to bring about concrete change to education needs to be maintained at all levels (see Table 6), but especially so in vocational education as this has the greatest capacity to provide marketable skills for those that might otherwise be on low-skill, low-wage trajectories.

Shortages of apprenticeship places are a key problem in vocational education. Most vocational training in Norway is provided by upper-secondary schools through the "professional" (*yrkesfag*) stream (the other track, the "general" stream *studiespesialisering* principally channels students into degree-level tertiary education). Apprenticeship courses are a central pillar of the *yrkesfag* stream, generally comprising two years study followed by two years placement with an employer. Yet around one third of students fail to find a placement (Norwegian Directorate for Education and Training, 2014) and this contributes to a long-standing concern of high rates of drop out from vocational education. The most recent initiative encouraging employers to offer apprenticeships, the "social contact for VET", met with partial success but more action is required. OECD analysis points to steeply

Table 6. **Implementation of past recommendations on human capital, jobs and welfare**

Recommendations	Action taken since the previous *Survey* (January 2016)
Improve education	
In primary and secondary education reform, consider: • Reduction in the number of schools • Making more data on school performance publically available • Reform of the teaching profession including: stricter selection and graduation criteria, more training, better structured career paths and wider use of performance-related pay.	Roll out of a programme to improve the status and quality of teachers continues. The programme includes increased support for teachers' continued education and the introduction of 5-year master's-level degree for new entrants to the profession. Curriculum overhaul is underway in primary and secondary schooling. The reform, *inter alia*, aims to clarify values and expectations and school responsibilities and facilitate in-depth learning. Reform to school management is underway. A white paper, sanctioned by parliament, includes recommendations for a system of in-service teacher training, stronger support for underperforming schools and enhanced early intervention for pupils.
In higher education: • Continue to promote mergers among providers • Pursue plans to include the graduation rates in the formula for performance-based funding • Further target incentives and financial support to students who complete their courses on time • Steer student choices, for instance, via loan discounts for subjects with high demand.	Significant progress on the merger process; most of the intended mergers have been completed. A three-phase performance-agreement process is underway: pilot agreements in five institutions in 2017, a further five agreements in 2018 and the remaining institutions in 2019. Policy efforts to improve the quality of higher education teaching have intensified with publication of a white paper in early 2017 that proposes channels for reform. More broadly a campaign focusing on skills is underway, including launch of the Strategy for Skills Policy 2017-21 in early 2017, which has widespread support from ministries and stakeholders.
Encourage labour-market participation	
Reduce work disincentives in the unemployment insurance system.	No major reform.
Reduce sick leave and tighten disability schemes, *inter alia* consider: • Lowering the replacement rate for long-term sickness absence • Clearer guidelines on disability assessment to general practitioners and monitor compliance.	Sickness leave: new medical assessment trialled, new guidance for doctors on the length of sick leave, stricter implementation of activation requirements (see Chapter 1 for more detail). Work Assessment Allowance (AAP): Several changes will be implemented from 1 January 2018 with an aim to increase the transition back to work. Among others the maximum period of receiving the benefit will be shortened and also there will be closer follow-up of recipients. Disability Benefit: no further reform since the major changes of 2015.
Remove biases favouring early retirement the old-age pension system.	No major reform.
Increase labour-market flexibility	
Increase flexibility in wage setting.	No major reform.
Lighten employment regulation.	No major reform.
Enhance efficiency of job placement services and active labour market policies (ALMP).	No major reform, though in 2017 a new initiative for youth was introduced. The initiative ensures that persons under the age of 30 years who after eight weeks of unemployment are not in a job, education or participating in labour market programmes, are provided with a work-oriented alternative.
Improve Health Care	
Past Surveys have focussed on aspects of financing and have suggested: • Re-structuring activity-based (including Diagnosis Related Groups, DRG) financing to avoid excessive incentives for low-priority activities • Greater use of co-payments by patients.	No major reform.

rising wage costs over the course of apprenticeships. This is likely not the only driver of the apprenticeship-place shortage, however. Shortfalls in the attributes sought by employers among apprentices may also be a factor, suggesting further adjustment to vocational (and earlier) education may be required.

Tackling environmental issues

Norway's carbon intensity of per unit of GDP is less than half the OECD average, yet per capita intensity is closer to the average. Also, Norway's carbon footprint is augmented more than in most countries by emissions embodied in imports (Figure 21, Panel A). Oil and gas production, along with chemical processes in aluminium production and alloys, account for a substantial share of greenhouse-gas emissions. Meanwhile, abundant hydropower means practically zero emissions from electricity production (Panel B). Other dimensions of air quality are generally good (Panel C). Norway's waste management involves comparatively little landfill and waste generation is below the OECD average (Panel D). Activity in environmentally related inventions appears somewhat below par (Panel F).

Wealth-fund management in Norway pays close attention to the environmental and social credentials of companies, where issues are often raised by the press and public. In 2016, two new ethically motivated exclusion criteria were introduced for the main wealth fund, the Government Pension Fund Global (GFPG). The first is aimed at companies whose acts or omissions, to an unacceptable degree, entail greenhouse gas emissions. The second targets mining companies and energy producers with a 30% threshold for revenues derived from, or operations based on, thermal coal.

Carbon pricing is extensive, with 80% of greenhouse-gas emissions either subject to a carbon-dioxide tax and/or included in the European Trading System (ETS). Norway's Paris commitment is to reduce greenhouse-gas emissions by at least 40% by 2030 compared with the 1990 level. Norway is in dialogue with the EU on joint fulfilment of the 2030 climate commitment. Transport and agriculture are the main emission sources in the non-ETS sector. Norway has provided wide-ranging electric-vehicle incentives, resulting in the highest number of electric vehicles per capita in the world. The incentives include exemption from VAT and registration tax, reduced annual motor vehicle tax, and free toll roads, national-road-network ferries, parking and access to bus lanes. Some of these have generated unintended consequences (e.g. congestion) and have been wound back.

Environmental taxation is a core pillar of Norway's efforts to reduce non-ETS greenhouse-gas emissions and in tackling other environmental issues. It has been given further impetus by a government appointed commission (Box 4 and NOU, 2015b), which underscores the importance of ensuring polluters take into account the damage inflicted on society and that taxation is an effective mechanism for achieving this. Some proposals from the Green Tax Commission have been followed up, for instance carbon-dioxide taxes on several items (see Table 7) have been made equivalent to those on vehicle fuels. Further efforts should be made into following the Commission's recommendations.

Integration of environmental issues in decision making has been given impetus by an expert-committee on green competiveness (Norwegian Expert Committee, 2016). The report, for instance, emphasises retaining business-sector competitiveness while pursuing environmental goals.

Figure 21. **Environment indicators**

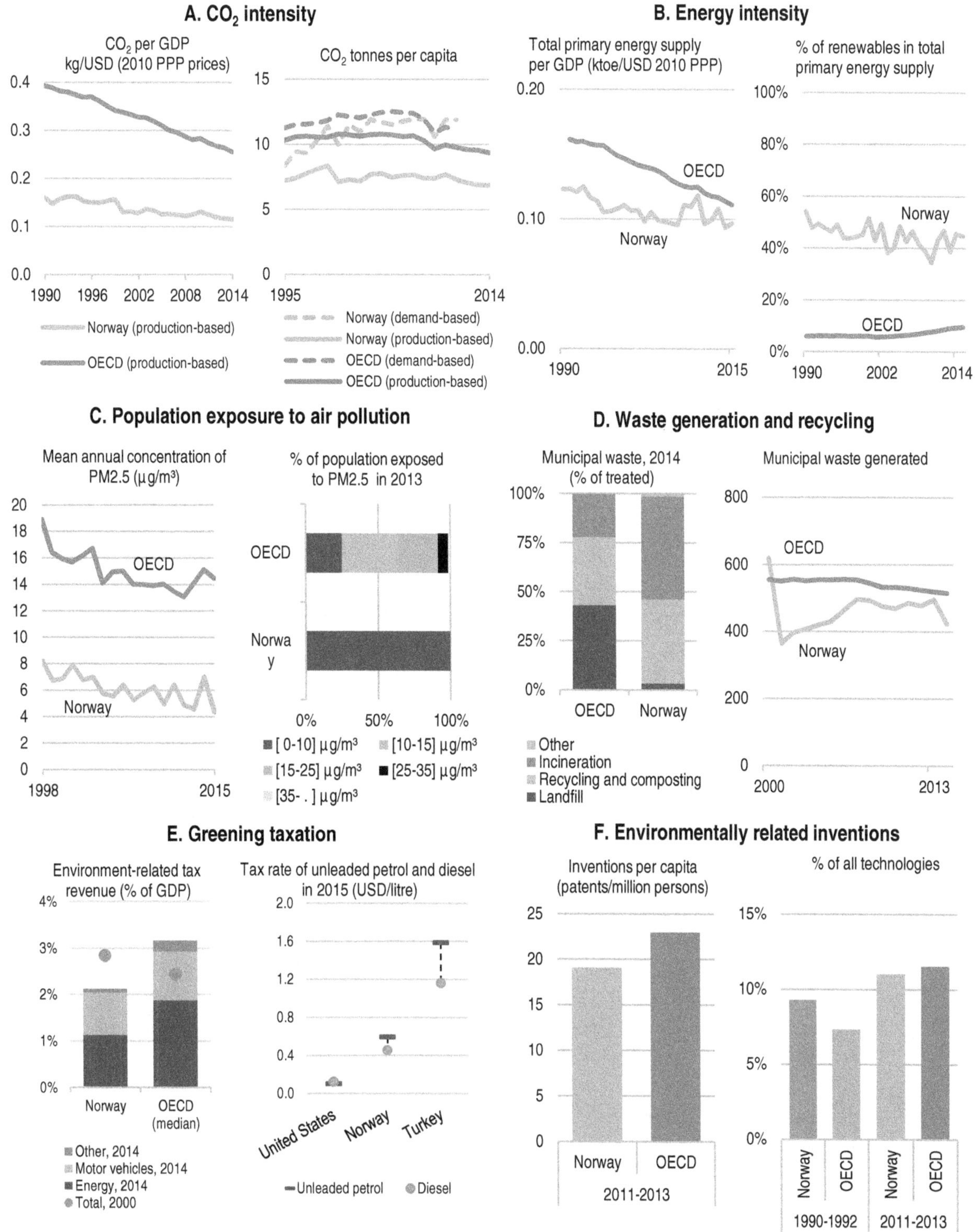

Source: OECD (2017), *Green Growth Indicators* (database).

StatLink http://dx.doi.org/10.1787/888933638885

Table 7. **Implementation of past recommendations on tackling environmental challenges**

Recommendations	Action taken since the previous *Survey* (January 2016)
Reforms should include: • Further limiting carbon-dioxide (CO_2) emissions, and greater uniformity in CO_2 taxation • More systematic inclusion of environmental considerations in cost-benefit analysis (e.g. by using an explicit shadow price for Greenhouse gas (GHG) emissions.	There has been partial follow-up to the Green Tax Commission, for instance by making the carbon-dioxide taxes on several items equivalent to those on vehicle fuels (the items covered mineral oil, natural gas, liquid-petroleum gas, hydrofluorocarbons, and per fluorinated chemicals).

Policy Recommendations

Box 4. **Recommendations from the Green Tax Commission – a selective summary**

- **Carbon-dioxide emissions.** Introduction of a uniform general tax on greenhouse gas emissions that are not covered by emissions trading, accompanied by abolition of reduced rates and exemptions.
- **Vehicle and fuel taxation:**
  - **Usage taxes.** For heavy vehicles road bring in pricing based on global navigation satellite system (GNSS) technology. For light vehicles introduce a combination of urban-area environment and congestion pricing, an "accident tax" and a fuel tax to cover external costs of road wear and tear
  - **Non-usage taxes.** Apply more uniform application of the environmental components in the motor vehicle registration tax across vehicle types and categories of user, accompanied by a reduced carbon-dioxide component
  - **Zero and low-emission cars.** Termination of several supports, including exemptions from VAT, motor vehicle registration tax and the annual motor vehicle tax. Bring in temporary grants for purchasing zero-emission cars, subject to an announced reduction and abolition schedule.
- **Other taxation.** Expand the sulphur tax to encompass coal and coke, introduce location-based tax on sulphur-dioxide and nitrous oxide and abolish tax exemption for waste oil.
- **Subsidy schemes and tax expenditure with environmental effects.** Put greater weight on environmental issues in: agriculture (e.g. reduced red-meat production grants), forestry (e.g. termination of grants for logging roads and cableways), transport (e.g. termination of preferential VAT rate for passenger transport and the income-tax allowance for commuting expenses).
- **Environmental technology.** Focus on using environmental taxation and financial grants for technological development, for instance temporary grants for environmental technologies.
- **Green tax shift.** Use increased environmental tax revenues to fund reductions in general taxation.

Bibliography

Finanstilsynet (2016), *Risk Outlook II 2016*, November 2016.

Hermansen, M. and O. Röhn (2015), "Economic Resilience: The Usefulness of Early Warning Indicators in OECD Countries", *OECD Economics Department Working Paper*, No. 1250.

Inkluderende Arbeidsliv (2017), *Målene om et mer inkluderende arbeidsliv – status og utviklingstrekk [The goals of an inclusive labour market – status and trends],* An expert report for the Inclusive Workplace (IA) Agreement, June 2017.

IMF (2017), *Norway Selected Issues*, IMF Country Report No. 17/181, July 2017.

McGowen, M.A., D. Andrews and V. Millot (2017), "The Walking Dead? Zombie Firms and Productivity Performance in OECD Countries", *OECD Economics Department Working Papers,* No. 1372.

Ministry of Finance (2017), *Revised National Budget 2017: A budget to promote, employment, welfare and security*, Ministry of Finance, Oslo.

Norges Bank (2016), *The Equity Share in the Benchmark Index for the Government Pension Fund Global*, Norges Bank's letter of 1 December 2016 to the Ministry of Finance.

Norges Bank (2017a), "Experience with the monetary policy framework in Norway since 2001", *Norges Bank Papers*, No. 1, 2017.

Norges Bank (2017b), *Financial Stability Report*, Norges Bank.

Norwegian Expert Committee (2016), *Green Competitiveness*, The Norwegian Government's Expert Committee for Green Competitiveness, October 2016.

Norwegian Ministry of Trade, Industry and Fisheries (2016), *State Ownership Report*, 2015, Oslo.

NOU (2015a), *Central government budgeting and accounting principles,* ("Børmer Commission"), Official Norwegian Report, NOU, 2015:14.

NOU (2015b), *Environmental Pricing – Report from a Green Tax Commission,* ("Borge Commission"), Official Norwegian Report, NOU, 2015:15.

NOU (2016), *The Equity Share of the Government Pension Fund Global,* ("Mork Commission"), Official Norwegian Report, NOU, 2016:20.

NOU (2017), *Sharing Economy-Opportunities and challenges,* ("Gabrielsen Committee"), Official Norwegian Report, NOU, 2017:4.

OECD (2010), *OECD Economic Surveys: Norway 2010*, OECD Publishing, Paris.

OECD (2015), *Indicators of Immigrant Integration*, OECD Publishing, Paris.

OECD (2016), *OECD Economic Surveys: Norway 2016*, OECD Publishing, Paris.

Rae, D. and P. van den Noord (2006), "Ireland's housing boom: what has driven it and have prices overshot?", *OECD Economics Department Working Paper,* No. 492.

Röhn, O., A. Caldera Sánchez, M. Hermansen and M. Rasmussen (2015), "Economic Resilience: A New Set of Vulnerability Indicators for OECD Countries", *OECD Economics Department Working Paper*, No. 1249.

© OECD 2018

ANNEX

Progress in structural reform

This Annex reviews action taken on recommendations from previous Surveys. They cover macroeconomic and structural policy priorities. Each recommendation is followed by a note of actions taken since the January 2016 Survey. Recommendations that are new in this Survey are listed in the relevant chapter.

Recommendations	Action taken since the previous *Survey* (January 2016)
Monetary and financial stability	
• Should house-price growth remain uncomfortably high, consider additional macroprudential measures while closely monitoring and reviewing their effectiveness. Specifically consider: • Further guideline loan-to-value ratios, reducing access to interest-only loans • Working with foreign regulators to close down any remaining loopholes ("regulatory arbitrage") that give foreign-owned branches and subsidiaries advantages in mortgage lending.	Tightening of macroprudential regulation continues. The latest measures became effective January 2017 and comprised: • Introduction of a limit on a borrower's total debt to five times annual gross income • A smaller allowance for loans that do not conform to macroprudential rules in the Oslo area (only 8% of lenders loans will be allowed to not adhere to macroprudential rules, instead of 10%) • Reduction in the loan-to-value ratio for home equity credit lines (the vehicle for interest-only loans) from 70% to 60%. A loan-to-value ratio of 85% continues to apply to mortgage loans, except for second homes in the Oslo area where the ratio has been reduced to 60%. Banking sector capital requirements. Phase in of new capital and buffer requirements for credit institutions and investment firms (based on Basel III standards and the CRR/CRD IV framework) was completed in July 2016. Insurance sector. The Solvency II framework was implemented January 2016, in parallel with the EU. This will imply significantly higher solvency requirements for Norwegian insurers.
Facilitate more responsive housing supply. In particular, reduce incentives of local authorities to withhold land for development, other than those related to clear externalities that cannot be compensated with revenue raised from sales.	No major reform.
Fiscal policy, public spending and taxation	
Review the "4% rule" Keep the deficit well below the fiscal rule to avoid unwanted fiscal expansion by providing guidance that sets a speed-limit on increases in the structural non-oil deficit.	The estimated real rate of return has been reduced from 4% of the value of the wealth fund to 3%. The lower rate will be first applied to the 2018 budget. The reduction in the drawdown rate obviates the need for additional guidance as recommended.
Increase public-spending efficiency, including through: • A stronger multi-annual approach to expenditure planning in the central-government budgeting • Ensuring impact analysis and cost-benefit analysis play a central role in decision making, notably in transport investment • Using more private-sector provision in public services, including in education and health care where outsourcing remains underutilised • Encouraging mergers among small municipalities.	Following recommendations of the 2015 commission on multi-year budgeting, the 2017 Budget more clearly communicates the multi-year revenue and expenditure outlook. "Efficiency dividends" continue to feature in budgeting. Establishment of the Digitalisation Council in 2016, an advisory service for government agencies engaged in ICT projects. Establishment of the Better Regulation Council, a body that scrutinises new laws and regulations with a view to minimising the impact on business. Following a central-government campaign, mergers are underway that will reduce the number of municipalities from 428 to 354 and the number of regions from 19 to 11.
Reduce taxation as a share of GDP and reduce tax distortions, including through: • Better alignment of taxation across asset classes in wealth tax and capital-gains tax, especially as regards housing assets • Further reduction in net wealth tax • Less generous tax treatment of housing. In personal-income tax, either incorporate imputed rental income or abolish mortgage interest deductibility.	Reductions in the "ordinary income" tax continue. This tax, which covers most forms of income, has been reduced further in 2017 to 24%. In VAT the 8% concessional rate was raised to 10% in 2016, narrowing the gap with other rate categories (which are 15% (food stuffs) and 25% (standard rate). Some further progress in alignment of taxation across asset classes. As of 2017: • The valuation for net wealth tax purposes of second homes is 90% and for businesses it is 80% (associated debt is valued accordingly) • There is a new valuation discount of 10% for shares and operating assets (to be increased to 20 % in 2018 (again, associated debt is valued accordingly). No major progress in reforming tax treatment of housing in personal income tax, though reduction in the tax rate on ordinary income reduces the tax value of the mortgage interest deduction.
Improving business conditions	
Improve framework conditions for business activity	
Address innovation and technology issues, including through: • Continued use of a competitive-bid approach for research grants and promoting framework conditions for clusters • Promotion of entrepreneurial skills such as project planning and STEM skills • Encouraging Technology Transfer Offices in universities • Strengthening the objectivity of evaluations of business-support programmes (notably innovation and R&D schemes).	The 2015 Budget proposed increasing support via the core programme, SkatteFUNN. The government has launched an evaluation of policy promoting university-business linkages, including assessment of whether technology transfer offices require more powers.

Recommendations	Action taken since the previous *Survey* (January 2016)
Improve transport services.	Road: A new company charged with planning, construction, operation and maintenance segments of the national road network has been established. Consolidation of road-toll companies continues. More extensive use of public-private partnerships is planned. Rail. A new infrastructure management company has been established.
Ensure strong market competition	
Adjust competition legislation and enforcement, including through: • Review of the "total welfare" criterion of competition policy • Increasing the regulatory power of competition authorities.	Assessment of mergers has shifted away from the "total welfare" approach towards a "consumer" approach.
Regarding state stakes in business: • Reduce the scope and size of stakes • Improve state–owned activities governance.	The state holding in one of Norway's largest real-estate companies, Entra ASA, was reduced from around 50% to 33% in 2016.
Strengthen competition in network industries (especially postal and rail services).	Postal services. A new Act came into force in 2016 that ends Norges Posten's monopoly on letters below 50 grams, and lightens the incumbent's universal service requirements. Parliamentary approval to reduce the state stake in Telenor has been granted. Rail services. A new infrastructure management company has been established.
Reduce barriers to entry in the retail sector.	No major reform recently.
Reduce state aid and subsidies	
Reduce support for agriculture and fishing sectors, including through: • Reduced import tariffs and direct subsidies to farmers • Removal of legislative biases that favour agriculture • Encouraging diversification of economic activity in rural areas by improving general framework conditions.	**Agriculture:** • Measures have been taken to encourage larger scale production, including higher ceilings on production quotas • Also, the removal of protective clauses in legislation so as to free-up price setting and permit corporate ownership is in the pipeline. • Parliamentary agreed to some limited reforms in April 2017. These include commitment for some simplification in policy and regulation, and rule changes on milk quotas. • The parliament has voted to phase out export subsidies for agricultural products by 2020.
Human capital, jobs and welfare	
Improve education	
In primary and secondary education reform, consider: • Reduction in the number of schools • Making more data on school performance publically available • Reform of the teaching profession including: stricter selection and graduation criteria, more training, better structured career paths and wider use of performance-related pay.	Roll out of a programme to improve the status and quality of teachers continues. The programme includes increased support for teachers' continued education and the introduction of 5-year master's-level degree for new entrants to the profession. Curriculum overhaul is underway in primary and secondary schooling. The reform, *inter alia*, aims to clarify values and expectations and school responsibilities and facilitate in-depth learning. Reform to school management is underway. A white paper, sanctioned by parliament, includes recommendations for a system of in-service teacher training, stronger support for underperforming schools and enhanced early intervention for pupils.
In higher education: • Continue to promote mergers among providers • Pursue plans to include the graduation rates in the formula for performance-based funding • Further target incentives and financial support to students who complete their courses on time • Steer student choices, for instance, via loan discounts for subjects with high demand.	Significant progress on the merger process; most of the intended mergers have been completed. A three-phase performance-agreement process is underway: pilot agreements in five institutions in 2017, a further five agreements in 2018 and the remaining institutions in 2019. Policy efforts to improve the quality of higher education teaching have intensified with publication of a white paper in early 2017 that proposes channels for reform. More broadly a campaign focusing on skills is underway, including launch of the Strategy for Skills Policy 2017-21 in early 2017, which has widespread support from ministries and stakeholders.
Encourage labour-market participation	
Reduce work disincentives in the unemployment insurance system.	No major reform.

Recommendations	Action taken since the previous *Survey* (January 2016)
Reduce sick leave and tighten disability schemes, *inter alia* consider: • Lowering the replacement rate for long-term sickness absence • Clearer guidelines on disability assessment to general practitioners and monitor compliance.	Sickness leave: new medical assessment trialled, new guidance for doctors on the length of sick leave, stricter implementation of activation requirements (see Chapter 1 for more detail). Work Assessment Allowance (AAP): Several changes will be implemented from 1 January 2018 with an aim to increase the transition back to work. Among others the maximum period of receiving the benefit will be shortened and also there will be closer follow-up of recipients. Disability Benefit: no further reform since the major changes of 2015.
Remove biases favouring early retirement the old-age pension system.	No major reform.
Increase labour-market flexibility	
Increase flexibility in wage setting.	No major reform.
Lighten employment regulation.	No major reform.
Enhance efficiency of job placement services and active labour market policies (ALMP).	No major reform, though in 2017 a new initiative for youth was introduced. The initiative ensures that persons under the age of 30 years who after eight weeks of unemployment are not in a job, education or participating in labour market programmes, are provided with a work-oriented alternative.
Improve Health Care	
Past Surveys have focussed on aspects of financing and have suggested: • Re-structuring activity-based (including Diagnosis Related Groups, DRG) financing to avoid excessive incentives for low-priority activities • Greater use of co-payments by patients.	No major reform.
Tackling environmental challenges	
Reforms should include: • Further limiting carbon-dioxide (CO_2) emissions, and greater uniformity in CO_2 taxation • More systematic inclusion of environmental considerations in cost-benefit analysis (e.g. by using an explicit shadow price for Greenhouse gas (GHG) emissions.	There has been partial follow-up to the Green Tax Commission, for instance by making the carbon-dioxide taxes on several items equivalent to those on vehicle fuels (the items covered mineral oil, natural gas, liquid-petroleum gas, hydrofluorocarbons, and per fluorinated chemicals).

Thematic chapters

© OECD 2018

Chapter 1

Maintaining a successful business sector in a changing world

Norway's success in maintaining high living standards, low inequality and good progress in gender balance owes much to its business sector. High-productivity business-sector jobs support high wages and profits, providing capacity to fund comprehensive public services and inclusive employment practices. Ensuring that the business sector thrives as globalisation and technologies evolve further and as the oil and gas sector enters long-term decline requires maintaining business-friendly conditions. This chapter examines framework conditions, notably competition legislation and policy affecting firm entry and exit ("firm dynamics"). It evaluates how best to encourage new business models, as well the growing issue of labour supply among older cohorts. Education policy's role in providing skills conducive to good lifetime earnings is also discussed.

Maintaining Norway's well-performing socio-economic model requires a strong business sector with capacity for exploiting opportunities in globalised markets, and for delivering goods and services domestically, in an environment of comparatively high wages and high taxes. Furthermore, capacity to shift the focus of economic activity is important to help Norway diversify away from oil- and gas-related activity over the longer term. This chapter first examines the composition of Norway's business sector and the challenges ahead. The subsequent sections consider key areas of policy.

Key features of Norway's business sector

Petroleum-related activity extends beyond offshore production; state stakes remain substantial

- **Activities related to oil and gas (together, "petroleum") sector remain an important segment of the mainland business sector.** Mainland businesses provide exploration and production services and investment goods not only in Norwegian offshore fields but also elsewhere in the North Sea, and beyond. Mainland petroleum activities are estimated to account for nearly 9% of total economic activity. Adding offshore activity to this, means total petroleum-related activity accounts for a little under one quarter of value added (Figure 1.1, Panels A and B). In employment terms the share is substantially smaller, reflecting high capital intensity in the petroleum sector.
- **State ownership in businesses remains substantial.** According to recent estimates, about 15% of business-sector employment is in companies with partial or complete state ownership. Stakes are held in a wide range of sectors, the most significant economically being a 67% in the oil and gas producer, Statoil.

Familiar sectoral shifts are underway in the mainland economy

- **Manufacturing's share of output has shrunk further.** The "machinery" and "other manufacturing" categories combined currently generate about 5.5% of mainland value added compared with 10.5% in the mid-1980s (Figure 1.1, Panel C). According to one input-output analysis (Prestmo et al, 2015), about 14% of manufacturing is linked to the petroleum sector.
- **Service activities occupy an increasing share of economic activity.** Businesses classified as "other services" today accounts for about 25% of value added (Figure 1.1, Panel C). In addition, Education, Health and social work have expanded significantly, which in Norway implies mainly an expansion of public-sector activity as private enterprise plays a comparatively small role in these sectors.
- Norway's "traditional" sectors, **farming and capture fishing, today account for only around 2% of output and employment.** For farming in particular, economic protection remains substantial reflecting longstanding priority in Norwegian policy to preserving rural and remote communities. Meanwhile, **capital-intensive aquaculture (mainly salmon) has expanded rapidly.** Exports now account for about 2% of GDP and the sector is second-largest export category after petroleum.

Figure 1.1. **The composition of Norway's economic activity**

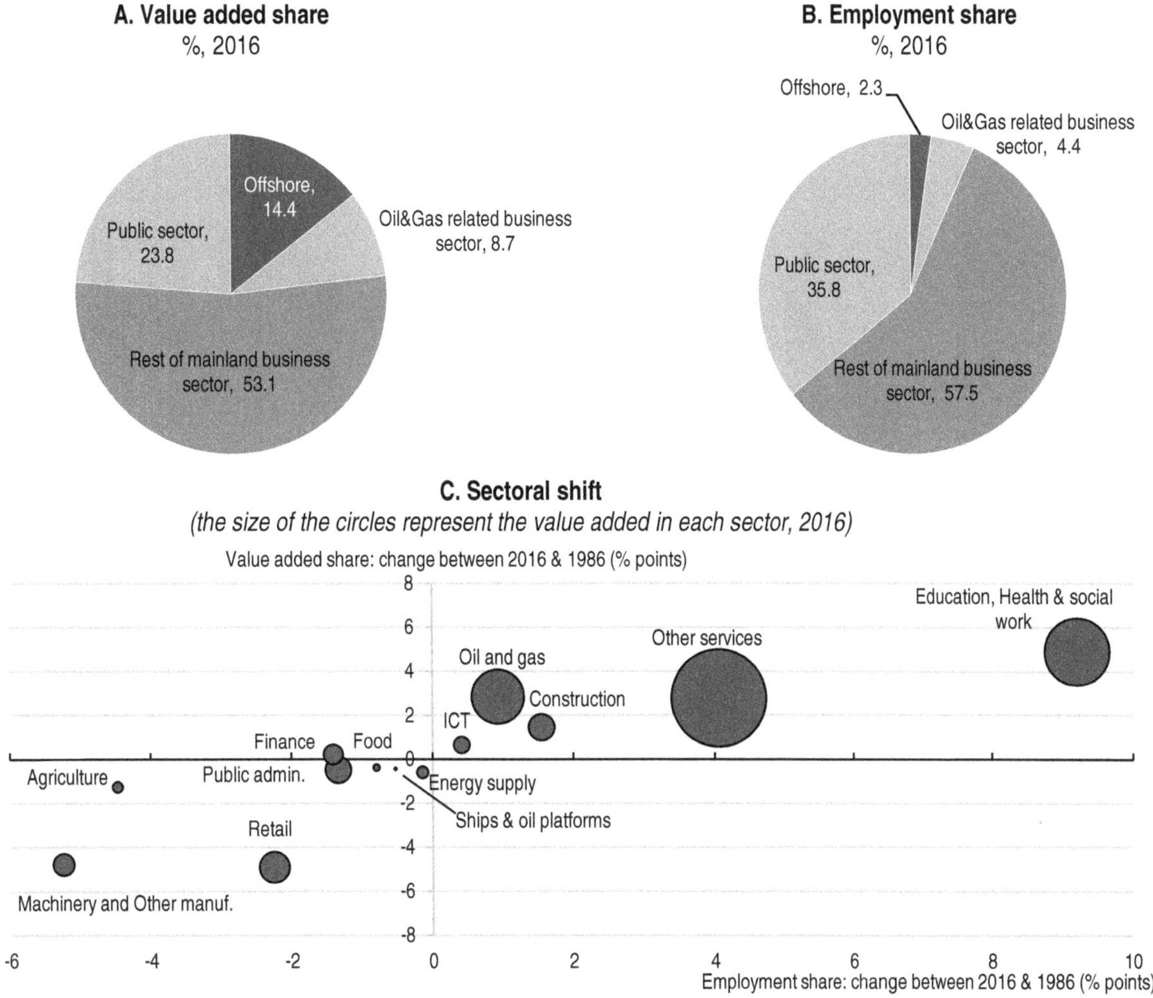

Notes: Panel A and B, Public sector comprises categories: Education, Health and Social Work, Public Administration and defence. The mainland Oil&Gas related business sector are estimates:

- "Value added" share is a Ministry of Finance estimate of the value of demand from the petroleum sector. As such it includes imports, which do not contribute to value added in the Norwegian economy.
- Oil-related employment reported by Statistics Norway (Økonomiske analyser 1/2017) as of 2016 around 185 000 jobs, or 6.7% of employment were directly or indirectly linked to the oil and gas sector.

Source: Statistics Norway; Statistics Norway; Ministry of Finance.

StatLink http://dx.doi.org/10.1787/888933638904

Business sector and employment practices are more inclusive than most

- **Business-sector employment practices have contributed significantly to the narrow gender wage gap and high rate of female employment.** Norway's gender wage gap is now 7% and women account for nearly 48% of employment (Figure 1.2, Panels A and B). Norway was an early mover in bringing in statutory quotas for women on the boards of public limited companies. Nearly 45% of board members are now women among large listed companies. Furthermore, gender balance is a key factor in Norway's narrow distribution of market income (Figure 1.2, Panel C) along with high educational attainment and a strongly centralised collective bargaining system.

Figure 1.2. **Much of Norway's inclusiveness derives from high employment rates and small gaps in earnings**

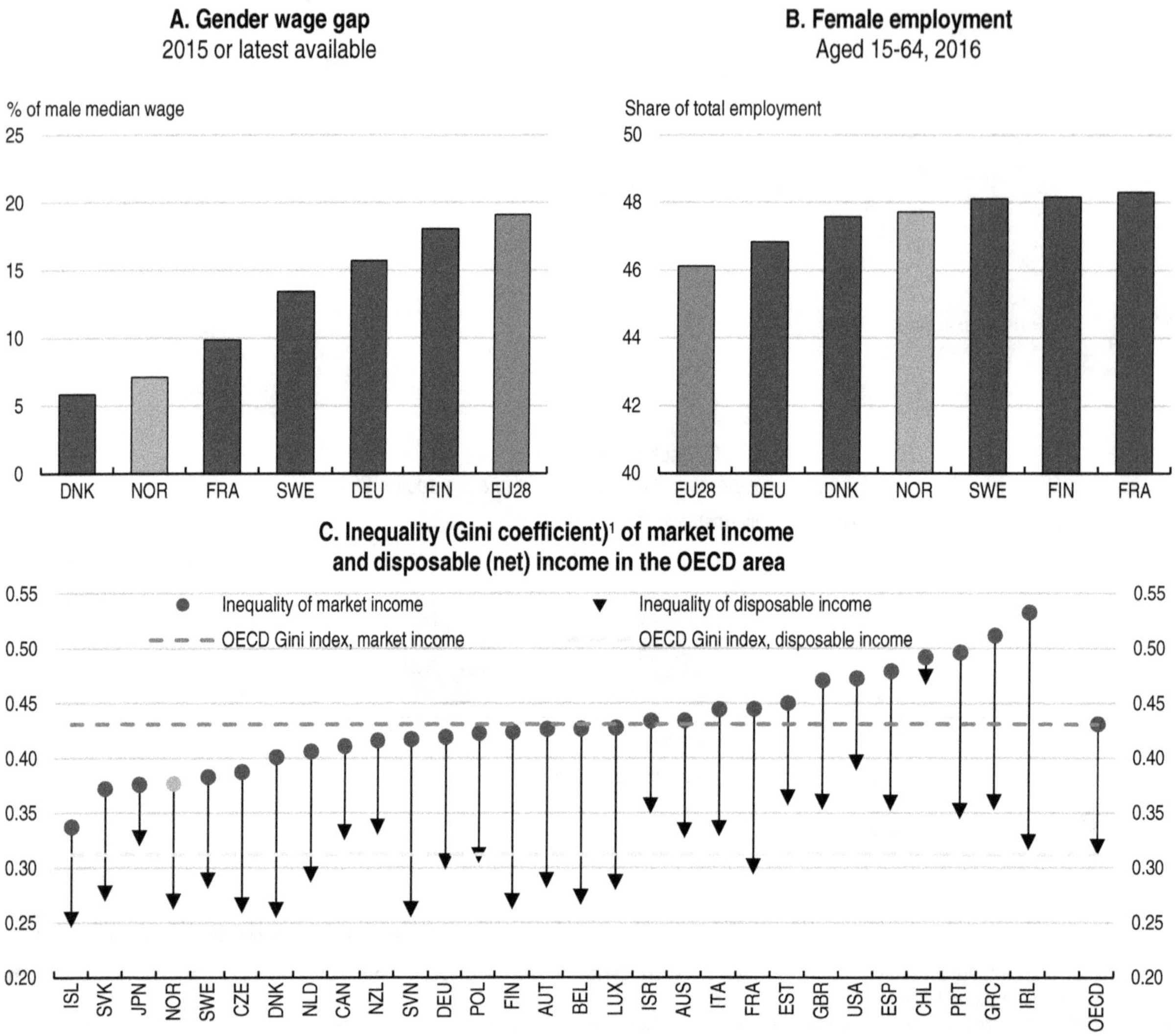

1. The Gini coefficient ranges from zero to 1, zero indicating all individuals have the same income; 1 indicating one individual receives all income.

Source: OECD Employment and Labour Market Statistics; and *OECD Income Distribution Database* (IDD).

StatLink http://dx.doi.org/10.1787/888933638923

- **Businesses score reasonably on environment-social-governance (ESG) indicators but lag behind leading countries.** Indicators based on Thomson Reuters data (Figure 1.3) score Norway above the United States on environment and social dimensions but not quite as well as its Nordic peers or the Euro Area. A comparison of oil-and-gas sector scores produces a similar story. Norway performs comparatively poorly on the governance component, possibly reflecting weak scores in state stakes in business.

Figure 1.3. **Norway scores reasonably in environment-social-governance (ESG) indicators**

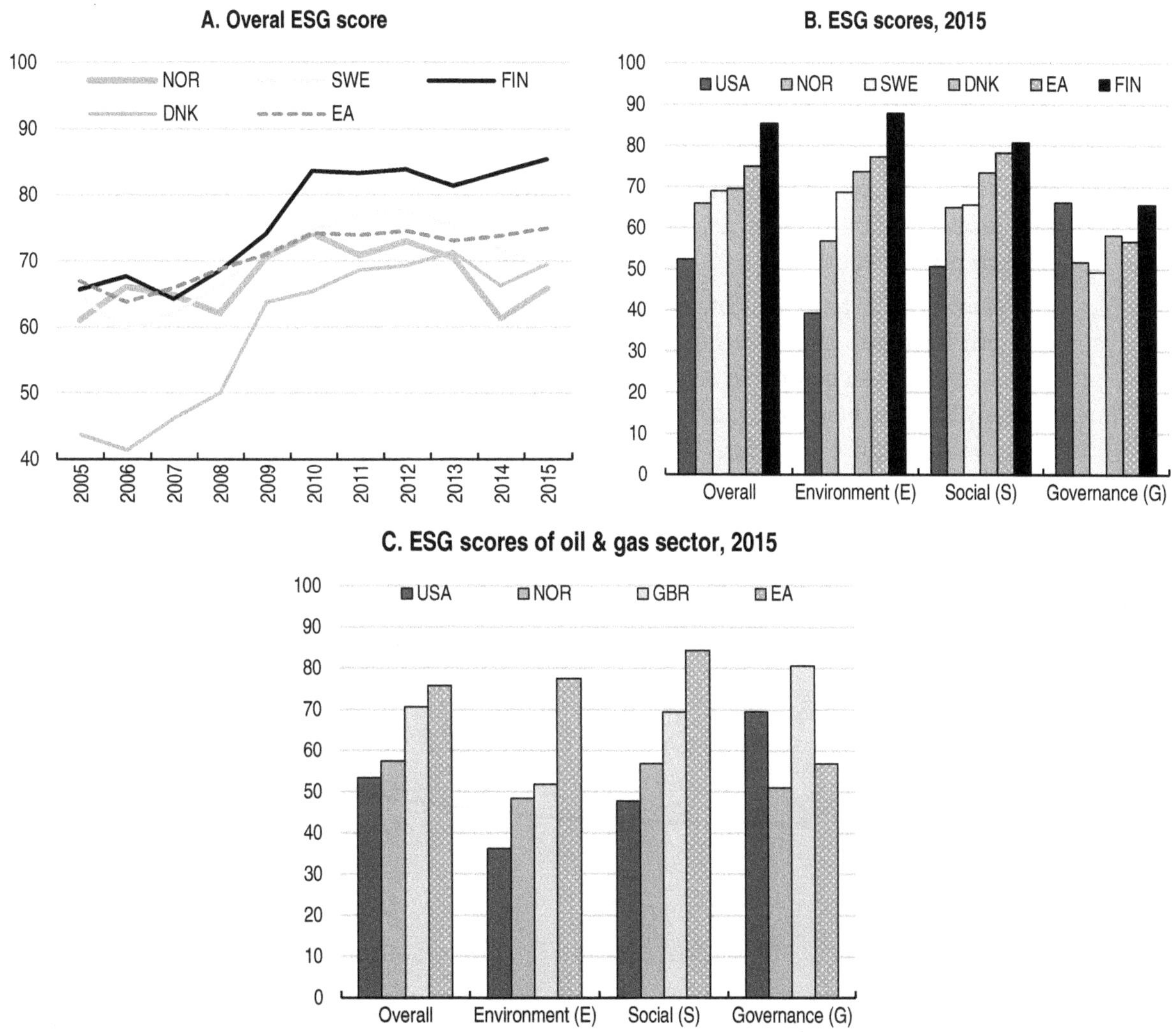

Note: The number of firms reporting environmental, social and governance (ESG) scores varies each year.
Source: Adapted from ASSET4 Thomson Reuters data.

StatLink http://dx.doi.org/10.1787/888933638942

Challenges and opportunities for Norway's business sector

Globalisation and technological change

Globalisation and technological change are re-shaping Norway in similar ways to many other advanced economies. New production and export capacity in emerging market economies, the internationalisation of supply chains ("global value chains") and the continuing digital revolution (and other new technologies) are generating compositional shift in economic activity and bringing dramatic change in the range and price of goods and services available to consumers (for a recent general discussion, see, for instance OECD, 2017a). Welfare gains have been significant. Emerging production bases, particularly in Asia, have reduced the price, and widened the range, of clothes, textiles and electronic goods in particular. In addition, globalisation and technological change have been an integral part of processes that have brought substantial improvement to the capacity and quality of existing products and the generation of new products and services.

Adjustment in Norway's economic activity arising from globalisation and technological change has been comparatively smooth. Employment and output have been shifting away from primary activities (such as agriculture) and manufacturing and towards service sectors. However, in Norway this process has left few people behind. This is partly because negatively affected sectors, such as manufacturing, do not account for a large share of employment. Furthermore, the generally healthy state of the economy, thanks notably to activity related to the petroleum sector has facilitated the reallocation of labour resources. Furthermore, comprehensive welfare support reduces the risk of local economies spiralling downwards when hit by plant closures.

High labour costs remain a core challenge. Businesses in all advanced countries are to some extent having to climb further up the value chain to remain viable. Norway's high production costs, even compared with other advanced economies, mean this pressure is more keenly felt. The euro-equivalent average wage calculated by Eurostat has come down in recent years (Figure 1.4, Panel A), largely due to exchange-rate depreciation and

Figure 1.4. **Norway's labour costs remain high in international comparison**

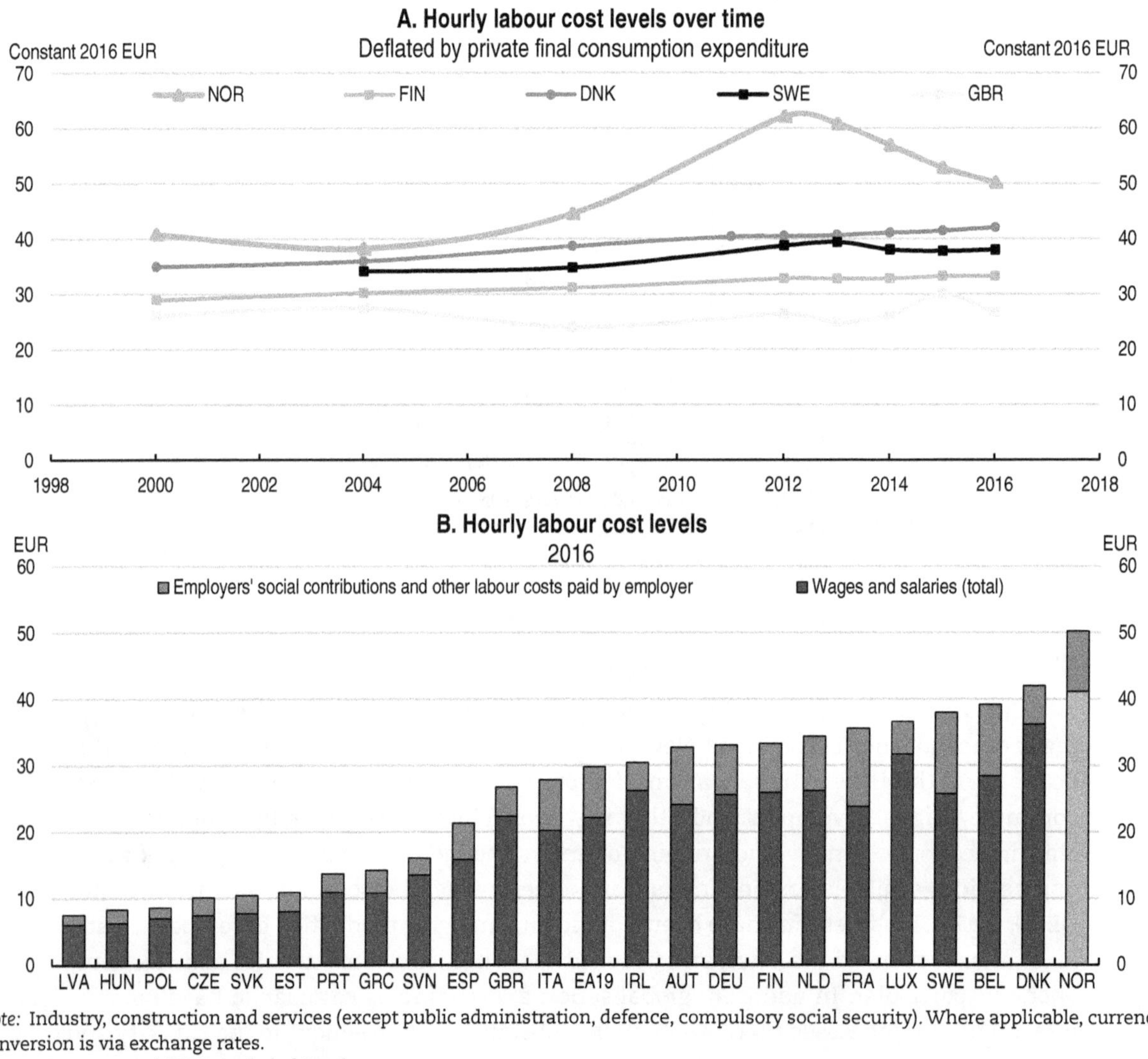

Note: Industry, construction and services (except public administration, defence, compulsory social security). Where applicable, currency conversion is via exchange rates.
Source: Eurostat; and *OECD Analytical Database*.

StatLink http://dx.doi.org/10.1787/888933638961

compositional effects from job-losses in the high-paying petroleum sector. Nevertheless, at around EUR 50 per hour, the average wage remains comparatively high. In Denmark and Sweden the hourly rate is around EUR 40 and there are many countries in Europe with rates below EUR 30 per hour (Figure 1.4, Panel B).

Norway's labour-cost challenge has been amplified by wage growth outpacing productivity growth in most years – i.e. unit labour costs have risen. This has happened in several OECD countries, but to a greater extent in Norway (Figure 1.5). This partly reflects employment linked to a wave of heavy petroleum-sector investment, which ramped up the wage bill in the "mining and utilities" category and inflated unit labour costs. However, unit

Figure 1.5. **Norway's unit labour cost (ULC) indices remain high despite recent falls**

In Euros

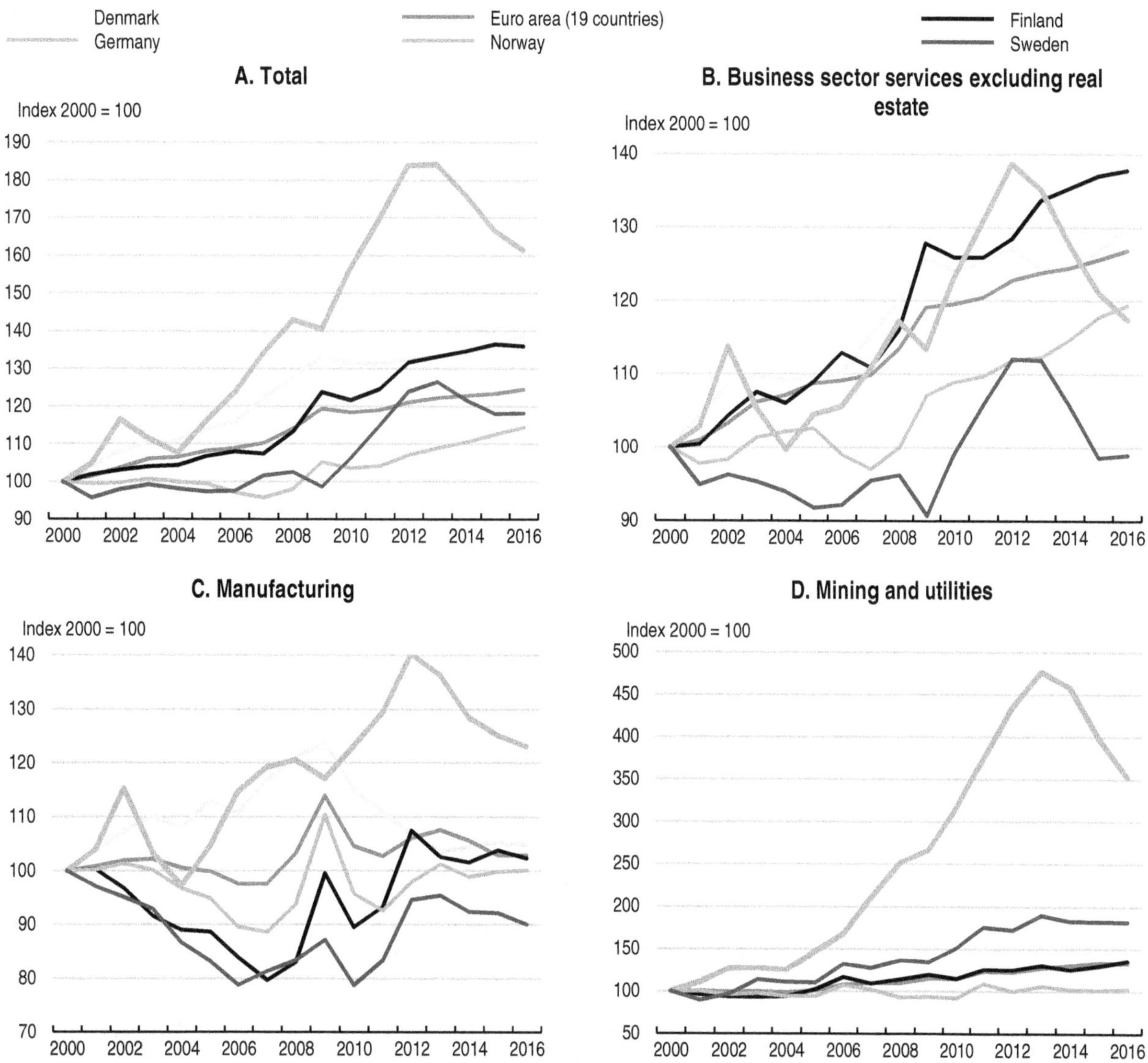

Notes: Unit labour costs (ULCs) measure the average cost of labour per unit of output. They are calculated as the ratio of total labour costs to real output. Annual ULCs can be expressed as the ratio of total labour compensation per hour worked to output per hour worked (labour productivity). Panel D, Denmark is omitted due to for sector comparability issues.

Source: OECD Productivity Statistics (database); and OECD *Analytical Database*.

StatLink http://dx.doi.org/10.1787/888933638980

labour costs have also risen quite strongly in manufacturing and in business-sector services. More recently, unit labour costs have fallen across the board due to currency depreciation. In the petroleum sector a fall-off in petroleum sector investment and cost-savings in response to the 2014 oil-price drop have also driven unit labour costs down.

Productivity slowdown

As in many countries, productivity growth has weakened (Figure 1.6). Weakening has occurred in trend labour productivity (which reflects the deepening of physical and human capital as well as innovation processes) and multi-factor productivity (MFP, which more closely reflects innovation). The step-down in the pace of productivity growth started around 2005. A leading explanation is that Norway is experiencing the low-growth trap phenomena seen elsewhere; a cycle of weak consumption demand, low output growth expectations, feeding to low business confidence and tempered investment. As elsewhere, breaking any such cycle is a core reason for the continuation of supportive macroeconomic policy, particularly monetary policy. Technological developments are almost certainly playing a role, as has been the case in past productivity trends (Box 1.1).

Figure 1.6. **Productivity growth has slowed**

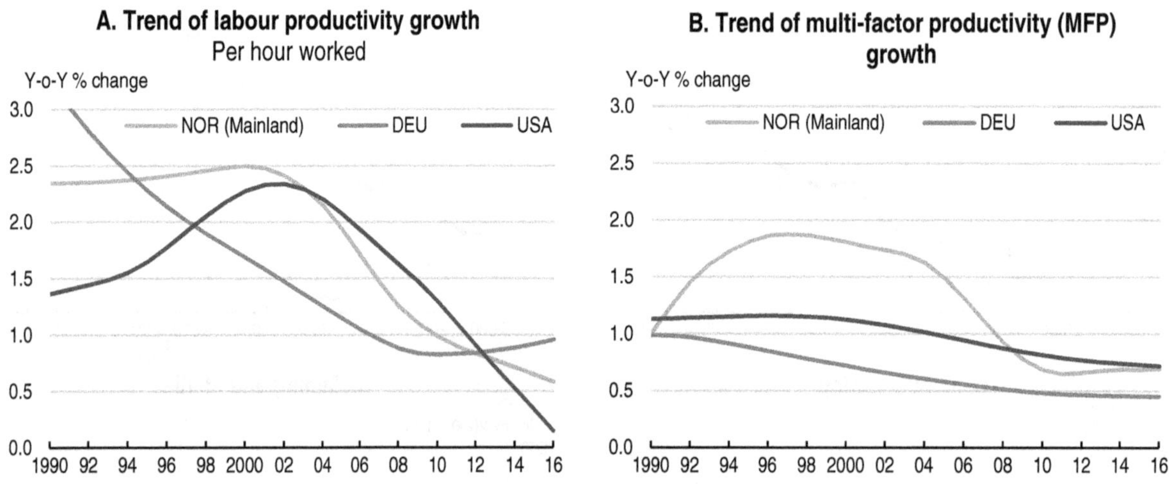

Note: Series are smoothed by a Hodrick-Prescott filter with a lambda of 100.
Source: *OECD Economic Outlook Database.*

StatLink http://dx.doi.org/10.1787/888933638999

Box 1.1. **Norway's productivity growth over the longer term**

Changes in trend productivity growth over the long term correspond to different phases of economic development. Norway's long-term pattern is in many respects a familiar one. A Norges Bank paper (Hagelund, 2009) identifies several phases of productivity growth, which can be summarised as:

- Strong productivity growth from post-World War II to early 1970s: "catch-up" with leading economies in investment and technology, particularly in manufacturing where machine-based automation generated large gains in labour productivity growth
- Weak productivity growth from mid-1970s to late 1980s: macroeconomic instability (including inflation), global oil crisis and tailing off from in gains from post-war catch-up

Box 1.1. **Norway's productivity growth over the longer term** *(cont.)*

- Resurgence from late 1980s to mid-2000s: competitive pressure from trade and product-market liberalisation, structural reforms in the 1990s, productivity gains from information-technology
- Step-down from mid-2000s onwards: prolonged weak investment growth linked to weak confidence and demand, possible weakening of productivity gains from information technology

Diversification away from petroleum activities

Norway's oil-and-gas related activities are driven by external demand as well as domestic production. In Norway's fields, oil production is already in decline, though this has been somewhat offset by increasing gas production (Figure 1.7, Panel A). However, at some point the latter will also peak. Norway's oil and gas production is echoed in the gap between total and mainland GDP; mostly in the form of exports (Figure 1.7, Panel B). Based on currently known reserves and estimates of new discoveries, along with likely production levels, experts generally expect Norway's oil and gas production will end in around 50 years. However, oil and gas production in offshore fields is only one segment of Norway's engagement with the petroleum sector. In addition, the future path of Norway's oil and gas activities depends on global developments. Echoing estimates described above, demand from petroleum activities in the mainland economy is currently estimated to be around 10% of mainland GDP, which is already below peak values and further decline is expected (Figure 1.8).

Norway's future oil-sector development is highly uncertain. This is illustrated in Table 1.1 which describes a "central" scenario plus possible upside and downside outcomes. The global oil price is a key influence. Changes in the current price of oil can shift expectations of future prices, which in turn shift the calculus of production and exploration activity. Higher expected prices can bring marginal fields into production and make new exploration and development activity worthwhile. Furthermore, the current price of oil influences activity because the major oil producers typically finance exploration and development out of profits, which are themselves strongly driven by the price of oil. The large downward shift in the price of oil since 2014, may or may not herald the "beginning of the end" for Norway's oil sector, much depends on the complex matter of production costs (Box 1.2). Whatever, the 2014 price drop has certainly illustrated the consequences of substantial price movements.

Diversification away from petroleum-related activities in Norway will probably be gradual, as described by the central scenario in Table 1.1. From a policy perspective, this suggests that policies should focus primarily on facilitating a business-led, market-driven resource reallocation through good "framework conditions" for business. In this context, framework conditions refer to the various structural policy areas that influence the general conditions that businesses operate in, notably areas such as taxation, competition legislation, regulatory requirements on starting-up, running and winding up business. These policy levers largely overlap with those that can also help Norwegian business engage with the challenges and opportunities of globalisation and technological change.

However, the "gradual transition" narrative may not play out. As Table 1.1 describes, a large and permanent negative shock to the oil sector is possible, for instance through a substantial acceleration globally in the switch to electric vehicles with consequent fall off in oil

Figure 1.7. **Combined oil and gas production has already declined**

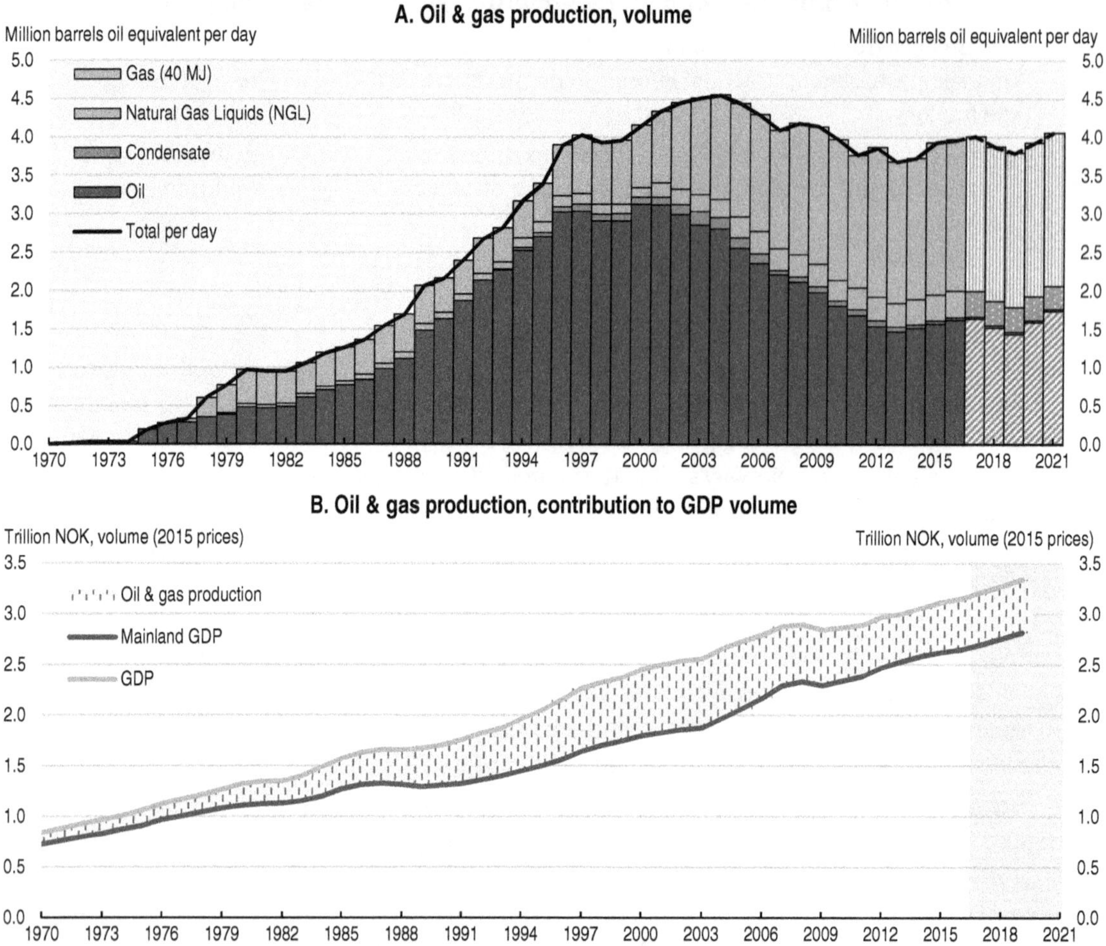

Source: Norwegian Petroleum Directorate and *OECD Economic Outlook 102 Database.*

StatLink http://dx.doi.org/10.1787/888933639018

Figure 1.8. **Mainland oil and gas are projected to decline steadily over the long term**

Estimated demand for oil and gas services, % of mainland GDP

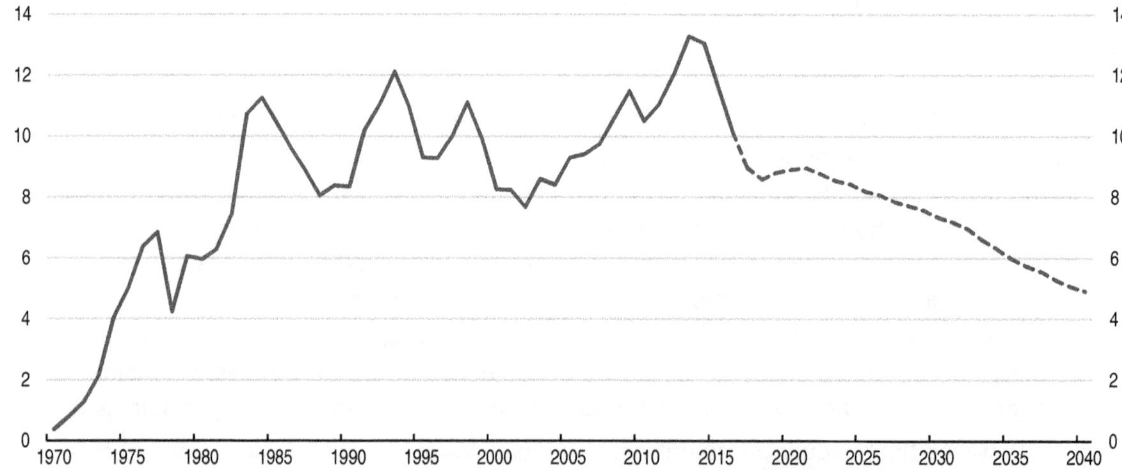

Source: Ministry of finance: Meld. St. 29 (2016-2017) – Long-term Perspectives on the Norwegian Economy 2017.

StatLink http://dx.doi.org/10.1787/888933639037

Box 1.2. **Production cost issues in oil and gas**

Norway's oil production has not fallen following the 2014 oil-price fall (Figure 1.7), suggesting that the marginal production cost for its offshore fields generally lies below the current global oil price. This is confirmed by some cost estimates; a consultancy company, Rystad Energy UCube, estimated Norway's average cash production cost at about USD 20 per barrel in 2016. However, this figure requires judicious interpretation. For a start, production costs vary widely from one field to another, so the range around the average value will be wide (for commercial reasons producers do no generally make public the details of field costs). Furthermore, production costs are not only influenced by the engineering aspects of production. In particular, the intensity of attention to costs by the producers varies with the oil price; for instance producers have reportedly found room for substantial cost savings since 2014. Furthermore, a full lifespan cost assessment needs to incorporate exploration and development costs and (increasingly in recent times), scrapping costs.

Table 1.1. **Possible scenarios for Norway's petroleum sector**

	Conditions that could give rise to the scenario	Likely consequences for the mainland economy
Central scenario: gradual decline in petroleum-related activity (domestic Norwegian production ends around 2060)	Oil-price remains at a level that supports a gradual decline in domestic production. No large new discoveries in Norwegian fields.	Mainland petroleum-sector activity steadily declines as demands from offshore Norwegian fields (and the global petroleum sector) gradually ease off. Transition is smooth. The slow adjustment away from oil sector means businesses, households and policies have time to prepare and adjust.
Downside scenario: accelerated decline in petroleum-related activity	Massive negative demand or supply shock to the global oil business (e.g. acceleration in the switch to electric vehicles or discovery of new large low-cost reserves globally). Oil price shifts permanently below production costs for much of Norwegian offshore production.	Norwegian offshore production is wound back rapidly, global demand for Norwegian oil-and-gas services weakens substantially. Severe economic downturn, particularly in certain regions. Transition to new activities is not fast enough to prevent entrenched socio-economic problems from long-term unemployment and skill redundancy.
Upside scenario: a substantial resurgence in petroleum-related activity	A surprise large new domestic discovery and/or sustained high oil prices.	Transition goes into reverse, oil-sector activity surges (marginal known reserves brought into production, new exploration activity), non-oil sectors diminish. Benefits and challenges of resource wealth once again take centre stage.

demand. Conversely, a string of surprise new petroleum-sector exploration possibilities and large new resource finds could put diversification into reverse, bringing to the fore the gains and challenges of a booming oil and gas sector. Particularly in the case of a negative shock, more interventionist policy may be warranted; for instance, additional regional support and more support for retraining to prevent the emergence of economically deprived areas.

Specific policy areas for Norway

Enabling Norway's business sector to thrive requires attention to a wide range of policy areas. The remainder of this chapter focuses on the following:

- **Scaling back and rebalancing taxation,** Norway's socio-economic model requires substantial revenues, so a large tax burden cannot be avoided. Yet, there are opportunities for some scaling back in the size of tax revenue relative to GDP and for re-balancing taxation to help business.
- **Promoting flexible markets and competition.** Ensuring competitive and flexible product markets is core to efficient resource allocation, and can be more challenging in small

economies because markets may be more easily dominated by a single enterprise or groups of enterprises engaged in tacit forms of collusion.

- **Improving resource reallocation through firm dynamics.** Bringing more firms close to best practice and frontiers in innovation and productivity through the entry, exit, expansion and contraction of firms is as significant for Norway as elsewhere.
- **Targeted support for innovation.** Much of Norway's productivity growth arises from global advance in technology and knowledge but encouraging domestic innovation is important and strengthens Norway's absorptive capacity for global knowledge.
- **Facilitating new forms of business.** As elsewhere, Norway is experiencing a wave of innovative business models based on internet platforms that challenge existing service delivery in a number of areas.
- **Maintaining strong and flexible labour supply.** As Norway's population ages the longstanding policy challenges linked to early withdrawal from the labour force (typically via the sickness and disability system) are gaining increased significance for the economy. Mobility within Norway and internationally is also important, as is supporting further advance in ensuring both female and male talent pools are utilised to the greatest effect.
- **Education and skills.** Ensuring workers have high skill levels is a core channel for making high labour costs viable for businesses and for ensuring economic inclusiveness for households.

Scaling back and rebalancing taxation

Norway's comprehensive public services, welfare support and investment require substantial fiscal revenue. Indeed, revenues (excluding petroleum-related) are equivalent to 45% of mainland GDP, which is among the highest in the OECD area. Past OECD assessment has underscored the room for efficiency gains in many areas of public spending in Norway. Achieving these gains can then be used to pare back the revenue-share of GDP.

Welcome shifts in the tax mix are underway. A commendable drive to move the tax burden away from income taxes and towards indirect taxes, including environmentally related taxes, continues. Income-tax reductions began in 2015 and are centred on rate reductions in the single-rate "ordinary tax", which applies to most forms of income (including corporate income in the case of enterprises, and capital income and wages in the case of individuals). The rate is 24% for 2017, down from 28% in 2014 (Figure 1.9) and there is parliamentary agreement for a reduction to 23% in 2018. The main goal has been to lower the burden of corporate-income tax. For individuals the reduction in the "ordinary tax" has been partially offset through increases in the progressive tax ("bracket tax") that applies to wage earnings. The tax changes maintain a narrow gap between the top marginal rate of tax on wage income and dividend income, which ensure personal business owners have little incentive to avoid taxation by reporting wage income as capital income. In addition, the changes retain neutrality with regard to portfolio choices (such as the choice between shares and bonds) via the dividend tax allowance.

Indirect-tax reform has included progress on narrowing gaps across VAT rates. In 2016 the concessionary rate of VAT on certain services (including passenger transport and accommodation) was increased from 8% to 10% bringing it closer to the concessionary rate applied to food stuffs (15%) and the standard rate (25%). The Government has proposed to further increase the 10 % concessionary rate to 12% in the 2018 budget. Further progress in reducing the differences in VAT rates would be welcome through further increase in the

Figure 1.9. **Norway's corporate tax rate has been lowered**

Statutory corporate income tax rate, 2017

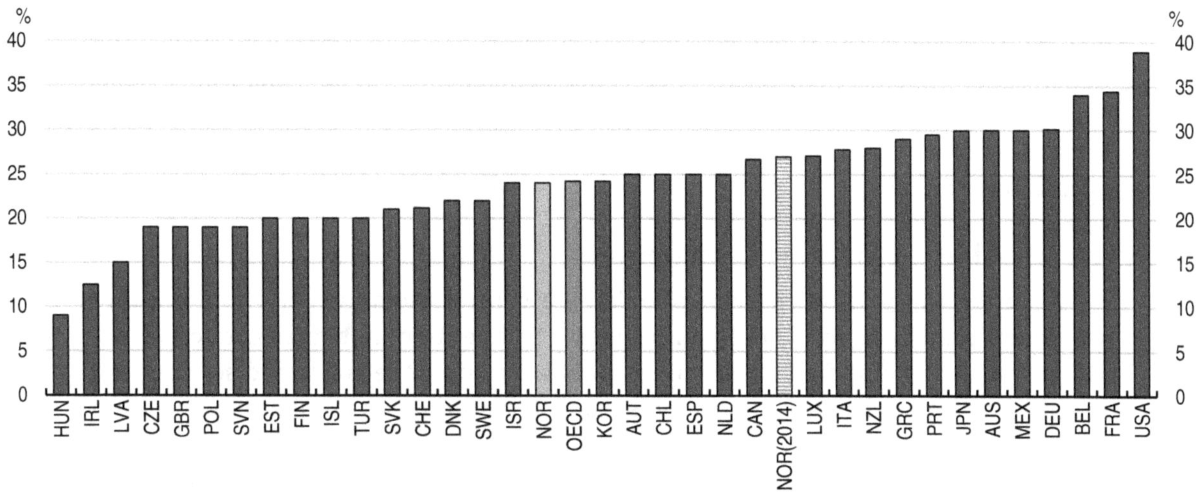

Source: OECD Revenues Statistics.

StatLink http://dx.doi.org/10.1787/888933639056

concessionary rates, along with reduction in the standard rate. Cost-of-living concerns from concessionary-rate increases could be packaged with greater targeted support to low-income households via the welfare and income-tax system. In the sphere of environmental taxation there has been partial implementation of recommendations by a green-taxation committee (see Assessment and Recommendations of this *Survey*).

Financial-services taxation has also received some attention. As for most countries, VAT is not imposed on financial services, largely because of challenges in measuring value added. Norway introduced a "financial activity" tax in 2017 as a substitute for this. The tax comprises a 5% additional employer levy on wages and a one-percentage-point higher rate of ordinary tax on corporate income in the financial sector (i.e. for 2017 the financial sector faces a corporate tax rate of 25%, compared with 24% for other sectors).

Taxes targeting wealth have been adjusted further. Wealth and inheritance taxes, in principle, shore up the redistribution provided through income-tax progressivity, helping address inequality issues. In practice, there are challenges. Indeed, Norway's inheritance tax was scrapped in 2014, partly because rules to counter avoidance (notably, rules on gifts) were complex and not very effective. Most notably, intergenerational transfers among the most affluent families in Norway are typically made by transfer of business interests, which was not captured by the inheritance tax (it only covers personal assets). As regards the wealth tax, the impact on incentives to invest is a key issue. The wealth tax, an annual tax levied on net wealth, has been lightened with reduction in the maximum marginal rate from 1.1% to 0.85% and with reduced weightings on business capital in the calculation of net wealth. Further reductions in the wealth tax rate would make sense as despite the recent reduction; the tax still implies a high marginal rate of tax on saving, especially in the current low-inflation, low-interest rate environment.

Norway's housing taxation continues to include generous concessions. Most notably, mortgage interest is deductible without corresponding inclusion of imputed rent in taxable income. The tax concessions fuel demand for home ownership and skew saving and investment more generally. Tackling this problem is politically difficult but should nevertheless remain an aspirational goal for policymakers. The optimal approach, in principle, would be to introduce imputed rent in income-tax calculation. A gradual phase-in process could make this more tractable. Or, property tax could be increased as a proxy for imputed rent. Alternatively, the interest-rate deduction could be phased out; though this would reduce the consistency of capital-asset treatment in the tax system (the system would less "symmetric"). Other avenues for housing taxation reform should be exploited, in particular through further increases in the weights applied to housing assets in the calculation of capital gains tax (and in net wealth calculation).

Promoting flexible markets and competition

Ensuring competitive markets should be a central theme in efforts to improve framework conditions for Norwegian business. Competition motivates cost-efficiency within firms and helps direct businesses towards providing the goods and services that intermediary producers and households want. In addition, as emphasised in recent research (e.g. Aghion et al., 2014), competition motivates innovation, especially among firms at the technological frontier because of its potential to bring commercial advantage (the "escape-competition effect"). This suggests policy that both encourages strong competition and increases the number of firms operating at technological frontiers is particularly powerful.

Norway's scale and geography, to an extent, shape the scope for competitive markets:

- The country's comparatively small economy and market size can mean that in some markets only small numbers of players are feasible due to economies of scale. This raises the risk of arrangements between firms (tacit or otherwise) which limit competition. This risk is amplified by Norway's geography, the largest population centres are quite distant from each other and there are extensive rural areas with low population density in which competition for some services is very limited (a recent OECD report examines the economies of Norway's northern areas, OECD, 2017b).
- Upscaling challenges in trade arise. Businesses founded in a small country can face challenges in expansion because there is less opportunity for growth domestically before entering international markets, which often involves substantial fixed costs and hurdles in regulation. This underscores the importance of membership of the EEA and Norway's extensive alignment with EU regulation in providing access to markets.

Norway scores reasonably in broad indicators of the environment for business (Figure 1.10). It has a middle-ranking position in the OECD's product-market regulation (PMR) indicator and performs very well in the World Bank's Doing Business indicator. Examination of the PMR indicator's sub-components shows Norway's score is negatively affected by the still extensive state stakes in business; scores in "public ownership" and "regulatory protection of incumbents" are comparatively poor (Figure 1.11). In other dimensions of the PMR indicator Norway generally ranks well.

However, regulatory indicators on services trade point to above-average restrictiveness in many sectors. Norway has longstanding and substantial trade in maritime transport and petroleum-related services. And, as elsewhere, information and communication technology means many services can now be provided at distance, bringing opportunity for lower cost and better quality domestic services, and new markets for exporting services. The OECD's Services Trade Restrictiveness Index shows Norway to have above-average restrictiveness in these sectors (Figure 1.12). This is partly due to state stakes, which as in the PMR, raise the

Figure 1.10. **Norway performs reasonably in top-level indicators of the business environment**

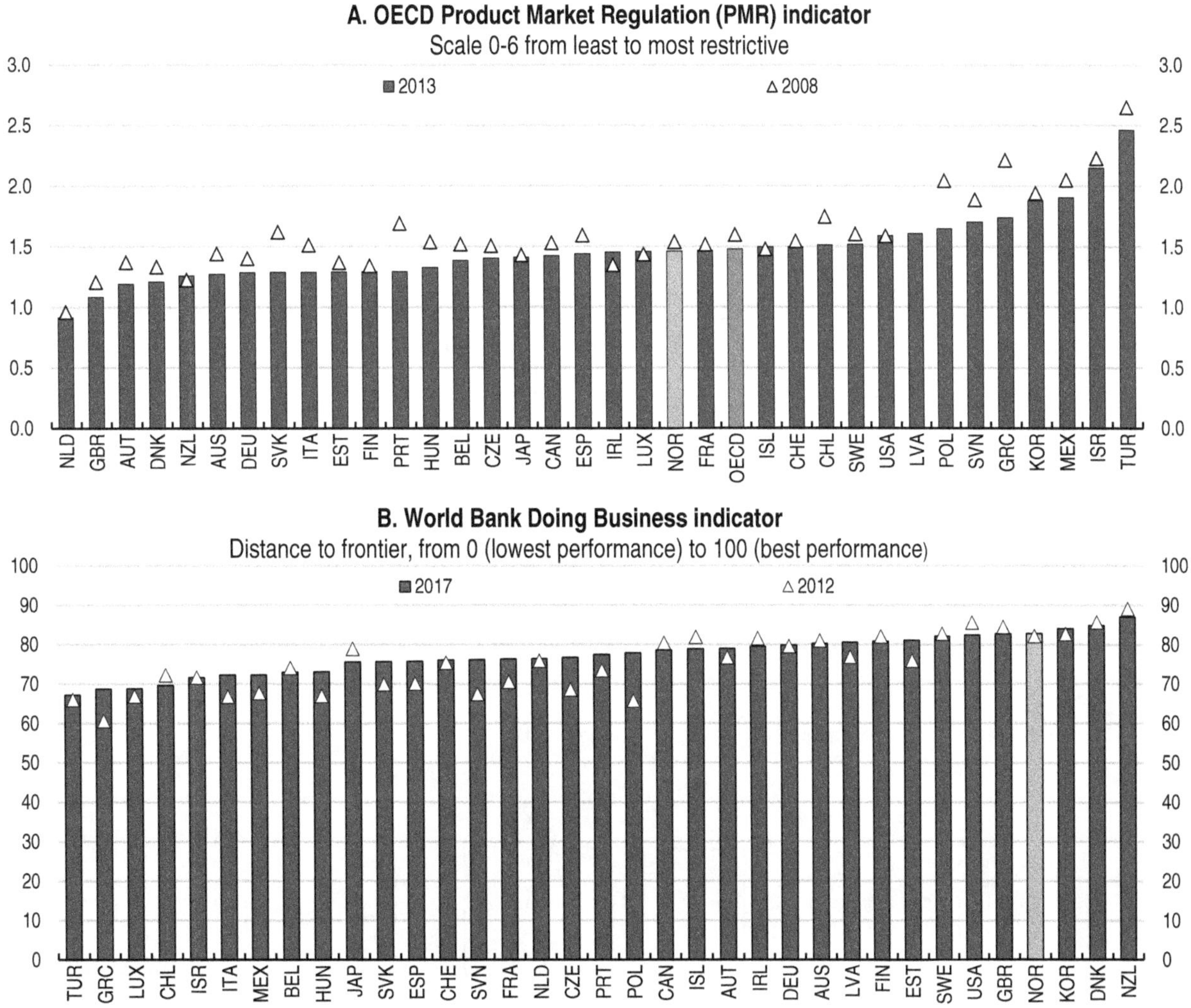

Source: *OECD Product Market Regulation Database* ; and World Bank Doing Business 2017.

StatLink http://dx.doi.org/10.1787/888933639075

restrictiveness score. However Norway is comparatively restrictive on some other fronts. Most notably, the Country Profile in the OECD's Services Trade Restrictiveness Index flags that Norway requires that at least half of the board members and the manager (CEO) in corporations must be residents of Norway or the European Economic Area (EEA). Similar restrictions apply in other Nordic countries but are rare elsewhere. Norway's other restrictions are typically more common, such as rules requiring wage parity rules for temporary foreign workers, capital deposit requirements for registering corporations and the incorporation of public procurement into regional trade agreements. Access to public procurement contracts by foreign businesses is expected to become more restrictive following the requirements that contractors must hire apprentices (the apprenticeship system is discussed further below). While positive for the supply of apprenticeships, apprenticeship programmes require companies to have qualified staff for training and links with upper-secondary schools, which foreign bidders for procurement contracts are unlikely to possess.

Figure 1.11. **Sub-components of the OECD PMR indicator flag Norway's state stakes in business**

Scale 0-6 from least to most restrictive

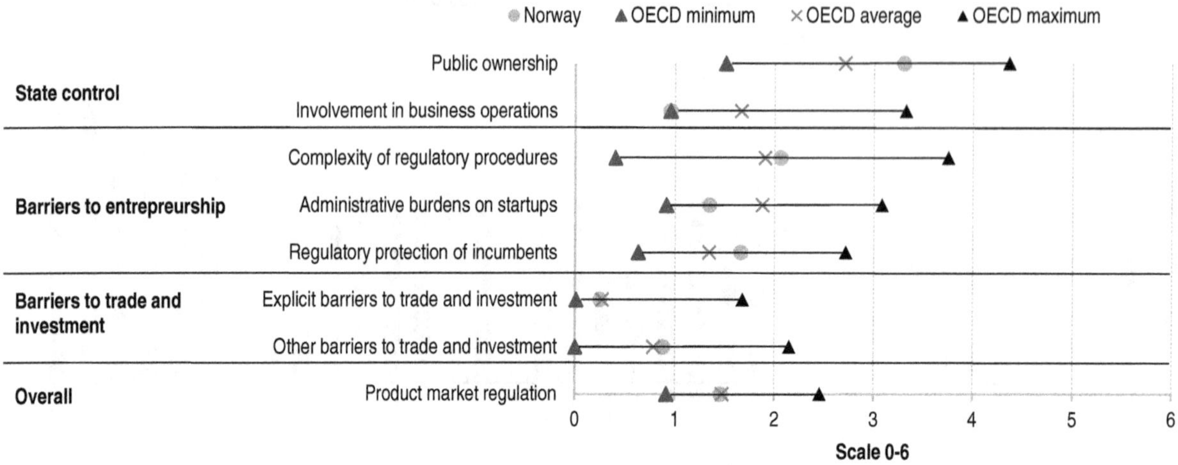

Source: OECD Product Market Regulation Database.

StatLink http://dx.doi.org/10.1787/888933639094

Figure 1.12. **The OECD's Services Trade Restrictiveness Index also flags issues in Norway**

The indices take values between zero and one (the most restrictive)

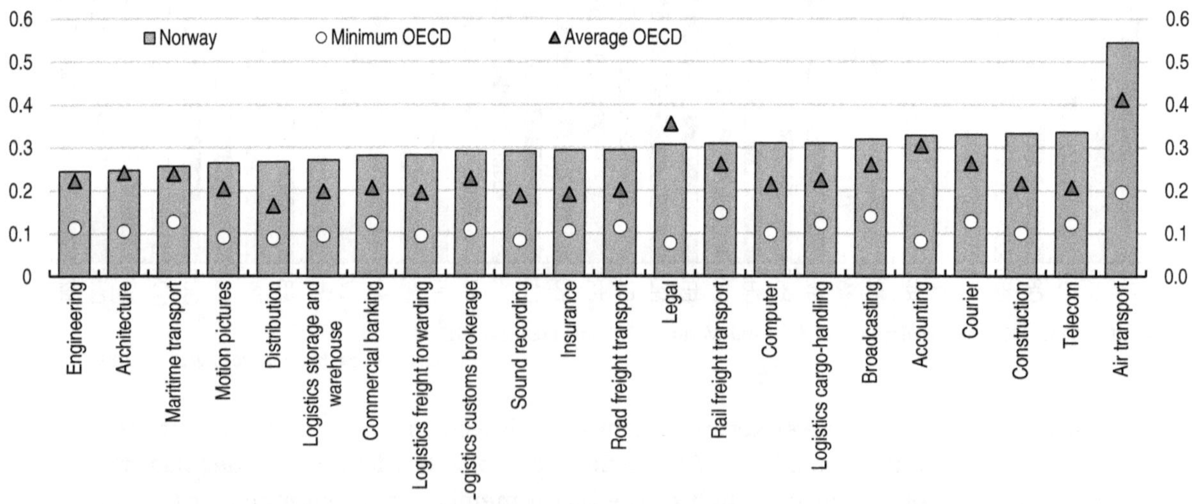

Note: The index includes regulatory transparency, barriers to competition, other discriminatory measures, restrictions on movement of people and restrictions on foreign entry. The STRI methodology takes into account different market and trade cost structures across sectors to ensure that they reflect the relative restrictiveness of each sector. Nevertheless, the indices may not be perfectly comparable across sectors. The indicators are for 2016 or the most recent year available.

Source: OECD Services Trade Restrictiveness Index (STRI).

StatLink http://dx.doi.org/10.1787/888933639113

Avenues for improving competition law

Norway's competition law and process is core to combating anti-competitive practices. The legislation is based on the Competition Act of 2004 and partially incorporates EU competition legislation. Amendments in recent years (Box 1.3) have focused on the treatment of mergers. For instance, Norway has moved away from a "total welfare" approach towards a consumer approach. A total welfare approach is sound in principle as it aims to maximise overall economic surplus by considering all gains and losses. However the authorities have decided that in the Norwegian context the approach was allowing too many deals that risk limiting market competition from a consumer perspective (Productivity Commission, 2015; OECD, 2014a).

Box 1.3. Recent amendments to Norway's competition legislation

In recent years amendments to the 2004 Competition Act have focused on two issues.

Measures to increase the efficiency of competition law (2014):

- Merger notification thresholds were increased, enabling the authorities to concentrate investigation; the investigative caseload has dropped from around 800 to 100 mergers
- Leniency rules have been simplified and harmonised with EU legislation.

Measures to increase independence and harmonisation with regard to mergers (2016/17), including:

- Establishment of a competition complaints board
- Removal of the Ministry of Trade, Industry and Fisheries as the appellate body for some types of National Competition Authority (NCA) decisions, including mergers
- Removal of government powers to overturn NCA decisions based on public interest considerations
- Adoption of the EU model for settlements in cartel cases
- Shift in merger-test approach from the SLC ("substantial lessening of competition") model to the SIEC ("significant impediment to effective competition") model
- Shift from a "total welfare" standard to a "consumer welfare" standard.

Past OECD *Surveys* have been critical of the sectoral exemptions from the Competition Act, which include agriculture, fishing and book retailing. The exemption for agriculture facilitates the operation of Norway's agricultural co-operatives and is one element of the wide-ranging support to preserve domestic agricultural production (much of which is uneconomic), along with extensive import tariffs and income-support payments to farmers.

Supermarket retail chains have attracted the attention of policymakers. As in a number of countries, the chains are criticised for being overly powerful in the grocery supply chain, exploiting monopsony powers over food producers and squeezing out small, independent retail outlets. Legislative measures have been suggested but none, so far, have garnered widespread support among competition experts. A report by the Ministry of Trade, Industry and Fisheries criticises a suggestion to allow the application of "abuse of unilateral behaviour" (under certain circumstances) even if the business in question has not been legally classified as being in a "dominant position". In addition, opinion is divided on the merits of a proposed "code of conduct" law for negotiations between the retail chains and suppliers.

Reducing government's direct role in business through public ownership

State ownership of business enterprise in Norway has diminished, but nevertheless remains extensive. Around 280 000 people, or 11% of employees (equivalent to around 15% of business-sector employees) are employed in companies that are partially or completely state owned according to the latest annual State Ownership Report (Ministry of Trade, Industry and Fisheries, 2016). Economically, the most significant holding is the 67% state stake in the oil and gas conglomerate, Statoil ASA. Other sectors with substantial state stakes include, notably telecoms (Telenor), energy and aluminium production (Norsk Hydro), chemicals (Yara International, ASA), a manufacturing conglomerate (Kongsberg Gruppen) and banking (DNB Bank). The frameworks for administering state-ownership are in many respects exemplary, aligning with good practice in governance. For example the annual *State Ownership Report* brings substantial transparency on the details of state holdings. However, good governance does not necessarily justify the retention of stakes. This is especially the case for stakes that are held in companies that operate in markets for goods or services that are competitive and well-functioning in other respects. It is therefore encouraging that a process of partial or complete sell-offs continues.

Improving resource reallocation through firm dynamics

Firm dynamics – the entry, exit, expansion and contraction of businesses – are core to resource reallocation, innovation and progress towards higher productivity. This is illustrated in a recent OECD publication that includes a study of firm dynamics among incorporated firms in Norway (OECD 2017c). The study confirms that, similar to other countries, firm dynamics can have a sizeable impact on overall productivity growth alongside within-firm productivity growth. Framework conditions that promote flexible and competitive product and labour markets provide an important backdrop for effective firm dynamics. There are more proximate policy influences. The following sections examine administrative procedures and regulatory requirements on business ("red tape"), and insolvency legislation and procedures.

Red tape associated with establishing and operating a business

Norway's red-tape burdens on business are lighter than most. Red tape often involves time and other costs for business, absorbing managerial resources. It also often reflects restrictions and regulations on business operation. Red-tape tends to affect start-ups more than incumbents (OECD, 2016a). This is partly because there are red-tape hurdles in establishing businesses but, in addition, small and young businesses often do not have strong capacity or experience in dealing with red tape. There are ways of ensuring processing and administration requirements are kept to a minimum and Norway appears to be doing reasonably on this front. The Entrepreneurship component of the OECD's product market indicator indicates low barriers to firm entry (see Figure 1.11). Furthermore, Norway ranks 21st highest out of 189 economies in the Starting a Business component of the World Bank's Doing Business indicator.

Welcome policy effort to reduce red-tape burdens further continues. A "better regulations council" similar to that in Sweden has been established (Government of Norway, 2013). Progress in specific areas has included lighter social-security reporting requirements for employers, simplification in building and planning legislation and simplified tax rules for business partnerships. In addition, efforts to simplify administration using digital solutions are underway. A new government portal for enterprise (Altinn) has been set up and a project revamping the ICT of the labour and welfare administration (NAV) is underway. Continued progress along these lines can only be encouraged.

Tuning insolvency legislation to better support innovation and risk taking

Insolvency legislation and procedure influence the efficiency of firm dynamics because they determine what happens to firms in difficulty. Insolvency systems need to offer opportunity to restructure and, where necessary, facilitate exit predictably and

Figure 1.13. **Norway's insolvency system is low cost and has a high recovery rate**

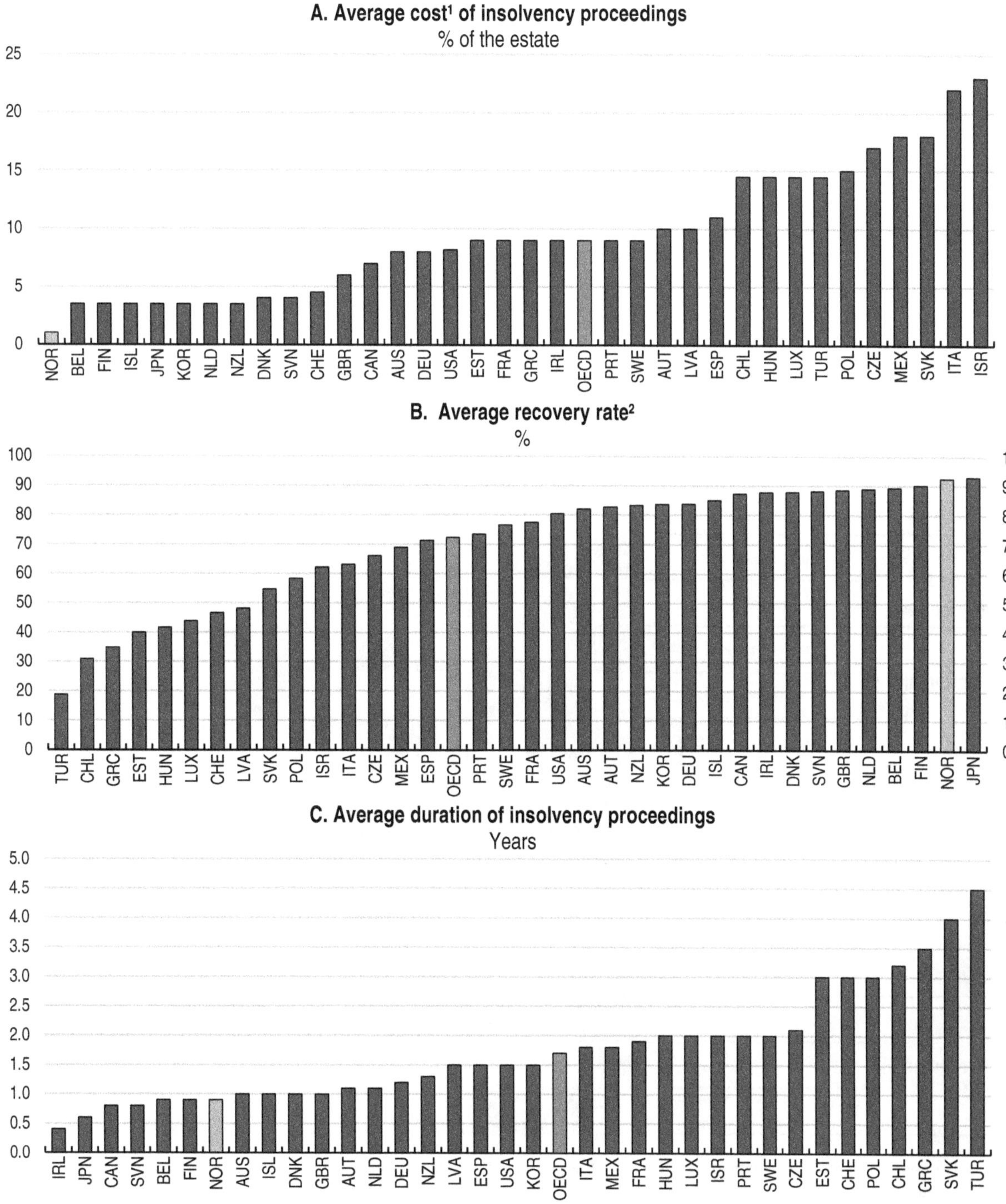

1. The cost of the proceedings is recorded as percentage of the value of the debtor's estate. The cost is calculated on the basis of questionnaire responses and includes court fees and government levies; fees of insolvency administrators, auctioneers, assessors and lawyers; and all other fees and costs.
2. The recovery rate is calculated based on the time, cost and outcome of insolvency proceedings involving domestic legal entities and is recorded as percentage of the amount recovered by secured creditors. The calculation takes into account the outcome: whether the business emerges from the proceedings as a going concern or the assets are sold piecemeal. Then the costs of the proceedings are deducted. Finally, the value lost as a result of the time the money remains tied up in insolvency proceedings is taken into account. The recovery rate is the present value of the remaining proceeds, based on end-2015 lending rates.

Source: World Bank, *Doing Business 2017 Database.*

StatLink http://dx.doi.org/10.1787/888933639132

Figure 1.14. **A new OECD indicator suggests weaknesses in insolvency restructuring and efficiency**

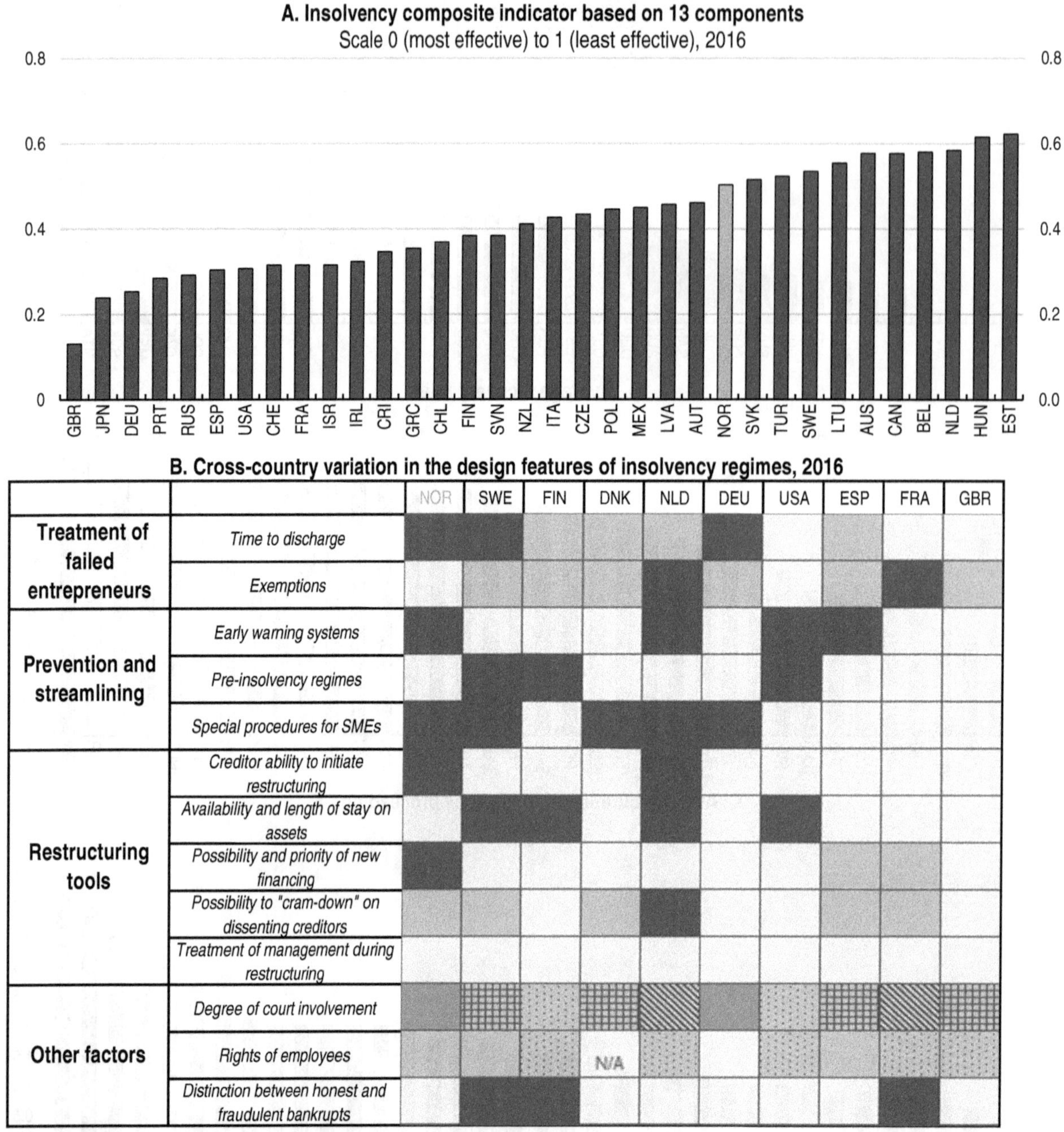

Notes: Darker shades denote the specific design features that are likely to delay the initiation of and increase the length of insolvency proceedings. Specifically, a white cell refers to the best practice and cells are ordered such that a black cell refers to features that are most likely to delay the initiation of and increase the length of insolvencyproceedings.
Source: McGowan et al. (2017).

StatLink http://dx.doi.org/10.1787/888933639151

expediently (Box 1.4) – as well as providing appropriate balance between the interests of the businesses (the "debtors") and those financing them (the "creditors"). A strong slant in favour of debtors can dissuade credit growth and prompt excessive risk taking. Conversely, strong creditor protection and heavy penalties on debtors can overly dissuade business enterprise and risk taking.

International indicators point to a mixed picture for Norway's insolvency system. Sub-components of the World Bank's Doing Business insolvency indicator show low financial and time costs (Figure 1.13). In addition, Norway's "recovery rate" is high, i.e. creditors are typically returned a substantial proportion of their investment through reorganization, liquidation or debt enforcement (foreclosure or receivership) proceedings. Meanwhile, Norway appears mediocre in a recently developed OECD indicator of insolvency that focuses on restructuring and efficiency (Figure 1.14, Panel A). Exploration of the individual components points to various weaknesses. Time to discharge (i.e. the number of years a bankrupt person must wait until they are discharged from pre-bankruptcy indebtedness) is relatively long (Figure 1.14, Panel B). Furthermore, there are shortfalls in prevention and streamlining, and in restructuring tools. There has already been some investigation of insolvency system, which is welcome. The Ministry of Justice and Public Security commissioned a report with a remit to propose changes to debt negotiation provisions ("reconstruction" provisions) in bankruptcy law. The government has yet to follow up on the commission's findings.

Box 1.4. **Key elements of insolvency**

There is no single best-practice model of insolvency due to variation in institutional and legislative contexts across countries. Nevertheless, an OECD review of insolvency (McGowan and Andrews, 2016) indicates there are several key elements:

- A clear trigger for initiating insolvency proceedings that encourages early remedial action towards restructuring
- Efficient liquidation options and fair opportunity for rehabilitation
- Checks against undesirable strategic behaviour
- Options for out-of-court settlement
- Provisions for cross-border insolvency and equal treatment for foreign and domestic creditors
- Attention to personal insolvency arrangements so that these align with the objectives of corporate insolvency.

Targeted support for innovation

Innovation, whether based on R&D activity or other investments in knowledge-based capital, drives much of productivity growth. This is especially the case in advanced countries such as Norway where productivity gains through capital deepening in well-established technologies are typically well-advanced. Key points for policy are:

- As a small open economy, much of Norway's productivity-enhancing innovation is "imported", in the form of tangible new products, machinery and equipment, or intangibles, such as software. The increasing internationalisation of production ("global value chains") has raised the role of innovation diffusion via supply chains. Imported innovation underlines the importance of cross-border trade, investment and business linkages, and consequently the importance of ensuring good framework conditions for business. Similar applies for exported innovation, where Norway has strengths in petroleum-sector technology and aquaculture.
- Nevertheless, domestic research and innovation has an important role to play. Furthermore, it can be strongly influenced by policy. Levers include, business R&D tax breaks, research

grants and influence via public funding of research in universities and research institutes (the 'research sector'). The research sector's linkage to business-sector productivity growth is complex. Substantial segments are not primarily focused on bringing gains for the business sector, for instance, this applies to areas of health research. The research sector most directly feeds into domestic productivity when this involves working with the business sector (for example through commissioned research or collaborative research). In addition, domestic research feeds through to global knowhow and then back through to domestic productivity gains. Also, "basic research" plays a key role, for instance through positive effects on the effectiveness of applied research (OECD, 2015a; Saia et al., 2015).

Norway's domestic research and innovation activity, as measured by R&D expenditure, is middle ranking. Overall R&D expenditure is just under 2% of total GDP and 2.4% of mainland GDP (Figure 1.15). In all three of its Nordic peers, Denmark, Finland and Sweden, R&D expenditure is closer to 3% of GDP. Norway's business-sector R&D expenditure is a couple of notches further down the international ranking while it ranks better in higher education expenditure. Cross-country differences in industry composition play a role in these comparisons; in Norway's case much business-sector R&D is in petroleum-related sectors. Furthermore, R&D spending does not capture all forms of innovation. Nevertheless, it seems that, broadly, Norway is below par in business-sector innovation, notably in relation to its Nordic peers.

Meanwhile, government expenditure on R&D is comparatively high (Figure 1.16). Given the middle-ranking overall R&D expenditure this may suggest that government R&D spending is not leveraging a lot of additional R&D activity in the business sector. To an extent this is not a concern, reflecting the non-business orientation of much government-backed research. Notably much government support for R&D is channelled towards improving the public health care system (OECD, 2017d).

Norway's primary policy levers on domestic research echo those used elsewhere. These essentially comprise: i) programmes that provide direct financial support, primarily, R&D tax breaks and research grants; ii) non-direct support for business, such as support for research incubators; and, iii) powers to influence university and research-institute behaviour most notably because block grants form a large part of most of these institutions' funding (Table 1.2). A recent OECD *Innovation Review* of Norway (OECD, 2017d) contains extensive coverage on the innovation activities of public-research institutes and the higher education sector. In addition it assesses the menu of support programmes. A selective summary of the Review's recommendations is shown in Box 1.5.

Support programmes for business R&D: overall coverage and mix of instruments

The recent OECD review recommends more strategic support (Box 1.5). It finds that the current menu of policies is comprehensive but geared to supporting existing strengths rather than emerging sectors for innovation. Some steps have been taken to address this. For instance the Research Council of Norway has introduced more strategic-type programmes that encourage the transfer of knowledge across sectors. The review underscores that more shift in this direction would be welcome.

Furthermore, the number of programmes raises concern. Funding growth in recent years has increased an already large number of programmes, which are managed by the Research Council of Norway and Innovation Norway. Reportedly, there is substantial overlap between some of these programmes, and the large number of different schemes

Figure 1.15. **Domestic R&D activity in Norway is middle ranking**

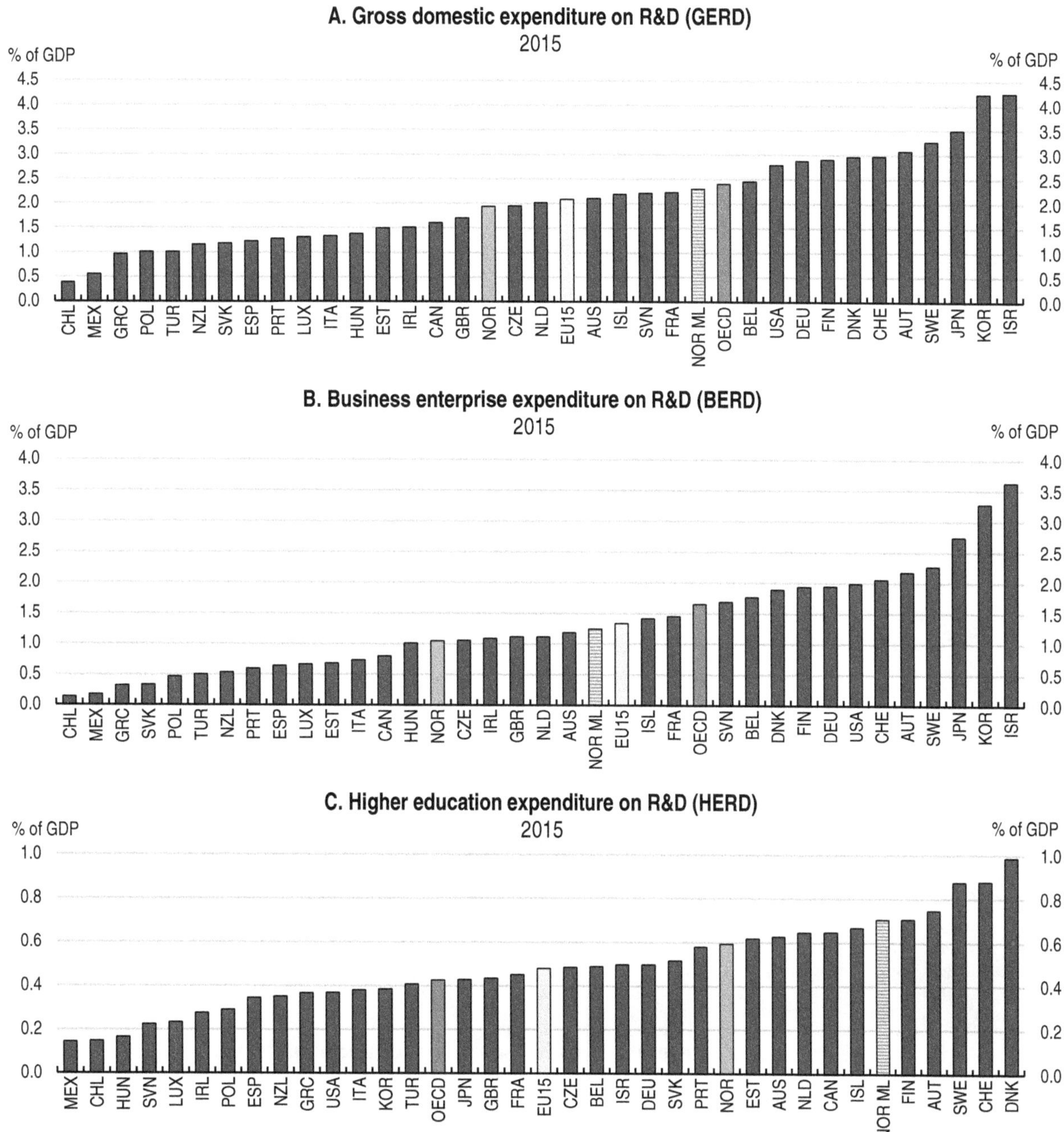

Note: For NOR ML the denominator is Mainland GDP.
Source: *OECD Main Science and Technology Indicators Database.*

StatLink http://dx.doi.org/10.1787/888933639170

makes it a complex system. The OECD's *Innovation Review* suggests incentivising the Council to reduce the number of programmes.

Support programmes for business R&D: the SkatteFUNN tax-break

The SkatteFUNN tax break is Norway's largest R&D support programme and its only innovation-related tax break. It is a tax credit calculated as a percentage of eligible R&D expenditures and provides more support to small-and-medium enterprise. When introduced

Figure 1.16. **Government expenditure on R&D is comparatively high**

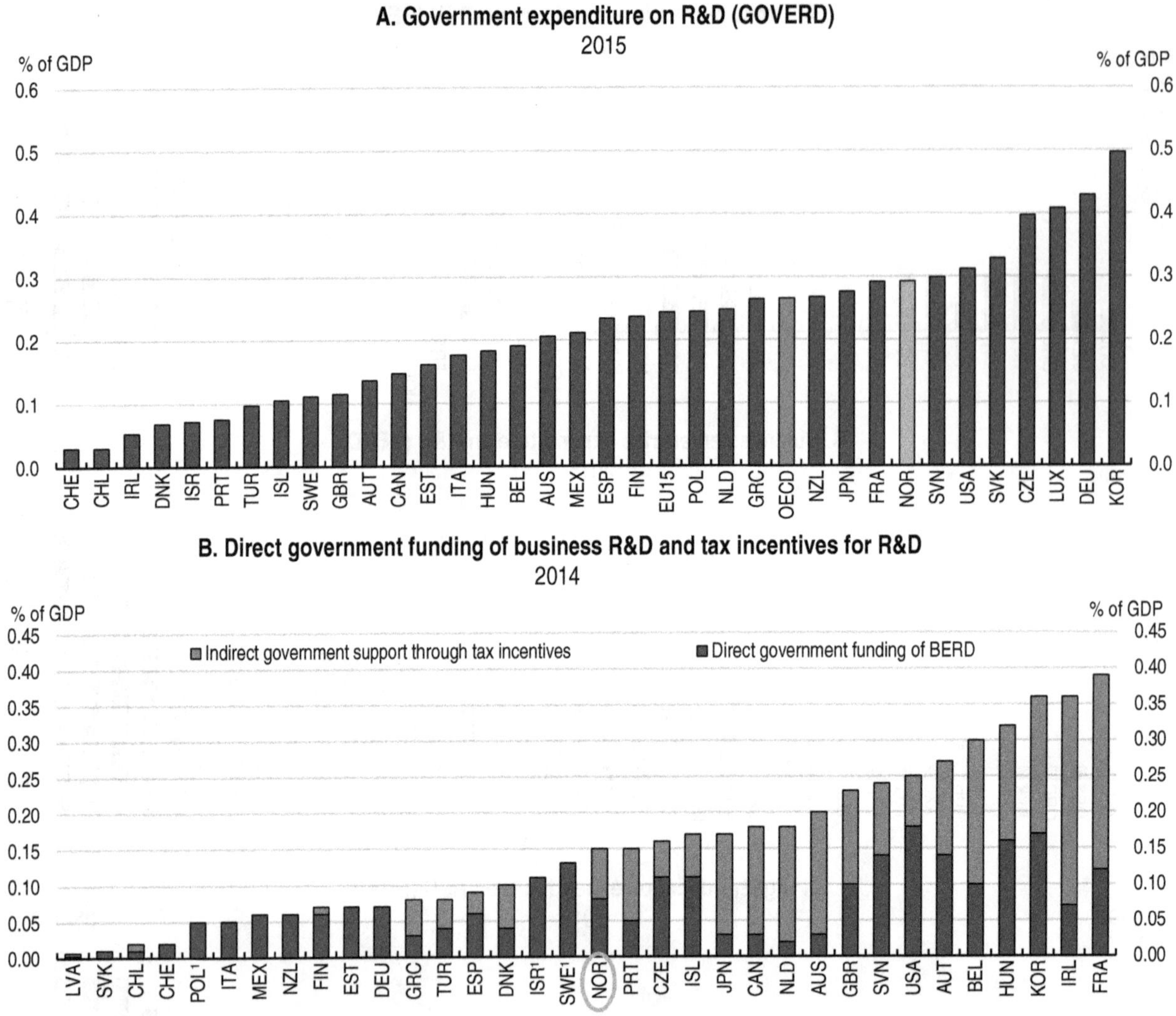

1. Data on tax incentive support not available.

Source: OECD Main Science and Technology Indicators Database.

StatLink http://dx.doi.org/10.1787/888933639189

Table 1.2. **Key elements in Norway's innovation support**

Policy area	Key aspects
Tax break for innovation-related expenditure (SkatteFUNN).	SkatteFUNN is a tax credit; 20% of R&D-related costs for SMEs and 18% for larger enterprises (with ceilings on the size of the credit). A tax refund is possible if the credit is greater than the firm's total tax liability.
Grant programmes run by the Research Council of Norway (an agency operating under the Ministry of Education and Research).	A large-scale grant programme. Competitive thematic research grant programmes.
Support via Innovation Norway (a state-owned enterprise under the Ministry of Trade and Industry).	Advisory and promotional activities. Public procurement for innovation programmes.
Support via the Industrial Development Corporate of Norway (SIVA, *Selskapet for industrivekst*, a state-owned enterprise under the Ministry of Trade and Industry).	Cluster programmes. Science parks, research parts, incubators, business gardens. Venture capital programmes.
Block funding for universities and public research institutes (administered by the Ministry of Education and Research).	Block funding comprises a mix of "basic" allocations, which are based on historical values, and criteria-based allocations.

Box 1.5. A selective summary of recommendations from the OECD *Innovation Review* (2017)

Innovation support programmes

- More strongly target innovation support towards identified priorities. For instance, cluster policies could be made more selective.
- Develop a holistic system of enterprise support that focuses both on R&D of established firms and renewal through start-up development.
- Reinforce collaboration across agencies and ministries around key priorities and opportunity-driven innovation policies.

Higher education sector

- Focus on excellence and critical mass: prioritise top-class recruiting and career models; further increase the capacity of higher-education leadership to reallocate resources towards excellence; continue funding centres of excellence.
- Promote further mergers between providers, mainly among university colleges. However, resist pressure to increase the number of universities; the functional stratification between regional or applied institutions and internationally competitive research-intensive universities should be maintained.

Public research institutes

- Use block funding to encourage good performance and incentivize (further) mergers between institutes and with universities.
- Ensure that the funds distributed directly by ministries to the research institutes are related to strategic projects.
- Encourage collaboration across institutes, include collaboration across institutes as a criterion for funding programmes.

Knowledge transfer

- Provide more diversified support to the "third mission" in universities, in addition to increasing the budget of the R&D commercialization programme, FORNY.
- Increase incentives for external engagement of academics with industry and other sectors, such as hospitals and the public and voluntary sector. Improve data collection on third-mission activities.
- Encourage knowledge-transfer activities of research institutes. Consider additional funding streams, including dedicated commercialisation funds, and/or the inclusion of knowledge-transfer indicators in existing funding.

Policy governance

- Use the long-term plan process to gradually enhance the level of multi-annual financial commitment and priority setting.
- Build upon the long-term plan process and institutional infrastructure to improve strategic and operational inter-ministerial co-ordination.
- Provide the Research Council of Norway with a more independent budget to run inter-ministerial strategic programmes.
- Incentivise the Council to further reduce the number of funding programmes.

the credit only applied to SMEs. Support has widened since then and there is now only a small gap between the credit rate applied to SMEs and large firms (the rate is 20%, compared with 18% for large firms). Ceilings on claimable R&D costs have been increased significantly from 2013 to 2017, which substantially increased support for larger-scale innovation (and increased the fiscal cost of the scheme). OECD calculations of the "B-index" show SkatteFUNN is middle ranking regarding the marginal incentive to investment in R&D, and, as expected given the structure of the credit, the index is lower for large firms compared with SMEs (Figure 1.17).

SkatteFUNN has positive features including refundability and a pre-approval system. Refundability in particular implies support for innovative enterprises at an early stage of development when, typically, revenue and profit streams have yet to fully develop. Under the pre-approval system firms apply (and, if successful, receive approval) for the SkatteFUNN credit in advance, which provides more certainty over systems where the tax-break is calculated *ex post*.

As for R&D tax breaks elsewhere, the impact on R&D activity and whether, overall, the tax expenditure is worthwhile are difficult to determine. While the tax break almost certainly has a positive impact on overall innovative activity, estimates of the value of this benefit range widely (in part because of hard-to-measure spill-over effects), so whether the benefits justify the fiscal cost is unclear. Creditably, the Norwegian authorities have initiated several impact studies. For instance Haegland and Moen (2007) estimated that the scheme had input additionality effects ranging from 1.3 to 2.9 per unit of support. A new government-initiated evaluation, due to be published in 2018, should shed new light on SkatteFUNN's effectiveness.

Support programmes for business R&D: access to finance is currently high on the policy agenda

As discussed in the context of firm dynamics (see above), administrative processes to set up businesses are quite smooth in Norway. However, access to finance is commonly a constraint on the establishment and growth of firms. Policy intervention can be used to address externalities, the "classic" reasoning for intervention being that there are public returns to research that are not factored into commercial financing decisions. Access to finance for innovative firms can be compromised, unintentionally, by the extensive regulation that governs financial markets.

Policy steps have already been taken. These include proposal in the 2017 Interim Budget for a tax-deduction for private individuals investing in young start-up companies, which essentially implies a 24% subsidy on the investment. The scheme is quite tightly targeted. The deduction is capped at NOK 500 000 (i.e. around EUR 55 000 at an exchange rate of 9 NOK per EUR) and eligibility requirements include that the company is less than six years old, has less than NOK 40 million in revenue and less than 25 employees. In addition, there are plans to make share-option compensation of employees more attractive. Currently, when the option is exercised, the employees and employers are required to pay, almost immediately, tax and social-security charges. This can be problematic when shares cannot be sold easily as it means finding alternative means paying these costs. The proposed measures reduce the immediacy of these payment demands. A committee (due to report in 2018) has been appointed to further examine access to capital, including those arising from prudential regulation. For instance, Norway's insurance-sector regulation forces asset portfolios to be highly conservative which means the sector invests little in shares or start-ups.

Figure 1.17. **Norway's R&D tax break is slanted to supporting SMEs**

2016

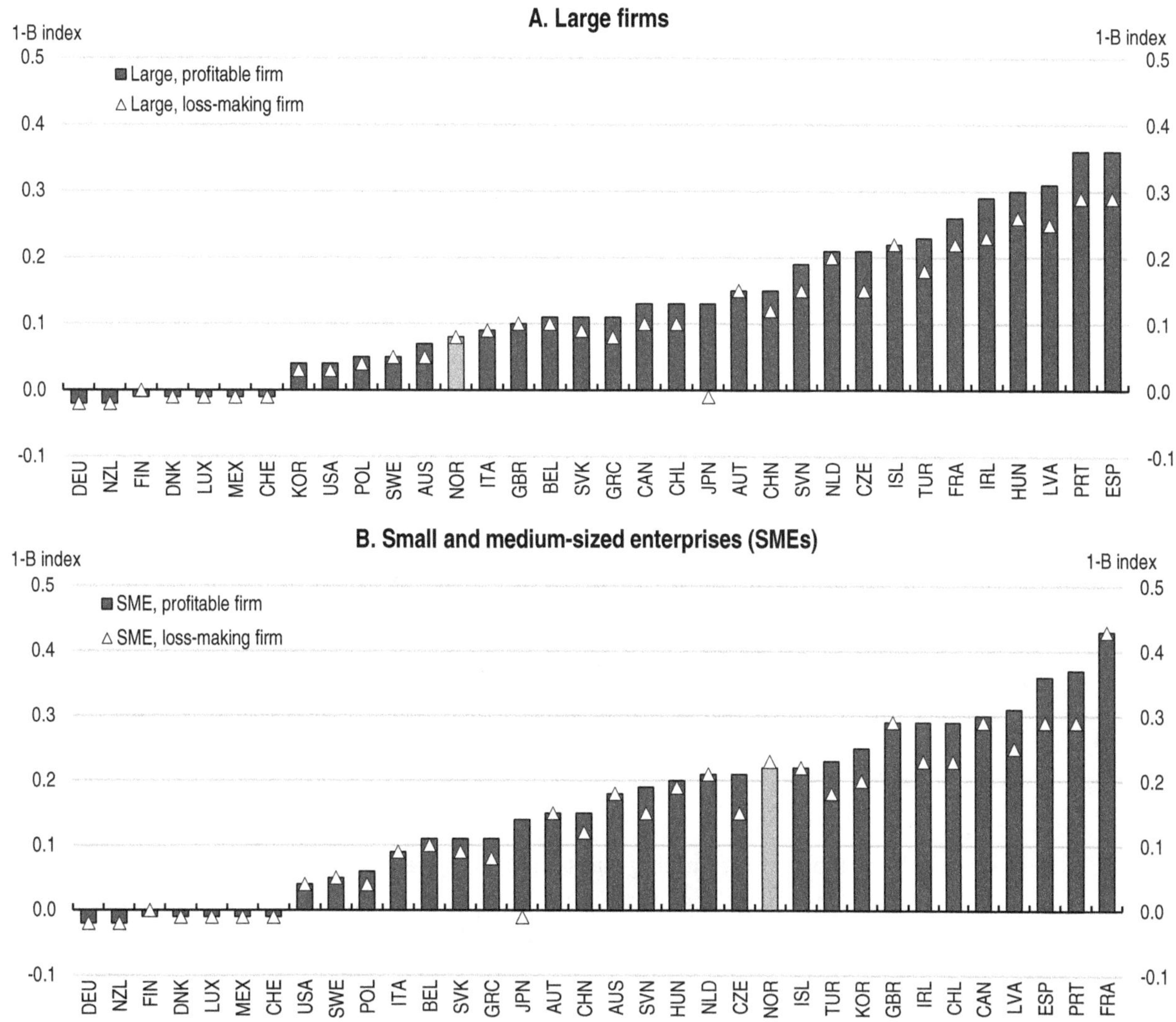

Note: The tax advantage is calculated as 1 minus the B index, which is a measure of the before-tax income needed to break even on an additional unit of R&D outlay. The index is calculated for a representative firm according to whether it can claim tax benefits against their tax liability in the reporting period. This is an experimental indicator and international comparability may be limited. See also OECD (2017, Science, Technology and Industry Scoreboard)

Source: OECD Science, Technology and Industry Scoreboard 2017.

StatLink http://dx.doi.org/10.1787/888933639208

Policy steerage on the higher education sector

Research capacities of universities and research institutes are core to domestic research. Good research capacity is an important draw for business investment and scale effects from collaborative research networks can generate high-productivity growth clusters. According to an OECD indicator, Norway scores quite well in collaborative research (Figure 1.18). Collaboration between public-sector research institutes and health trusts is, reportedly, particularly strong (OECD, 2017d). Yet industry funding of higher-education expenditure is moderate in international comparison, suggesting perhaps weaker collaboration in this sphere.

Scale of operation is a key issue for research in Norway's higher education sector (which comprises universities and more vocationally oriented "university colleges"), particularly that required for internationally recognised centres of excellence. Mergers underway mark a positive step. Indeed, the response to the government's inducements to merge (see 2016 *Survey*) was broadly successfully. As of autumn 2017 the number of higher education institutions had been reduced from 33 prior to the merger programme to 21. The final impact of these mergers will depend importantly on the degree to which there is follow-through in mergers between faculties and departments.

Figure 1.18. **Norway scores reasonably in collaborative research**

Firms collaborating on innovation with higher education or research institutions, by size, 2012-14

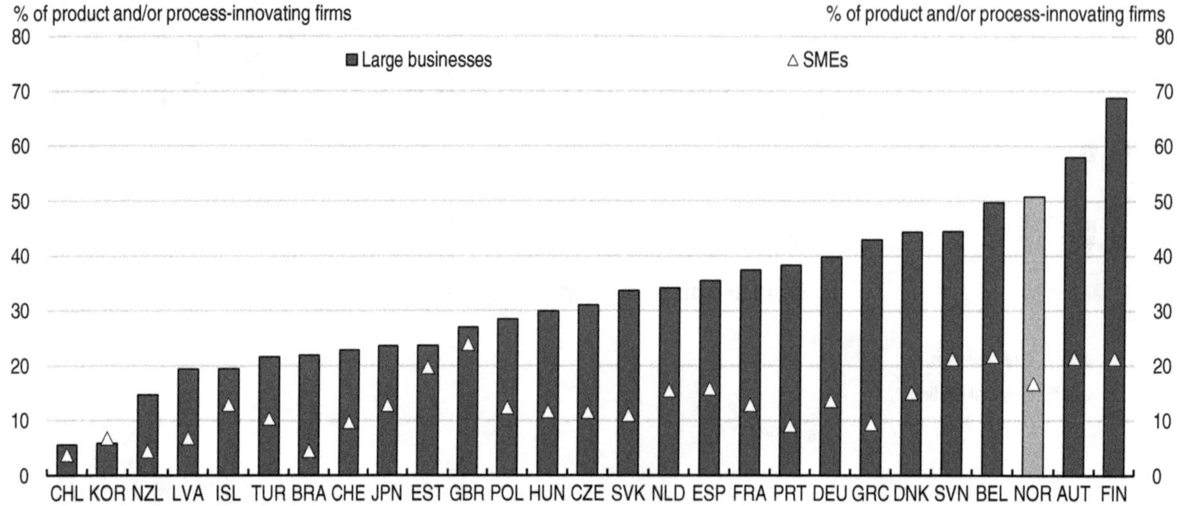

Source: OECD Science, Technology and Industry Scoreboard 2017.

StatLink http://dx.doi.org/10.1787/888933639227

Recent reforms to block-grant funding aim to improve research incentives. The reforms partly aim to re-shape research incentives with new components added to the block allocation linked to research activity (Table 1.3). In addition, a roll-out of performance agreements is underway that will see further alteration of research incentives via the funding system.

Policy steerage on research institutes

Norway's research-institute sector is comparatively large. There are over one hundred institutes, of which 44 are recipients of state block grants (OECD, 2017d). Areas of specialisation include aquaculture and health care. There are some large players among the over one hundred institutes. For example, SINTEF (*stiftelsen for industriell og teknisk forskning*, "foundation for industrial and technical research"), a research institute headquartered Trondheim has around 2000 employees. Nevertheless, many institutes are small, arguably too small in many cases. There have been voluntary mergers in recent years and there is a case for inducing more though a similar government program to that implemented in higher education. In addition, stronger encouragement for exploiting synergies between institutions should be considered.

Similar to higher education, funding reform is being used to induce change in the research-institute sector. Funding of research institutes is complicated because several ministries are involved. A common performance-based mechanism for one segment of budget allocation aiming, *inter alia*, to strengthen scientific quality and collaboration was

Table 1.3. **Block-grant funding for higher education following the reforms of 2017**

Component of funding	Share of aggregate higher-education revenues (approximate and will vary across institutions
Block-grant funding continues to account for around 80% high-education provider revenues (in aggregate), 20% from various other sources	80%
Of which: A) roughly 70% remains based on an institutions historical budget level ("Basic Component")	56%
B) the remaining 30% of block-grant funding comprises:	24%
1. **"Open-ended component"** (85% of the 30%). This budget allocation is "open ended" and the allocation formula now comprises: • Credit points (64%) • Graduation rates (15%) (new) • PhD graduates (5%) (new) • Exchange students (1.2%)	20%
2. **"Fixed-limit budget components"** a fixed limit budget equivalent to roughly 15% of the 30% remainder). The allocation formula now comprises: • Publication Credits • Research Council of Norway funding • EU funding and similar • A contract research indicator.	4%

introduced in 2009. However this still does not apply across all research institutions and room remains to harmonise the performance indicators used (OECD, 2017d).

Policy strategy and governance

The OECD *Review of Innovation Policy* considers strategic steerage in innovation policy. Since 2014, strategic guidance has begun to operate through four-year rolling "long term plans" that look one decade ahead. At present the emphasis is on guidance, as the plans do not lay down binding commitments. The review recommends these plans include more defined financial commitment and provide a stronger inter-ministerial and operational co-ordination. In addition, the review underscores the challenges faced by the Research Council of Norway as the central conduit for the programmes of several ministries. It runs more than 30 major programmes and many smaller ones. The review suggests the Council is provided with a more independent budget for running inter-ministerial programmes and incentives to reduce the number of programmes (Box 1.5).

Facilitating new forms of business

As elsewhere, internet-platform businesses (so-called "disruptors") are growing in scale and scope in Norway (for general discussion see OECD 2015b). Disruption in personal transport and short-term accommodation has so far attracted most attention. Disruption on other fronts is emerging, for instance in financial and legal services. In a welcome move, the Norwegian Government established a committee to look into the "sharing economy", which accounts for much of the new wave of business models. The committee delivered its report in February 2017 (NOU 4, 2017).

Policy needs to embrace disruption, though not unconditionally. As other OECD *Surveys* have pointed out (for instance OECD, 2017e), disruption can bring widespread benefits to households (and businesses) through lower-cost and better quality goods and services. Smoothing the way for disruption may require countering incumbents' attempts to stifle new entrants. Furthermore, there can be unintended obstacles to disruption in legislation and regulation that could be removed without negative consequence. However, support for disruptors should not be universal, as some business models bring downsides for consumers and service providers or may be based on undesirable exploitation of regulation or taxation.

Labour dimensions of disruption are particularly challenging in the Norwegian context

Sharing economy business models are typically founded on using internet platforms to create a point of exchange for supply and demand. In some cases the service providers (e.g. drivers of taxi-like services) operate under some form of non-standard work category; such as self-employment and temporary employment contracts (for a general discussion see OECD, 2016b). For service providers this can bring welcome independence and flexibility but involves greater risk and less protection than regular employment, prompting debate as to the relative merits of some sharing economy businesses (OECD, 2016b).

Norway's legal framework regarding non-standard work arrangements is provided by the Working Environment Act of 2005 (*Arbeidsmiljøloven*). Key elements in the definition of "employee" are whether the individual has a) a personal and ongoing duty to work and b) a duty to submit to another person's management, instructions and control. The nature of the relationship between the service providers and the management and owners of digital platforms in areas such as taxi-like services indeed suggests the situation is by no means clear cut. For instance, the digital platforms, to an extent, set rules about the service provided, which can be interpreted as being under managerial control. In terms of policy action, the key question is whether the existing system of legislation and procedure can handle these new questions regarding status as an employee. The majority of the members of the committee on the sharing economy concluded this was the case.

Recommendations have been made to strengthen sub-contractor rights. Network effects in the sharing economy can result in markets dominated by a handful of operators (or even just one), leaving the (sometimes numerous) subcontractors with little bargaining power. Norway's sharing-economy committee discussed giving subcontractors the right to negotiate collective agreements in situations where the internet platform sets the services prices. Making service-provider ratings portable could also help.

Taxation of service providers in the new business models

Differences between service providers in incumbent and disruptor business models often mean differences in the way they are taxed. The small scale (and low revenue amounts) of service providers often contrasts with incumbent providers and this drives differences in tax treatment. For instance, based on data provided by internet-platform providers, the annual income from taxi-like services or short-term rentals in Norway is typically around NOK 20 000 (i.e. around EUR 2 200 at an exchange rate of 9 NOK per EUR). Small-scale income based on one-time services per client is typically treated as freelancer labour income and not as business income. Such small-scale income service providers are entitled to a tax free income of NOK 1 000 (NOK 6 000 in the case of work in client's home or holiday home) per client. This entails a tax advantage compared to the self-employed, whose surplus is taxable from the first krone. The Sharing Economy Committee suggested simplifying tax treatment of small incomes from services, including service provision that would otherwise not be taxed.

In Norway some of the most thorny tax questions relating to disruption are in the accommodation market:

- Similar to some other countries, rentals of private accommodation are not subject to VAT, representing a tax advantage over "traditional" accommodation providers. This relates to a wider issue of VAT thresholds (see below).
- Various exemptions on non-commercial accommodation rental income further add to differences in tax treatment with traditional providers. The income from renting out up to half of a person's own home is free from tax. If more than half of the home is let out rental income is also free from tax up to NOK 20 000 per annum. A majority of the Sharing Economy Committee suggested that income from short-term tenancy agreements should be taxable also for residential landlords. In the 2018 Budget the government has proposed that rental income from tenancy agreements lasting less than 30 days will be taxable capital income.
- Classification as a commercial activity (which brings heavier tax and reporting duties) is unclear. For instance, rental activity combined with significant input in the form of private work (such as cleaning) can justify re-classification.

Increasing numbers of small-scale providers have brought VAT thresholds under the spotlight. Thresholds for VAT collection, if set low, can impose heavy administrative burdens on small-scale operators in return for little fiscal revenue. Meanwhile, high thresholds can put substantial sub-groups of providers at an advantage. The Norwegian threshold, equivalent to only around EUR 5 500 per year (Table 1.4), implies a lot of small-scale activities are obligated to report VAT.

Table 1.4. **Selected tax details relevant for the sharing economy**

Area of taxation	Selected detail (EUR values approximate, based on an exchange rate of 9 Norwegian Krone per Euro)
Value-added tax (VAT)	• VAT threshold: operations with sales of more than NOK 50 000 (EUR 5 500) during a 12-month period are subject to VAT. • Real-estate rental is exempt from VAT legislation (the Value Added Tax Act).
Income-tax treatment of small jobs/services	• General rule: labour income up to NOK 1 000 (EUR 110) per client is generally exempt from taxation. If remuneration is higher than NOK 1 000, then the whole remuneration is taxable. • Labour income from work performed in a client's home or holiday home (e.g. cleaning services) is exempt up to NOK 6 000 (EUR 650) per client.
Income-tax treatment of revenue from non-commercial rental (e.g. of houses, vehicles)	• General tax-free threshold of NOK 10 000 (EUR 1 100) per taxpayer per year. Renting out up to half of own home is free from tax. If more than half of own home is let out, up to NOK 20 000 (EUR 2 200) is free from tax.
Other	• Taxis are subject to lower motor-vehicle registration tax and lower annual vehicle tax (though all electric vehicles, taxis or otherwise are entirely exempt).

Also as regards small-scale provision, the committee on the sharing economy suggests introducing "third party disclosure rules" to sharing-economy platforms akin those that apply to traditional businesses. For instance, the platforms could be obliged to report details on the independent operators using their system, including details of revenues. The latter could then be automatically fed into tax administration data on individuals' incomes. Small-scale providers can be further helped by information campaigns on their tax situation. This has already been addressed in Norway; the tax authorities have published information regarding the taxation of short-term rentals and other sharing economy activities.

Transportation-sector disruption has not got that far in Norway

Personal transport services such as Uber are in most cases illegal in Norway due to compulsory taxi licencing. The situation is akin to that in some other countries. In Norway, the legality of the drivers rests on whether they can be considered to operate as a transport service under the Professional Transport Act. In principle, applicability of the term "operate" is determined according to various factors such as frequency of operation and whether the vehicle is systematically used for commercial purposes. The Norwegian taxi regulation contributed to the termination of Uber's unlicensed service (UberPop) in October 2017.

Meanwhile, Norway's taxi licencing system remains largely unreformed. Similar to taxi regulation in many countries, the licencing system includes regulations endeavouring to ensure service availability, passenger safety and protection from abusive charging practices. However these regulations often also serve to protect incumbent operators. The numbers of licences are set by county governments according to an assessment of need but the challenges in doing this invariably means there is mismatch between supply and demand. Among the various criteria, licence holders (who may be taxi drivers, or employers of drivers) must be a member of an approved taxi dispatch centre, and the provision of taxi services must be their principle occupation. The taxi drivers themselves are subject to a range of additional criteria, including (in some localities) tests of geographical knowledge. Though the taxi sector has modernised to an extent (for instance options for booking online have been developed), there is little justification for retaining the system in its current form. As recommended by the committee on the sharing economy, wholesale replacement of the current taxi-licencing system with less restrictive regulation to address availability and consumer-protection would be welcome. Pressure for change has already come from the EFTA Surveillance Authority, which in February 2017 delivered a "reasoned opinion" questioning the legality of limiting the number of taxi licences in the context of EEA laws on freedom of establishment.

Disruption in the accommodation market has been less contentious

Short-stay rentals via companies such as Airbnb, occupy a small but growing market share. For instance, as of 2015 Airbnb accounted for nearly 2% of the total number of overnight stays (NOU, 2017). As elsewhere, short-term rentals are probably expanding the accommodation market because the services are somewhat different from traditional accommodation providers (hotels, guest houses). Nevertheless, these services will have taken some business away from traditional providers, though exactly how much is not known.

Short-term rentals do not face major controversies in Norway but there are issues. In particular:

- Building regulation. Short-term rentals are typically private homes, and therefore subject to different (usually lighter) building regulation compared with traditional accommodation in areas such as fire safety and electrical systems. In Norway, much building regulation lies in the hands of municipalities and so any policy response to this issue will be heterogeneous and may be a vehicle for protecting vested interests.
- Legal provisions to protect neighbours. Under Norway's legislation, home owners can be required to apply for a change in use if is deemed that accommodation is used for activities resembling a hotel or commercial operation and that this results in increased traffic noise or other inconvenience. Such provisions provide useful protection for local residents but, as with building regulation, can end up as an instrument for those opposed to short-term lets.
- Threat to the ordinary rental market. In some cities in Europe and the United States restrictions on short-term rents have been introduced that reflect concerns for the negative impact on the ordinary rental market (higher prices, reduced availability). So far

this problem has not become prominent in Norwegian cities. This is partly because the long-term rental market is comparatively small (rates of home ownership are very high).

Policy can help ensure a balanced development in short-term rents. Ensuring good information on the rules and regulations that apply to private rents helps reduce uncertainty for renters and clients. In addition, there is value in monitoring and encouraging an exchange of experiences across local government on building regulation and the application of laws. This can help improve practice (and prevent regulatory changes from being used unreasonably to protect commercial or local interests).

Maintaining strong and flexible labour supply

Norway scores well in many aspects of labour supply. High levels of labour-force participation, especially among women, high educational attainment, and low rates of long-term unemployment mean there are few groups with weak skills or little work experience. Furthermore, Norway's membership of Europe's core agreement on the free movement, the European Economic Area, facilitates international labour migration (notably from eastern-European countries, such as Poland), providing an important source of supplementary labour supply. Retaining these channels for labour migration will be important for helping Norway's economy cope with business-cycle fluctuations in the future. This said, Norway's high rates of home ownership, fuelled by unusually favourable tax treatment, may to an extent be limiting household and labour mobility; providing another reason for reform (see Assessment and Recommendations). In addition, labour-market withdrawal among older cohorts remains a challenge for policy.

Sickness and disability benefit reform

Norway's sickness and disability system has become a channel for *de facto* early retirement. The authorities face the difficult challenge of ensuring the system provides individuals with appropriate support for disability, while encouraging those with capacities for employment to remain in the labour force. The route to early retirement typically entails individuals transitioning from paid sick leave (which lasts up to one year), to a rehabilitation-type benefit, the Work Assessment Allowance, AAP, which can be provided for up to four years (from January 2018 the main rule will be three years) and then to the national-insurance funded Disability Benefit. The latter may be supplemented by income from occupational disability pension schemes.

Progress has been made in reducing recipiency, but concerns remain. For instance the proportion of 50-67 year-olds receiving the Disability Benefit has been declining (Figure 1.19). Nevertheless, the recipiency rate in this cohort is nearly 30% and the decline is recipiency is partly due to increased numbers receiving the rehabilitation benefit. Around 5% of the working-age population receive the latter benefit and about 3.5% receive the sick-pay allowance. Furthermore, there has been increase in the share of Disability Benefits among young and middle-aged cohorts. Though the recipiency rates remain low, the development is of some concern.

Past and ongoing reforms have significantly improved the sickness and disability system. There are provisions for gradual return to work, a fine grid of partial disability benefits along with comprehensive rehabilitation, training and work placement services. Recent reforms to sick leave (Table 1.5) include efforts to strengthen medical assessment. In addition, changes in the Work Assessment Allowance will be implemented from January 2018.

Figure 1.19. **Recipiency of Disability Benefit is declining among older cohorts but rising in young age groups**

People on Disability Benefit, % of age category

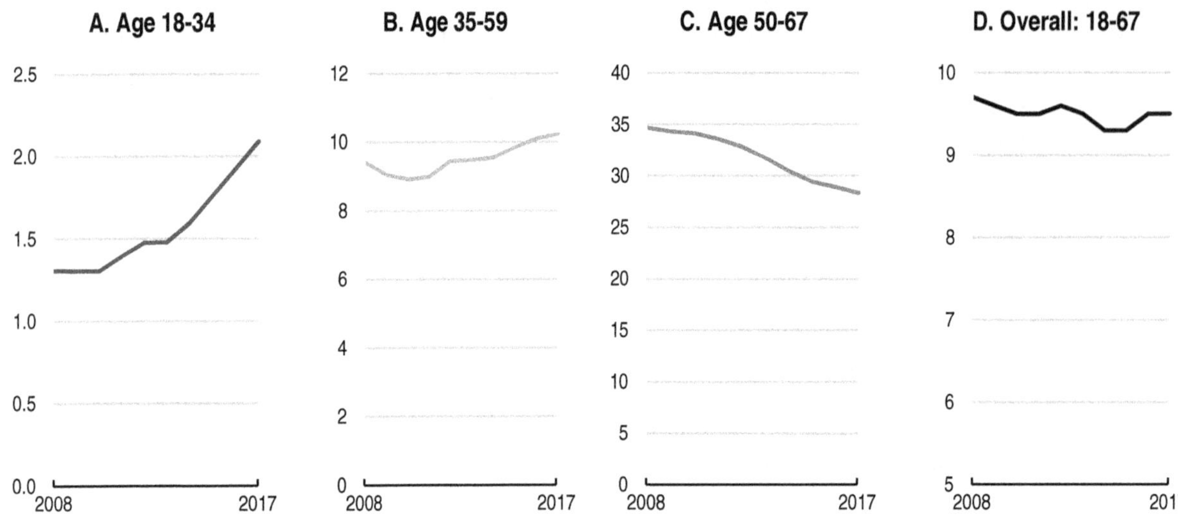

Source: Norwegian Labour and Welfare Administration (NAV).

StatLink http://dx.doi.org/10.1787/888933639246

The long-standing series of agreements between the government, employers and unions, the Inclusive Working Life Agreements, which aim to reduce sick leave continue. *Prima facie*, these agreements help prosecute reform. Yet despite operating since 2001, the impact of the agreements on sick leave has been underwhelming. One reason may be that, to date, the Agreements have contained a clause that prevents government-initiated changes to the sickness system while the Agreement is in operation. Disability-Benefit changes introduced in 2015 included steps making that make it easier to take on paid work and there is evidence that these moves have increased labour supply (Alne, 2016).

The ongoing efforts to improve the sickness and disability system can only be applauded. As urged in previous *Surveys*, reform should consider:

- Prolonging the employer-financed phase of sick leave so as to strengthen incentives for businesses and public-sector employers to take preventative measures.
- Reducing the generosity of payment. Tackling generosity may require reining in pay outs provided by the supplementary disability schemes, as well as the publically funded components to be effective.
- Tightening medical assessment procedures, especially through more third party medical assessment. Medical assessment has been the subject of reform in the past. Most recently a new medical assessment after six months of sickness benefit has been trialled. However, the medical-assessment process still relies heavily on input from the individual's GP which can raise the risk of leniency to help individuals remain on benefit.
- Re-thinking the Inclusive Working Life Agreements, especially regarding the clauses that restrict alteration to the sickness leave system.
- Increasing the minimum age at which the Disability Benefit can be accessed to 30 years or higher, accompanied by the strengthening of efforts to bring and keep these young adults in the labour market through multidisciplinary, integrated services. Denmark has experimented with this approach in recent years with considerable success.

Table 1.5. **Norway's sickness and disability system: Key features and recent initiatives**

	Sick leave
Key features	• Employer pays sickness benefit for the first 16 calendar days, the benefit can be paid for a total of one year. • Follow up requirements include: formulation of a return-to-work plan by employer and employee within four weeks, an expanded medical certificate and requirements regarding activity after eight weeks. • As a main rule, a compulsory dialogue meeting after 26 weeks between NAV, the employer and the person receiving sickness benefits.
Recent measures	• A trial new requirement for a medical assessment after six months of sick leave has been completed. • Introduction of guidance for doctors on the appropriate length of sick leave. • Ramped up implementation of rules requiring that those on sick leave beyond eight weeks are subject to activation requirements.
	Work Assessment Allowance (AAP)
Key features	• Principally aims to get individuals into employment, targets those who have been assessed as having at least 50% impairment in work capacity. • Receipt of the benefit is conditional on following an agreed activation plan. • Those reaching the end of one-year of sickness leave may apply to the scheme.
Recent initiatives	• New rules will be implemented from January 2018, including the rules governing the duration of the scheme.
	Disability Benefit
Key features	• Provides long-term disability support for those of working age (i.e. 18 to 67 years) and can be supplemented by a disability pension from a public occupational scheme. • Income from employment is permitted though benefit is partially withdrawn for income levels above certain limits.
Recent initiatives (2015 reform)	• The disability pension system is no longer part of the old-age pension system. This, inter alia, has resulted in disability benefit being taxed as wage income. • Combining disability and work income has been made easier.

Supporting further advance in workplace gender balance and improving child care

While Norway scores well in terms of gender balance and businesses are tapping more effectively into the female talent pool than many countries, this does not preclude the need for further policy action nor the presence of weak points in existing systems.

Norway's progress on strengthening women's role at the top-end of businesses has been impressive but there is still room for further advance and progress has proven slow. It has taken considerable time to achieve the nearly 45% share of women on the boards of the largest companies (Figure 1.20). A legislated gender quota of 40% applied to listed companies in 2003 but was only met with a substantial response following the introduction of sanctions. Furthermore, the response was, in part, negative; about a third of the approximately 560 companies concerned delisted in response to the sanctions. Therefore progress has been less substantial than appears in Figure 1.20. In addition, the impact on enhancing women's careers more generally appears to have been limited (Bertrand et al., 2014), although further positive effects may emerge in the coming years. There remains ground to cover, given it would appear small and private companies are not yet tapping fully into female talent. Extension of quotas may not be the right tool in this context, or indeed feasible, due to the legal rights of private companies. Instead, continued policy efforts to identify, nurture and promote female talent are probably a more fruitful way forward.

Norway's system of parental leave and child care is generally comprehensive, but not without room for improvement. Parental leave provisions are generous in Norway, facilitating the initial months of child care and providing stability of employment and income (Figure 1.21). As discussed in the 2016 *Survey*, parental-leave provisions took a

Figure 1.20. **Norway has been a leader in getting women on company boards**

Female share of seats on boards of directors in publicly listed companies, 2016 or latest available year

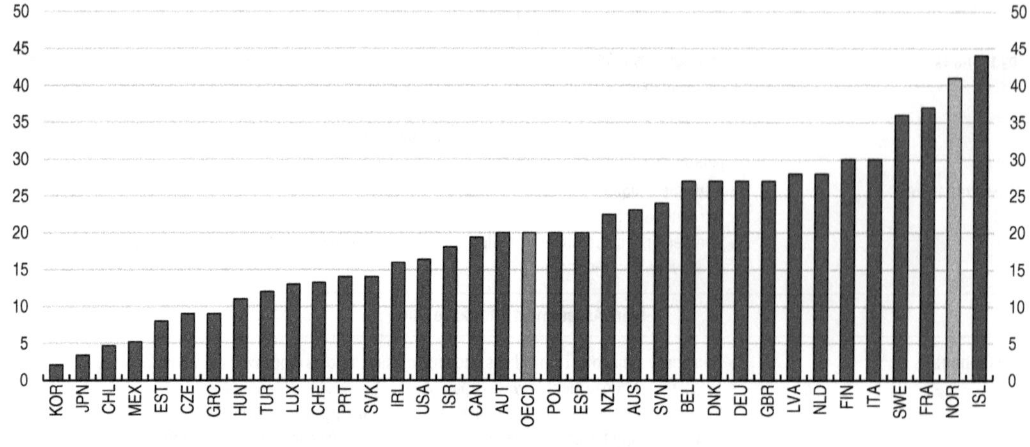

Source: For EU countries, Iceland, Norway and Turkey, EC Database on Women and Men in Decision Making, (*http://ec.europa.eu/justice/gender-equality/gender-decision-making/database/index_en.htm*); for all other countries, Lee et al. (2015).

StatLink http://dx.doi.org/10.1787/888933639265

Figure 1.21. **Paid parental leave is comparatively long**

2016

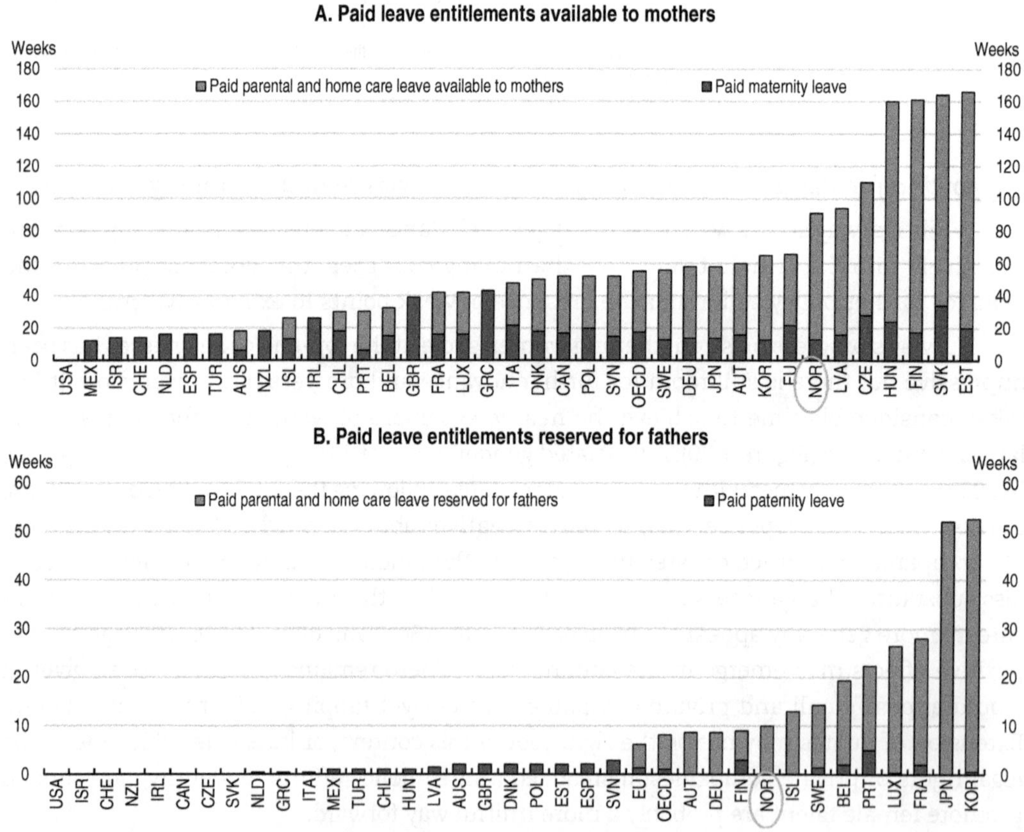

Notes: Panel A: Information refers to parental leave and subsequent periods of paid home care leave to care for young children (sometimes under a different name, for example, "childcare leave" or "child raising leave". Panel B: Information refers to entitlements to paternity leave, "father quotas" or periods of parental leave that can be used only by the father and cannot be transferred to the mother, and any weeks of sharable leave that must be taken by the father in order for the family to qualify for "bonus" weeks of parental leave.

Source: OECD (2017), *OECD Family Database*.

StatLink http://dx.doi.org/10.1787/888933639284

potentially backward step with regard to gender balance with reduction in the leave that is reserved for the mother and father individually (with corresponding increase in the "shared period"). This is likely to have reduced use of parental leave by men as less leave is reserved exclusively for them, thereby diminishing women's labour-market opportunities. As regards child care, a recent general OECD assessment (OECD, 2016c) underscores that it is often low-income groups that make the least use of childcare, largely linked to mothers not working, but children from these groups often have the greatest potential benefit from childcare in terms of cognitive development. IMF assessment (IMF, 2017) makes a specific suggestion to improve coverage. A child-care place is guaranteed for children who turn one no later than the end of November in the year they apply for a place. Those turning one after end November are entitled to a place in August the following year. Thus, parents with children turning one-year old just after the end of November in effect are not guaranteed a child-care place until the child is nearly two years old.

Education to help business and households thrive under globalisation

Education and training (human capital development) fundamentally drive Norway's capacity to thrive on the changes brought by globalisation and to cope with challenges of long-term shrinkage in petroleum-related activities and population aging.

Reform efforts in compulsory education and degree-level education head in the right direction

Ensuring primary and secondary education provides, *inter alia*, sound basic skills. As underscored in the Assessment and Recommendations of this review, Norway scores reasonably in the OECD's PISA tests, but there is room for improvement. Primary and secondary education reforms currently include a major curriculum overhaul (the previous major review was in 2006) and efforts to improve the management of schools.

In higher education the labour-market relevance of courses and length of study are frequently the subject of debate. Enrolment in tertiary education in Norway has long been high, helped by generous support for students (generally, there are no tuition fees and students receive support for living expenses). However, as discussed in the previous *Survey*, this support may be unhelpfully weakening the influence of vocational and career considerations in the choice of subjects and intensity of study (students in Norway tend to be older on graduation than those in other countries). There is little appetite in Norway for a substantial downgrade in student support. Nevertheless, there is room for policy action. The previous *Survey* suggests, for instance, altering living-expenses support for students and block-grant funding formulae with criteria that encourage course completion. This approach could also be used to influence subject choices by students and course offerings by providers.

In addition to improving choices on the demand side in higher education, there is opportunity for supply-side improvement. Welcome progress is being made to improve the quality of teaching and courses in higher education, a topic raised in the previous *Survey*. A white paper was published in early 2017 (Ministry of Education and Research, 2017) that identifies a range of weaknesses, including uneven academic standards, cases of poor course design, insufficient use of active teaching methods (e.g. tutoring). The paper proposes several routes for improvement, including more use of peer review and monitoring in teaching and developing a competitive arena for teaching (in a similar way to research).

More broadly, a welcome campaign focusing on skills is underway. Over the past two years the government has engaged in a major effort to develop a policy for improving skills, partly prompted by the OECD's Skills Strategy project with Norway, which led to diagnostic and action reports (OECD 2014b and 2014c). In February 2017 the Norwegian Strategy for Skills Policy 2017-2021 was launched with wide support from ministries and stakeholders. In addition, a committee examining future skills needs has been established. Such efforts to address skills can only be applauded, given the pay-off for businesses as well as households.

Challenges in Norway's upper-secondary vocational education

Globalisation reinforces the importance of skill-based education. The markets for jobs requiring little or no post-compulsory education are shrinking and are increasingly concentrated in areas with a strong supply of workers that have comparatively low reservation wages (in Norway's case often via labour migration). Vocational education is the chief channel for raising the employment and earnings capacities for those that would otherwise be on low-skill, low-wage trajectories, and for providing employers with ready-to-go skills for many types of work. Assessment of Norway's vocational education is part of an upcoming OECD *Investing In Youth* study (OECD, 2017f) and the following paragraphs draw on this analysis.

Most vocational training in Norway is provided by upper-secondary schools. The schools are the responsibility of county-level government and are inclusive in that students have the right to attend for three years, irrespective of previous schooling performance (the students are generally aged 16 to 19). Practically all students completing compulsory education enrol in upper-secondary courses and it is a national policy that all students attain an upper-secondary diploma. Upper-secondary education is also "integrated" in that students of all backgrounds and abilities are taught within each school. Within each school there are two tracks, an academic ("general") stream (*studiespesialisering*) that principally channels students into degree-level tertiary education and a vocational stream (*yrkesfag*, meaning "professional"). Apprenticeship courses are a central pillar of this latter stream. These are generally structured on a 2+2 basis; i.e. two years of full-time study is followed by two years of training and work experience with an employer.

The inclusiveness of Norway's upper-secondary education is positive, but brings challenges. Particularly in the vocational stream, there is a diverse intake in terms of student abilities, motivation and background. This is reflected in the wide range of paths followed by the vocational-stream students. According to a data published by the Norwegian Directorate for Education and Training (Figure 1.22), 20% of second-year students transition into the general stream in the third year of study (transition is possible through one-year conversion courses). Meanwhile, nearly 25% of students are no longer in the system by the end of the third year, apparently "dropping out".

Non-completion of vocational-education courses has long been a policy concern. It is partly explained by Norway's tight labour market; job opportunities prompt some to leave upper-secondary school before graduating. While this has positive dimensions, there is a risk that early leavers are putting themselves onto a trajectory of low-paid, unstable and unfulfilling jobs for the longer term. Non-completion is particularly high in restaurant and food processing programmes, and the reasons are telling. Students entering these programmes typically have poor grades from lower-secondary school and many have special needs (Norwegian Directorate for Education and Training, 2017), which indicates that many early leavers are indeed vulnerable to poor socio-economic outcomes for the longer term.

Shortages in the two-year apprentice placements with employers are a key problem. Around one third of students do not find a placement (Norwegian Directorate for Education

Figure 1.22. **Many vocational-stream students do not complete courses**

Transitions from the second year of upper secondary vocational strudy programmes to the third year of education. 2014, %

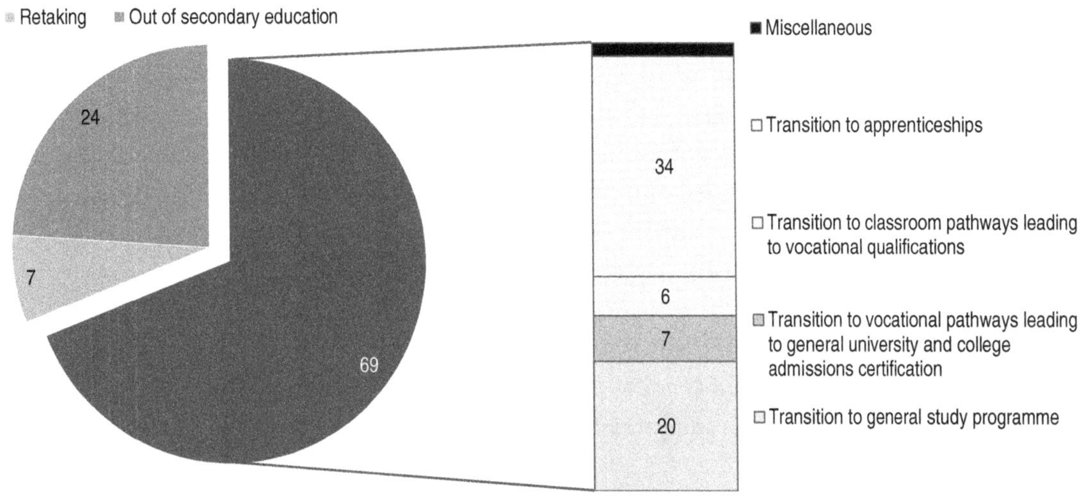

Source: The Norwegian Directorate for Education and Training 2016: The education mirror 2016.

StatLink http://dx.doi.org/10.1787/888933639303

and Training, 2014). Furthermore, though schools provide one-year courses for students that cannot find placements, few students take them up. Of around 6 000 students who failed to find apprenticeships in 2013, only about 350 took up the school based alternative. According to one study (Mogstad Aspoy and Nyen, 2015), the one-year courses are unpopular because of the lack of work-based training; the absence of apprenticeship earnings is likely to be an additional factor. The vast majority of those that do not get an apprenticeship place either drop out or pursue routes to higher education. The most recent major policy initiative to encourage employers to offer apprenticeships, the "social contact for VET", aimed to increase the number of places by 20% between 2011 and 2015. The scheme comprised a range of measures including a cash bonus equivalent to around EUR 6 200 for businesses taking on apprentices for the first time. The scheme was partially successful, increasing apprenticeships by an estimated 10% (OECD, 2017f). In addition, as mentioned above in the assessment of business regulation, there are now requirements for public procurement contractors to run apprenticeship programmes – a plus for apprenticeship places but potentially limiting access to public procurement contracts for foreign companies.

Apprenticeship wages are one factor dissuading the supply of apprenticeship places. The wages are set as part of collective agreements. According to calculations in the upcoming OECD *Investing in Youth* study, first-year apprentices cost around 16% of a skilled workers salary (with government subsidy included in the calculation) but this rises to 60% in the second year due to the increase in the regulated wage. The OECD study further points out that apprentice wages in Germany and Switzerland start at roughly the same relative cost but only increase to around 30% of the skilled worker wage. This would suggest that Norwegian reform should either seek to flatten the apprentice wage award and/or increase subsidies to employers. As regards the latter, the OECD study suggests reintroduction of a bonus to employers on the graduation of apprentices along the lines of a scheme that operated in the late 1990s.

Apprenticeship wages are unlikely to be the sole explanation for the shortage of apprenticeship places. The apparent shortage may reflect that employers have tapped optimally into the talent pool and that students who cannot find apprenticeship places are not considered suitable. This would suggest a need for further work on improving student abilities and their relevance for the workplace. Furthermore, an OECD analysis of apprenticeships in the sparsely populated Nordland region (OECD, 2017g), emphasises that greater flexibility on how apprenticeships are scheduled (i.e. alternative arrangements to the current 2+2 approach) could allow course structures that suit both students and employers better. The report also underscored the role of training offices in deepening linkages between schools, students and employers and the importance of supporting transport (and accommodation) for apprentices in remote regions.

Policy recommendations

Recommendations on maintaining a successful business sector in a changing world

Further cultivate business framework conditions that promote flexible markets and competition:

- Continue addressing weak points in competition legislation, in particular re-consider sectoral exemptions, such as those in agriculture
- Slim down the wide-ranging portfolio of state stakes in business through privatisation, especially where these are held in companies operating in competitive and well-functioning markets.

Scale back and rebalance taxation:

- Complete the programme of income-tax rate cuts, and consider further reductions
- Reduce the tax distortions in housing. Either carefully phase out mortgage-interest relief or increase property taxes on housing as a proxy for implicit rental income while paying attention to symmetries in the tax system
- Consider further wealth tax reduction given its substantial impact on the returns to saving in the current low-return environment, while paying attention to inequalities.

Ensure policy settings encourage good firm dynamics:

- Strengthen routes to recovery in the insolvency regime for businesses in difficulty, through lighter penalties for failed entrepreneurs, better prevention and streaming mechanisms and more restructuring tools.

Ensure Norwegian business makes the most of innovation:

- Maintain a free-trade policy and facilitate cross-border investment and business linkages
- Work further on ensuring impact from the R&D tax credit given its central role in supporting innovation
- Reduce the number of targeted innovation support programmes and review their focus as per the OECD *Innovation Review*
- Tackle regulatory barriers to the supply of credit to high-risk, small-scale enterprise
- In higher education and in research institutes, and as per the OECD's *Innovation Review*, focus on excellence and critical mass, including through use of block-funding to re-shape research incentives and through supporting institutional mergers.

Encourage market entry by innovative business ("disruptors") while also checking for downsides:

- Use competition-policy tools to combat resistance by incumbents and reduce disparities between incumbents and disruptors in the tax system, and in business support mechanisms
- Adjust sectoral regulation quickly as new business models and services emerge
- Replace the taxi-licensing system with less restrictive regulation to address availability and consumer-protection.

Recommendations on maintaining a successful business sector in a changing world *(cont.)*

In labour supply:

- Press on with reform to sick leave and disability benefit including through an employer-financed phase of sick leave and tighter medical assessment
- Continue policy efforts to identify, nurture and promote female talent for positions at the top-end of business
- Address shortfalls in the availability of child-care provision particularly in care facilities for infants.

In education policy, ensure reform of upper-secondary vocational education is core pillar of policy:

- Strengthen incentives for employers' to offer apprenticeship places by lowering costs, either through lowering apprentice wages or through providing additional subsidies
- Make courses more attractive and relevant to students.

Bibliography

Aghion, P., S. Bechtold, L. Cassar and H. Herz (2014), "Causal effects of competition on innovation: experimental evidence", *National Bureau of Economic Research Working Paper*, No. 19987.

Alne, R. H. (2016), "Jobber de uføretrygdede mer etter uførereformen i 2015? (Has employment increased following the disability reform of 2015)", Arbeid og Velferd nr. 3, 2016.

Bertrand, M., S. Black, S. Jensen and A. Lleras-Muney (2014), "Breaking the Glass Ceiling? The Effect of Board Quotas on Female Labor Market Outcomes in Norway", *National Bureau of Economic Research Working Paper*, No. 20256.

Government of Norway (2013), Political Platform for a government formed by the Conservative Party and the Progress Party, October 2013.

Hægeland, T. and J. Møen (2007), "Input additionality in the Norwegian R&D tax credit scheme", *Statistics Norway Reports* 2007/47.

Hagelund, K. (2009), "Productivity Growth in Norway, 1948-2008", *Norges Bank Economic Bulletin*, 2/2009.

IMF (2017), *Norway Selected Issues*, IMF Country Report No. 17/181, July 2017.

Ministry of Education and Research (2017), *Quality Culture in Higher Education*, White Paper Meld. St. 16 (2016-17).

Ministry of Trade, Industry and Fisheries (2016), *State Ownership Report*, 2015, Oslo.

McGowan, M.A. and D. Andrews (2016), "Insolvency regimes and productivity growth: A framework for analysis", *OECD Economics Department Working Paper*, No. 1309.

Mogstad Aspøy, T. and T. Nyen (2015), *Godt, men ikke for godt – Evaluering av forsterket alternativ Vg3 for elever som ikke får læreplass* [Good, but not too good – an evaluation of the reinforced alternative VG3 for students who did not secure an apprenticeship], FAFO-report 2015:46.

Norwegian Directorate for Education and Training (2014), *The Education Mirror*, 2014.

Norwegian Directorate for Education and Training (2017), *The Education Mirror*, 2017.

NOU 4 (2017), *The Sharing Economy*, Official Norwegian Report (NOU), 2017:4.

OECD (2014a), *OECD Economic Surveys: Norway 2014*, OECD Publishing, Paris.

OECD (2014b), *OECD Skills Strategy Diagnostic Report: Norway*, OECD Publishing, Paris.

OECD (2014c) *OECD Skills Strategy Action Report: Norway*, OECD Publishing, Paris.

OECD (2015a), *The Future of Productivity*, OECD Publishing, Paris.

OECD (2015b), "Hearing on Disruptive Innovation", *Issues paper by the Secretariat*, June 2015, OECD Publishing, Paris.

OECD (2016a), "No Country for Young Firms? Start-up Dynamics and National Policies", *OECD Science, Technology and Industry Policy Papers*, No. 29. OECD Publishing, Paris.

OECD (2016b), "New Forms of Work in the Digital Economy", *OECD Digital Economy Papers*, No. 260, OECD Publishing, Paris.

OECD (2016c), *Who Uses Childcare? Background brief on inequalities in the use of formal early childhood education and (ECEC) among very young children*, OECD Publishing, Paris.

OECD (2017a), OECD *Economic Outlook*, OECD Publishing, Paris.

OECD (2017b), OECD *Territorial Reviews: Northern Sparsely Populated Areas*, OECD Publishing, Paris.

OECD (2017c), OECD *Business Dynamics and Productivity*, OECD Publishing, Paris.

OECD (2017d), OECD *Reviews of Innovation Policy: Norway* 2017, OECD Publishing, Paris.

OECD (2017e), OECD *Economic Surveys: Australia* 2017, OECD Publishing, Paris.

OECD (2017f), "Raising school completion rates and providing high-quality professional training", Chapter 4 in *Investing in Youth, Norway*, 2017, OECD Publishing, Paris

OECD (2017g), *Engaging Employers in Apprenticeship Opportunities: Making It Happen Locally*, OECD Publishing, Paris.

Prestmo, J.B., B. Strøm, and H.K. Midsem (2015), "Spillover Effects from the Offshore Petroleum to the Mainland Economy," *Statistics Norway Report* 2015/8.

Productivity Commission (2015), "Underpinning Growth and Welfare", *Official Norwegian Reports*, NOU 2015: 1.

Saia, A., D. Andrews and S. Abrizio (2015), "Productivity Spillovers from the Global Frontier and public Policy", *OECD Economics Department Working Papers*, No, 1238.

© OECD 2018

Chapter 2

How to improve transport-infrastructure investment

Norway makes substantial public investment in transport and this has intensified in recent years. There is potentially large economic benefit from such investment, particularly as good transport infrastructure can help Norway's transition away from oil-related activities. However, realising these gains requires sound processes for selecting and delivering projects. This chapter assesses the investment process from initial proposals through evaluation, discussion, selection, approval, implementation, and ex post *evaluation. It finds that, although the policy process at each stage is clear, and the planning framework has central oversight, final choices of project are often sub-optimal. The chapter identifies a need for stronger top-down influence in the planning process and more influence of economic-efficiency considerations in project selection. It also calls for efforts to broaden* ex post *assessment of transport investment projects and reduction in project delays.*

Transport-infrastructure investment can substantially improve the environment for business and raise living standards. New or improved transport links alter the economic geography for businesses and households; reducing journey times, facilitating trade, connecting communities and widening access to jobs. Norway's oil wealth has meant substantial fiscal capacity to realise these returns. Spending on transport infrastructure as a share of GDP is indeed comparatively high, and has increased in recent years (Figure 2.1). Looking forward, fiscal room for such investment is likely to narrow under the adjusted fiscal rule (the move from a "4% rule" to a "3% rule", see the Assessment and Recommendations of this *Survey*), making it all the more important that good investment choices are made. This chapter focuses on the processes whereby new transport infrastructure projects are

Figure 2.1. **Norway makes sizeable investment in transport infrastructure**

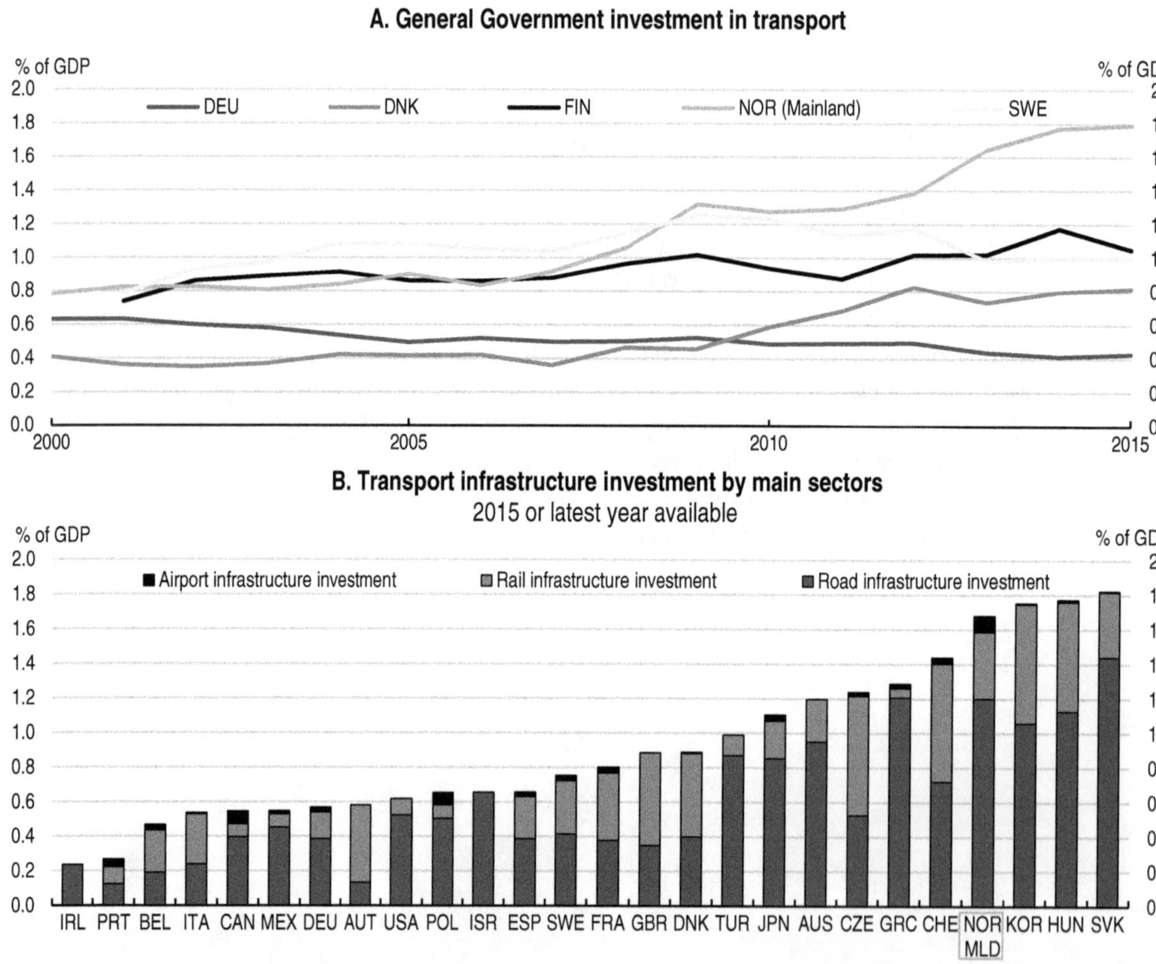

Source: OECD National Accounts and ITF Databases.

StatLink http://dx.doi.org/10.1787/888933639322

selected and delivered and suggests ways of strengthening the efficiency of investment. The analysis focuses on road infrastructure given that this accounts for most of investment (Figure 2.1).

Geography and socio-political priorities strongly influence Norway's transport investment

As in other countries, the nature and density of transport networks in Norway are partially shaped by population density. Norway has 17 persons per square kilometre, which is among the lowest population densities in the OECD area (Figure 2.2, Table 2.1) and similar to those of Finland and New Zealand. Low population density is loosely echoed in road density. Norway and Finland are particularly alike on this front, with around 25 km of road per square kilometre of land (and both countries consequently have a similar road-length per inhabitant, Table 2.1). Rail density, meanwhile, is substantially below that in Finland, and closer to that in Canada and Chile. Population density also influences other dimensions of transport networks; low-population-density countries involve longer linkages but these typically have lighter usage and fewer junctions and accommodations for other land uses and transport systems compared with high-density countries.

Figure 2.2. **Low transport-network densities partly reflect low population density**

2015 or latest year available, selected low-population-density countries

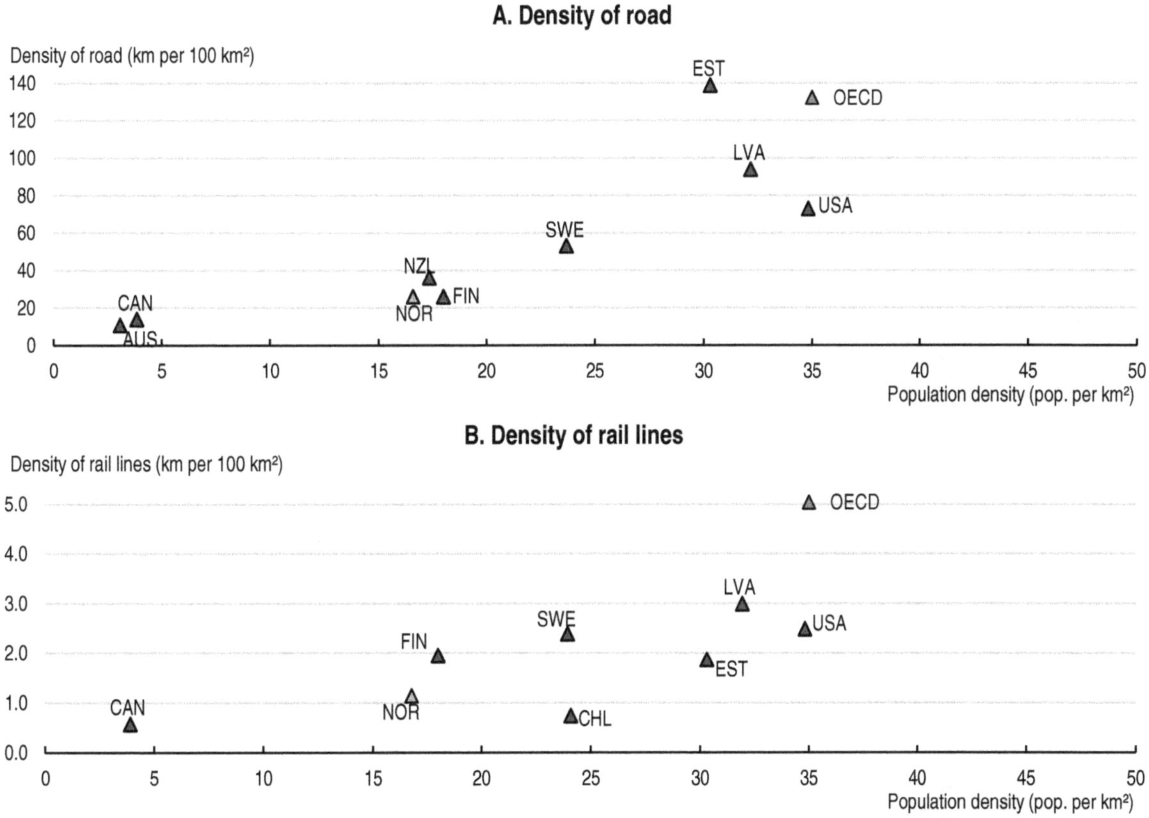

Source: OECD ITF Database.

StatLink http://dx.doi.org/10.1787/888933639341

Table 2.1. **Population and transport-network densities in selected countries**

2016 or latest year available

	Population density (per km²)	Density of road (km per 100 km²)	Road length per capita (km per 100k inhabitants)	Density of rail track (km per 100 km²)	Rail track per capita (km per 100k inhabitants)
Australia	3.1	11	3 560	0.11	38
Canada	4.0	14	3 618	0.57	146
Norway	17.1	26	1 566	1.14	68
New Zealand	17.7	36	2 075	-	-
Finland	18.1	26	1 444	1.95	108
Sweden	24.2	53	2 238	2.39	100
Estonia	30.3	139	4 587	1.87	62
Latvia	31.7	94	2 922	2.99	94
United States	35.3	73	2 097	2.49	72
Denmark	133.0	176	1 335	5.02	38

Source: OECD ITF Database.

Norway's elongated shape, mountainous topography and many steep-sided fjords also influence the density of transport networks, and, importantly this generates challenges in construction and maintenance, and affects costs. The Norwegian road network of 93 000 kilometres (km) contains approximately 1 000 tunnels and 18 200 bridges (Table 2.2). The Lærdal road tunnel is the world's longest, at 24.5km. In the rail network's 4 000km of track (mostly single line) there are nearly 800 tunnels and about 3 000 bridges. In addition the long land border with Sweden involves cooperation on transport issues. Constructing new cross-country road and rail connections or improving existing linkages in Norway involves higher costs in some dimensions of engineering than in other countries, for instance terrain-related costs are often high. Meanwhile some dimensions of costs are likely to be lower. For instance in Norway costs relating to land purchase and compensation for new routes, and additional costs linked to putting transport routes through habited areas, are likely to be lower in Norway compared with those in high-population-density countries. However, certain efforts to compare project costs with other countries indicate cost differences narrow once such differences are taken into account. Norway's geography also means the country relies heavily on air and maritime transport. Indeed, Norway has 13 international airports, or roughly 3 per million inhabitants, which is by far the highest ratio in the OECD area (Figure 2.3).

Table 2.2. **Norway's transport network: selected figures**

Public roads, total km	93 000
of which National roads	10 500
County roads	44 000
Municipal roads	38 500
Road tunnels (number of)	1 000
Road bridges (number of)	18 200
Rail network, km	4 000
Rail tunnels (number of)	775
Rail bridges (number of)	3 000
Airports (number of)	
International	13
State-owned	46
National ports	32

Source: Norwegian Public Roads Administration, Norway State Railway (NSB), SSB.

Figure 2.3. **A comparatively large number of airports**

International airports per million population, 2015 or latest year available

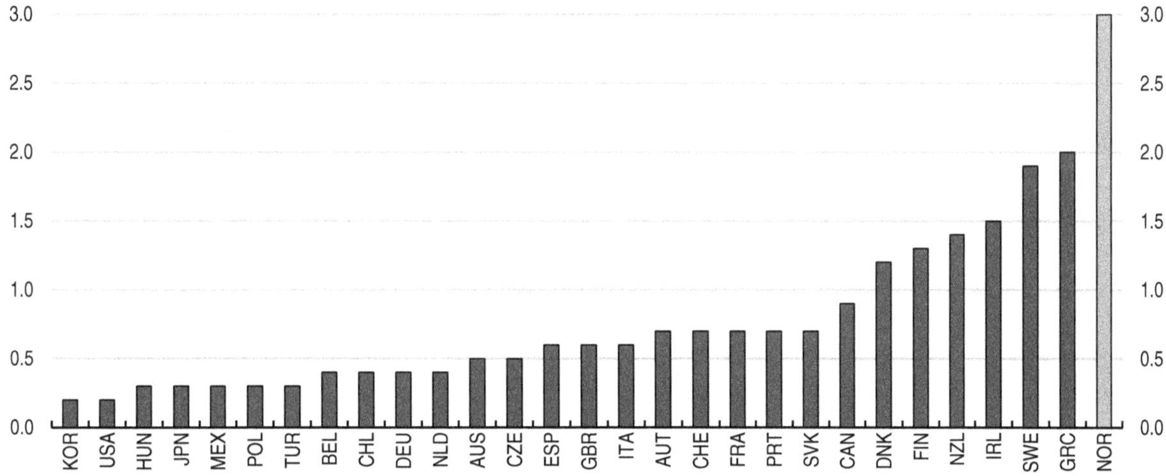

Source: OECD ITF Database.

StatLink http://dx.doi.org/10.1787/888933639360

Norway's policy emphasis on sustaining rural and remote regions plays an important role in transport infrastructure development. There has long been substantial political support for sustaining communities in rural and remote areas, which often face challenges in economic viability and depopulation. The support for rural and remote areas features in a wide range of policies including subsidies for transport and telecommunication requirements as well as health and cultural facilities and in economic activities (notably agriculture support). These supports have been successful at maintaining a relatively high share of rural population (47% of the population live in predominantly rural areas versus an OECD average of 25%, OECD 2016). In addition, the support for rural and remote areas has important implications for the prioritisation of projects in transport infrastructure.

Despite comparatively high spending, Norway's transport network does not rank highly according to some indicators. In the World Economic Forum (WEF) indicator system Norway is middle-ranking among OECD countries for transport infrastructure overall (it ranks 32 out of 138 among all countries covered by the WEF) and scores poorly on the road-quality component (Figure 2.4). The WEF rankings reflect views expressed by samples of business managers and so are unlikely to represent a universal view on the quality of transport infrastructure. Nevertheless the scores suggest room to better match infrastructure development with demands and expectations, at least as far as the business community is concerned.

Figure 2.4. **Mediocre scores in the World Economic Forum transport indicators**

2016-17

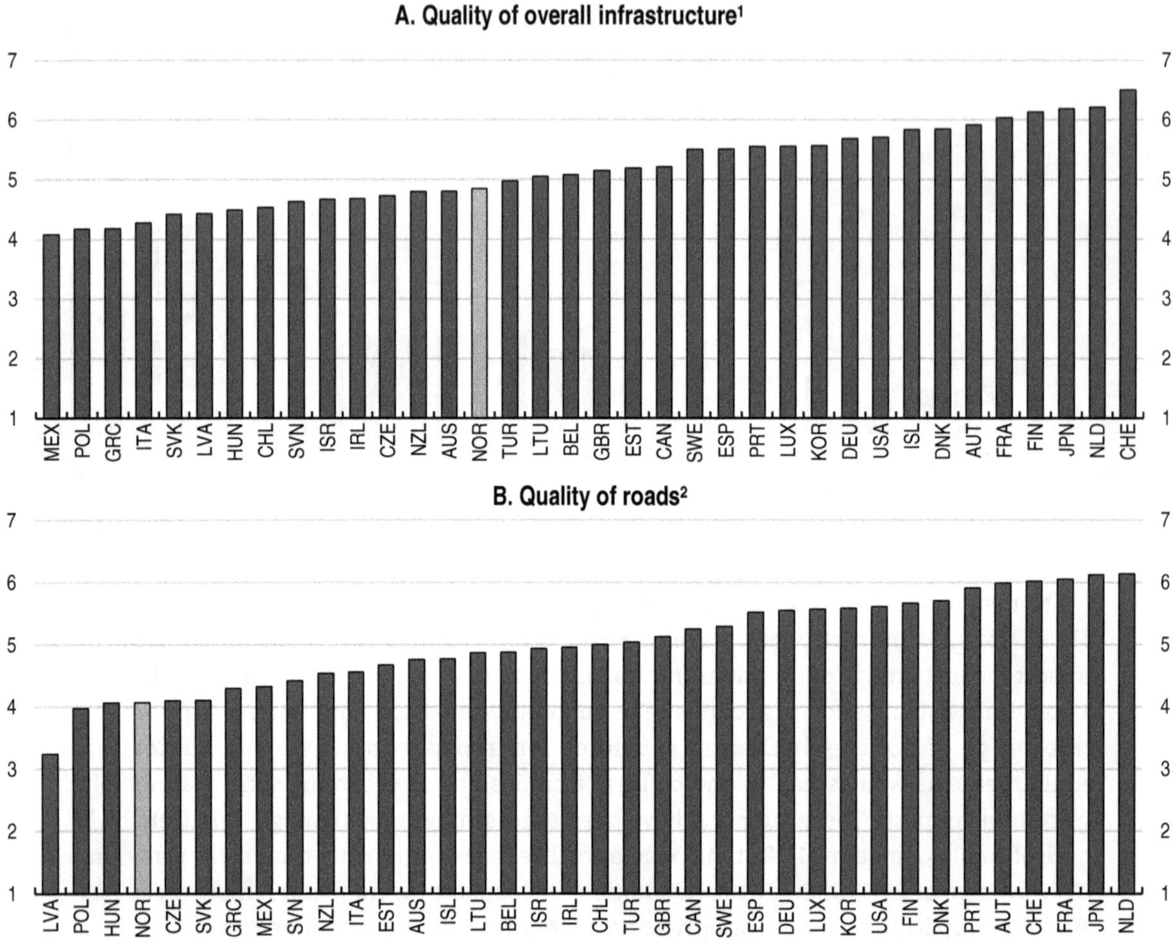

1. The score is based on the assessment of business leaders operating in the country in response to the question: how do you assess the general state of infrastructure (e.g. transport, communications and energy) in your country? [1 = extremely underdeveloped – among the worst in the world; 7 = extensive and efficient – among the best in the world].
2. In your country, how is the quality (extensiveness and condition) of road infrastructure [1 = extremely poor – among the worst in the world; 7 = extremely good – among the best in the world].

Source: World Economic Forum Global Competitiveness Index dataset.

StatLink http://dx.doi.org/10.1787/888933639379

Funding and responsibility for transport infrastructure

In Norway, central government is responsible for building and maintaining the national road and rail networks as well as fairways and state-owned ports and airports. Meanwhile, counties are responsible for building and maintaining regional roads as well as local and regional transport; and, municipalities for roads and all other ports in their areas. Transfers from central government finance a significant share of regional and local transport infrastructure. Special arrangements for cities have been introduced recently, with central government providing earmarked financial support to cover half of large transport-infrastructure investments, such as the Oslo metro extension. County roads are covered by expenditure equalization schemes that are determined in part by factors such as road length and operating costs. In addition to central and non-central government financing, transport-systems receive funding from various sources. Notably, tolls systems have increased during the last years as a method of partial financing of new road projects;

as of September 2017 there were approximately 60 toll systems operating. Some of the toll systems operate on a number of urban ring roads and on some projects where tunnels or bridges have been built as a replacement for ferries.

The government cabinet is the core decision maker for transport policy. In a formal sense, decisions about implementation are thus "top-down". In practice, and as in most OECD countries, responsibilities (and influence) are highly dispersed. By the time projects come before the cabinet for approval, they have typically got there by a "bottom-up" process. The Norwegian government model is characterised by core line ministries that develop new policy, and executive agencies that are responsible for executing policy (OECD, 2013). Transport infrastructure conforms to this model with the Ministry of Transport and Communications having overall responsibility for the sector, but with planning and implementation devolved to four executive agencies covering the different transport modes. There are three government-administered executive infrastructure agencies in the transport sector, the Norwegian Public Roads Administration (NPRA, Statens Vegvesen), the Norwegian Railway Directorate (Jernbanedirektoratet), and the Norwegian Coastal Administration (Kystverket). For air transport the agency role is performed by the government-owned company Avinor AS.

Recent reforms have included establishment of new road and rail companies

A restructuring of the transport sector was carried out in 2016 and early 2017. It focused on improving the delivery and implementation of projects and involved the creation of two new state-owned companies: a rail infrastructure company (Bane NOR SF) tasked with building and operating the rail network, and a New Roads Company (Nye Veier AS).

The rail-sector restructuring has separated out strategic and operational roles. The previous rail authority has been split into the Rail Directorate, responsible for developing policy and the long-term strategy for the sector, and a unit responsible for delivering and managing rail infrastructure (Bane NOR). Bane NOR is by far the larger in terms of staff numbers; it has inherited most of the employees from the previous organisation. The Rail Directorate's responsibilities include preparation of inputs into the National Transport Plan (NTP, see below). Furthermore, it handles the budget for the sector and strikes agreements with Bane NOR and the other actors in the rail sector. The agreements determine the priorities and timing of investment in new lines, and specify performance and service levels. The Rail Directorate has primary responsibility for concept-stage studies for new investment, but may order such studies from Bane NOR. In addition, Bane NOR engages with local authorities during the planning process, conducts stakeholder consultations, and secures land for projects.

Road-sector reform saw establishment of the New Roads Company (NRC) for delivering new motorways (Box 2.1). It has been allocated a portfolio of 530 km of motorways to build and operate over the next 20 years for a budget of NOK 148 billion. The NRC is principally funded from the state budget and tolls, but can also access a state funded credit facility (up to one year duration). While the NRC has no leeway on the selection of road projects it delivers, it does have discretion with regard to the timing and sequencing. The aim is that this operational flexibility will enable it to generate cost savings. Reportedly, the Company's first road project was estimated at NOK 4 billion but will be delivered for NOK 3 billion, providing encouraging initial evidence that this new approach can deliver substantial savings. The fact that governments have already used public-private partnerships (as an alternative to regular procurement) for some new road infrastructure (and intend to use more), is likely to incentivise efficiency in the NRC.

Box 2.1. The role of the Norwegian Public Roads Administration

The Norwegian Public Roads Administration (NPRA) is responsible for planning, building, operating, and maintaining all national and county roads. It comprises five regional units plus the Directorate of Public Roads, whose responsibilities include strategic planning, international activities, and traffic safety (NPRA, 2016). Of the over 90 000 km of roads, about 10 000 km are national roads and about 44 000 km are county roads. The NRPA is responsible to the Ministry of Transport and Communications for national roads and to county councils for matters related to the county roads. The remaining 39 000 km are municipal roads, for which the NPRA is not responsible (NPRA, 2013).

Such corporatisation can enhance efficiency if it introduces appropriate incentives and targets, and provides sufficient managerial and operational freedom to the infrastructure company. Given that the reforms came into effect only in 2016 and early January 2017, it remains to be seen whether these new structures will be effective at improving value for money in infrastructure delivery.

Transport-infrastructure investment is driven by multi-annual National Transport Plans

An infrastructure investment programme should be underpinned by a long-term strategy that defines future needs and identifies solutions for meeting those needs as efficiently as possible. Large infrastructure investments involve different policy areas and sectors, resulting in complex decision-making processes involving multiple stakeholders and levels of government. The OECD's Framework for the Governance of Infrastructure underscores the principles of good practice (Box 2.2) and the OECD's *International Transport Forum* has identified best-practice principles in strategic planning (OECD/ITF 2017a).

Box 2.2. OECD Framework for the Governance of Infrastructure

1. Developing a strategic vision. Establish a national long-term strategic vision that addresses infrastructure service needs. The strategy should be politically sanctioned, coordinated across levels of government, take stakeholder views into account and be based on clear assumptions.
2. Managing threats to integrity. Corruption entry points should be mapped at each stage of the public infrastructure project, and integrity and anti-corruption mechanisms should be enhanced.
3. Choosing how to deliver infrastructure. When choosing how to deliver an infrastructure service, i.e. delivery modality, government should balance the political, sectoral, economic, and strategic aspects. Legitimacy, affordability and value for money should guide this balancing.
4. Ensuring good regulatory design. Good regulatory design and delivery are necessary to ensure sustainable and affordable infrastructure over the life of the asset.
5. Integrate a consultation process. The consultation process should be proportionate to the size of the project and take account of the overall public interest and the views of the relevant stakeholders. The process should be broad-based, inspire dialogue and draw on public access to information and users' needs.

Box 2.2. **OECD Framework for the Governance of Infrastructure** *(cont.)*

6. Coordinate infrastructure policy across levels of government. There should be robust co-ordination mechanisms for infrastructure policy within and across levels of government. The co-ordination mechanisms should encourage a balance between a whole-of-government perspective and sectoral and regional views.
7. Guard affordability and value for money. Governments must ensure that infrastructure projects are affordable and the overall investment envelope is sustainable. The asset should represent value for money. This requires the use of dedicated processes, a capable organisation and relevant skills.
8. Generate, analyse and disclose useful data. Infrastructure policy should be based on data. Governments should put in place systems that ensure a systematic collection of relevant data and institutional responsibility for analysis, dissemination, and learning from this data.
9. Make sure the asset performs through its life. Ensure a focus on the performance of the asset throughout its lifespan by putting in place monitoring systems and institutions.
10. Public infrastructure needs to be resilient. Infrastructure systems should be resilient, adaptable to new circumstances and future proof. Critical risks materialise and technological change can fundamentally disrupt sectors and economies.

Source: OECD (2017).

Norway's system of rolling National Transport Plans (NTPs) is intended to address these challenges. The Plans are submitted by government to parliament in the form of a white paper. Until recently, the Plans were made every four years and spanned a 10-year planning period (in effect, each plan comprised four "core" years plus six "out" years). The latest Plan (Box 2.3) has a 12-year period (six core years plus six out years). Under the four-year cycle, preparation of the NTP usually began soon after a new government took office with the final selection of projects taking place in the run-up to the next general election. The change of timing under the latest Plan potentially has some significance for governance (discussed in later sections). The Plans are developed jointly by the three transport agencies, plus Avinor, and this is a core mechanism for ensuring a multi-modal approach to transport development. The joint development includes, for instance, cooperation in determining the key macroeconomic assumptions to be used for future transport projections and in the development of common methodologies. The Plans cover all transport infrastructure with substantial central-government funding, which in practice means almost all major projects. The Plans cover national roads (but not municipal or county roads), rail, and state-owned airports and ports. The Plans can also include urban transport infrastructure and increased capacity and reliability in central telecom infrastructure (see Box 2.3).

The submission, selection and delivery of infrastructure via the Plans essentially run as follows:

- The transport agencies (plus Avinor) propose projects for incorporation into the Plan according to guidelines delivered by the Ministry of Transport and Communication and after internal discussion and consultations with the relevant local and regional authorities, which themselves often have projects that they wish to promote.
- Large projects (defined as those with estimated costs exceeding NOK 750 million) that require central-government financing are put through the first of a two-stage "quality

Box 2.3. **The new National Transport Plan**

The new NTP, covering 12 years 2018-2029, was submitted to parliament in April 2017 (NTP, 2017). The strategy for mobility between regions focuses on improving connectivity in the road and rail networks, while for urban areas the focus is on developing public transport, cyclist and pedestrian systems. In addition, the plan focuses on achieving zero-emissions growth. It envisages that by 2025 all new cars, city buses and light vans will be zero-emissions vehicles, and that walking, cycling and public-transport usage will have substantially increased. Central-government funding for urban infrastructure will be conditional on "urban environment agreements" struck between the central government, county authorities and municipalities. Furthermore, the plan specifies that land-use plans for the larger urban areas must also be aligned with the zero-growth objective.

Plans for rail envisage continued development of InterCity routes with double track lines. The Stad Ship Tunnel maritime transport project, boring a ship-going tunnel through a peninsula, has been proposed in the plan, though it has been scheduled to start at the end of the first planning period.

The specific guidelines given by the Ministry of Transport to the three transport agencies, plus the state-owned airport company, Avinor, included calls for greater emphasis on "socioeconomic profitability", civil protection and further work on making standards consistent. As usual in the NTP process, the Ministry specified that certain projects must be included in the plan, in some cases because they are already initiated.

The proposed budget for the 12-year plan is NOK 1 064 billion, including toll revenue. This is a substantial increase over the previous plan (NOK 664 billion in the 2014-2023 NTP), implying an average allocation of NOK 90 billion per year, or around 2.7% of current annual GDP. Road-transport spending accounts for 57% of the proposed budget, and rail transport 35%.

Source: NTP (2017).

assessment" appraisal process (this first stage is referred to as "QA 1"). The process is overseen by the Ministry of Finance and incorporates quality assurance by independent reviewers.

- The Ministry of Transport and Communication prepares the National Transport Plan as a white paper. As part of the process of preparing this plan, a shortlist of priority projects is selected at the political level by the government of the day, with economic appraisal as part of the project information feeding into this choice. This is a critical step in the selection process. The formulation of the latest plan was unusual in that, rather than the government selecting projects following internal discussion, there was open political negotiation among the governing coalition via the Parliamentary Committee for Transport and Communications. As mentioned above, to date, finalisation of the white papers has taken place in the run up to general elections, but this may not be the case for the next plan.
- The National Transport Plan is then submitted as a white paper to parliament for discussion. Large projects are put through the second stage of the quality assurance process ("QA2"). Projects are rarely rejected at this point in the process as they have considerable (political) momentum, with typically several years of deliberation, transport appraisal as well as gathering both local and national support (see Welde and Odeck, 2017 for discussion).
- Projects enter the construction phase and a subset of projects is subject to *ex post* evaluation.

Infrastructure planning in metropolitan areas has an extra degree of complexity because it typically involves multiple municipalities, as well as county- and state-level government (the city of Oslo is an exception since it constitutes both a county and a municipality, Box 2.4). Negotiations between central and sub-national governments relating to metropolitan infrastructure development are based on the National Transport Plan. In the largest metropolitan areas long-term vertical collaboration has been facilitated in recent decades by co-financing agreements for transport infrastructure, called "packages" (Bypakker). Past efforts to strengthen co-ordination include, for instance, the adoption of a joint regional land-use and transport plan between Oslo and the county of Akershus in 2015. Urban growth agreements (formerly urban environment agreements) have been introduced to strengthen coordination, and to ensure that the growth in passenger traffic in the urban area shall be covered by public transport, cycling and walking.

Box 2.4. **Infrastructure planning and financing in the city of Oslo**

The city of Oslo is the largest metropolitan area in Norway, and is both a municipality and a county. The Oslo authorities have a "climate budget" and the authorities' vision is for a car-free inner city, and for all growth in passenger traffic to be covered by walking, bicycling and public transport, instead of private car use.

The metropolitan transport authority (Ruter As) is responsible for planning, building and operating Oslo's public transport. It is 60% owned by Oslo County and 40% owned by neighbouring Akershus county. Public transport planning is performed jointly between the Rail Directorate, the Norwegian Public Roads Administration, and Ruter As. Long-term transport planning is currently guided by the "Concept Study Oslo Hub" of 2016, which is also designed to be consistent with land-use strategy for the city.

A regional transport model developed by the road and rail authorities identifies future transport needs, and the project planning methodology is the same as that used by the central government. Stakeholder consultations play an important role and take place at an early stage in the project lifecycle.

Public transport development and operation in Oslo is partly financed from the city's ring-road tolls (neighbouring municipalities also receive some of the toll revenue). Central government provides financing too, notably for national road projects, cycling lanes and public-transport projects. As mentioned in the main text, vertical collaboration is facilitated by "packages" (Bypakker) – long-term transport plans covering both public and private transport. In the case of Oslo, the Bypakke Oslopakke 3 is an important part of urban planning. This Bypakke is part of Oslo's Urban Environment Agreement, which endeavours to strengthen co-ordination of development of housing, land use and the transport system.

Project appraisal and selection processes

Statutory appraisal and selection procedures are comprehensive. In line with best international practice, most transport projects in Norway undergo a thorough assessment of their positive and negative impacts, both directly on transport users but also on the wider economy and society (see for example OECD/ITF, 2017b). The requirements in terms of analytical work are set out in the government's Instructions for Official Studies of Central Government Measures (DFØ, 2016) which apply to all public spending measures. The Instructions require that central government bodies conduct impact assessments during the development of measures, and economic analyses for measures that are expected to give rise to major benefits or costs. Most national transport projects fall into this category. As mentioned above, in addition there are "quality assurance processes" (QAs) for major transport projects (further discussion below).

As in most OECD countries, cost-benefit analysis (CBA) is used as to rank alternative projects and alternative versions of the same project. In Norway, the CBA guidelines are embodied in an impressively comprehensive document, "Circular R-109" (see Box 2.5). The guidelines include requirements to account for the wider ramifications of transport projects using supplementary estimates and analysis, including environmental impacts. Work on improving CBA continues. For instance, a common methodology for assessing the wider economic benefits (and costs) is currently being developed by the transport agencies.

Substantial consultation goes into submissions to the NTP white paper. Project proposals emerge from a process involving inputs from ministries and a wide range of bodies and stakeholders. These are evaluated via "Concept Evaluations" by the three transport agencies plus Avinor, following guidelines provided by the Ministry of Transport and Communications. The evaluations include assessment of the needs addressed, specification of project requirements, identification of alternative solutions and consultation with stakeholders (county and municipal authorities, businesses and industry organisations). In addition, the evaluations issue guidance for the pre-project phase and include cost-benefit analysis.

Box 2.5. **Norway's "Circular R-109" guidelines for cost-benefit analysis**

Cost-benefit analysis depends critically on underlying assumptions and forecasts of both costs and benefits. For transport investment, past experience usually provides sufficiently accurate estimates of engineering costs and land acquisition, as well as maintenance costs in future years. However, the measurement of benefits is typically more challenging. Some benefits can be ascribed a monetary value, typically time and lives saved, but there is a wide range of methods, and therefore outcomes. Similar issues apply to the choice of discount rate. Thus, having the same benefit-calculation and discount-rate methodologies are applied across CBA calculations is critical.

In Norway, cost-benefit analysis for appraising public investment projects is governed by "Circular R-109", which is a set of recommendations on CBA presented to the Ministry of Finance by a government-commissioned committee in 2012. It provides an impressive account of the theory and evidence on cost and benefit measurement and raises key issues on a wide range of issues, including:

- **Timespan of cost and benefit calculation:** the committee recommended 40 years (instead of 25 years), which is the same period used in EU project appraisal.
- **Work time valuation:** the Committee noted that although in theory, shorter travel times could lead to longer working hours, and higher production and incomes, in practice, working hours are not usually flexible and assessment is complicated by the fact that employees often do some work while travelling.
- **Leisure time valuation:** the Committee noted that, in theory, the real net wage measures the value of leisure at the margin, but in practice, because of inflexible working hours, fixed annual salaries, and other considerations, the value of leisure could be higher or lower than this.
- **GDP growth and valuing time:** the report underscores that GDP growth implies growth in the value of time in work or leisure and that this needs to be reflected in CBA.

Box 2.5. **Norway's "Circular R-109" guidelines for cost-benefit analysis** *(cont.)*

- **Environmental goods valuation:** The Committee concluded that information on willingness to pay for environmental goods was too weak to be of use but that health and mortality impacts of environmental goods could be taken into account.
- **Social discount rate:** the Committee recommended that for projects in direct competition with those in the private sector, the discount rate faced by private enterprises should be used; otherwise a real risk-adjusted rate starting at 4% for impacts in the first 30 years with declining values in later years.
- **Measurement of wider impacts:** the Committee found room to widen the impacts covered in CBA. For instance, it recommended supplementary assessment of interaction between transport project and urban productivity, and the reporting of wider impacts on labour supply, incomes and land values.
- **Road tolls:** the Committee recommended that public-road tolls should not be imposed if there is no evidence of queuing or if the cost of collecting tolls exceeds their revenue.

Source: Norwegian Public Roads Administration.

The two-stage quality assurance process for large projects

Projects with estimated costs in excess of NOK 750 million are subject to additional scrutiny via a two-stage quality assurance process (see Samset and Volden, 2013) (Figure 2.5). The process includes input from independent reviews; reflecting Norway's comparatively wide use of external review in assessing government-led project compared with many other countries. The quality assurance process was initially implemented to combat cost overruns (Odeck et al., 2015):

- QA1 focuses on quality assurance of choice of concept. It is conducted prior to the government cabinet's selection of projects for inclusion in the National Transport Plan;
- QA2 focuses on quality assurance of the management base and cost. It applies to projects that are included in the National Transport Plan but have yet to be submitted to parliament for approval and funding.

The central purpose of QA1 is to check, at a relatively early stage, that the project has undergone a process of "fair and rational" choice. It is conducted by the responsible ministry or government agency and includes investigation of alternative solutions, socio-economic impacts and relevance of the project to transport needs. There is emphasis on environmental and social impacts, land-use implications and regional development. This evaluation, *inter alia*, must include a "do-nothing" option ("zero option") and at least two alternative and conceptually different options. The external reviewers' role includes analysis as well as review of documents. For instance the external reviewer is required to undertake a cost-benefit analysis of impacts that incorporates risks (Figure 2.5).

The purpose of QA2 is to check the quality of the inputs to decisions, including the cost estimates and uncertainties associated with the project, before it is submitted to parliament to decide on funding allocation. It includes assessment of cost estimates derived from basic engineering work and assessment of at least two alternative contracting strategies. Notably, however, QA2 does not include revisiting and updating the cost-benefit analysis performed in QA1, unless the project seems to have been significantly altered from the option chosen at QA1. In addition, QA2 focuses on project management in the implementation phase.

According to Odeck et al. (2015), there is evidence that QA2 has successfully reduced cost overruns but it also appears to have prompted cost overestimation.

Figure 2.5. **Norway's Quality Assurance regime for major public investment projects**

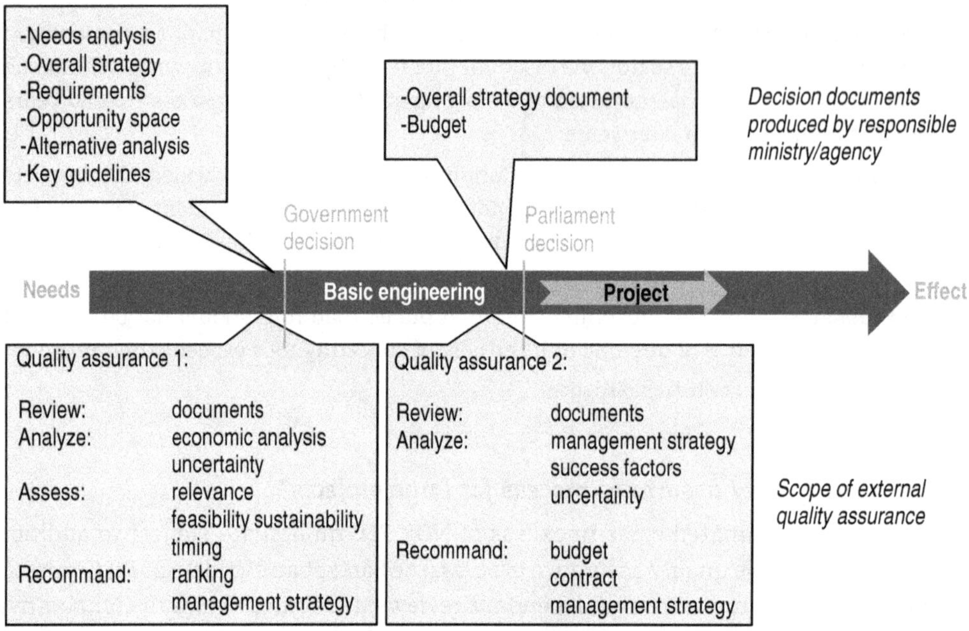

Source: Norwegian University of Science and Technology (*www.ntnu.edu/concept/qa-scheme*).

Challenges in the project appraisal and selection processes

Economic efficiency considerations do not have enough influence

The process described above has admirable features. There is considerable early-stage consultation and discussion between the agencies and lower levels of government, as well as with other interested parties. This facilitates stakeholders' ability to influence projects as modifications are easier and less costly to make. The requirements for CBA in the project appraisal and selection process and other objective analyses are comprehensive.

Despite these sound features, economic efficiency considerations often have only weak influence in actual project selection. Instead, selection is typically dominated by practices that reflect interested parties pushing projects for approval that are of particular benefit to them. This surfaces in:

- Lowballing of early-stage cost estimates (cost estimates that are made prior to official CBA analysis). Some reports claim that presentations of projects in the initial stages of the process often use cost estimates that are widely known to be inaccurate (Andersen et al., 2016).
- Projects selected with poor CBA scores. Often, projects are selected onto National Transport Plans despite their poor CBA ratings. The political negotiations that make the selection of project for the Plans have a reputation for attaching little importance to the CBA analysis. This has been confirmed in research. Sager (2016), for instance, illustrates that costs exceed benefits for most of the major road projects reports initiated in the period 2014-17 (Table 2.3). Analysis by Eliasson et al. (2015) of projects selected for the

National Transport Plan 2014-23 confirm there is little consideration of project efficiency (Figure 2.6). For example, the net benefits of the projects in the portfolio hardly differs from that expected under random selection, despite there being no shortage of projects with good CBA outcomes among the candidates for selection.

- Cost growth in latter stages of the selection process, specifically between the two stages of the quality assurance process (QA1 and QA2). Indeed, project costs sometimes rise substantially above those calculated in the CBAs (Welde and Odeck, 2017). The cost increases typically involve specification upgrades ("gold plating") or project modifications, for instance arising from discussions with local government. Furthermore, late-stage cost inflation is likely to be more prevalent where costs have been lowballed earlier on. Cost increases mean cost-benefit calculations conducted at later stages of the process typically show lower net benefit compared with earlier calculations.

In sum, the outcome of Norway's project selection process, too often, results in elegant but costly solutions to seemingly minor problems from an economy-wide perspective, such as tunnels under fjords in sparsely populated regions. The underlying politics of these choices often reflects, as noted above, Norway's longstanding policy emphasis on sustaining communities and industries in rural and sparsely populated regions.

Table 2.3. **Benefit-cost summary for major road corridor projects initiated in the period 2014-17 (NOK million)**

Corridor	Number of projects	Net benefit	Cost	Net benefit to cost ratio
1. Oslo-Svinesund-Kornsjø	1	-860	1 830	-0.47
2. Oslo-Ørje/Magnor	2	-1 790	4 750	-0.38
3. Oslo-Grenland-Kristiansand-Stavanger	7	12 080	33 890	+0.36
4. Stavanger-Bergen-Ålesund-Trondheim	4	18 020	26 800	+0.67
5. Oslo-Bergen/Haugesund. Branch via Sogn to Florø	4	-2 320	8 950	-0.26
6. Oslo-Trondheim. Branches to Måløy, Ålesund, and Kristiansund	3	5 210	6 500	+0.80
7. Trondheim-Bodø. Branches to the Swedish border	2	-1 740	5 670	-0.31
8. Bodø-Narvik-Tromsø-Kirkenes. Branches to Lofoten and the national border	2	-530	1 890	-0.28

Source: Sager (2016).

Land-use planning often adds complications and delays

Discontinuity between national-level infrastructure planning and local-level land-use planning often leads to implementation delays. In Norway municipal governments have considerable steerage on land-use strategy and planning (country-level government has some legal powers to impose plans on municipalities but in practice these are not much used). Municipal-government land-use plans are legally binding documents that detail permitted buildings, installations and activities. In addition, land-use legislation explicitly promotes preservation of farming activities and family farms. Transport infrastructure (including the national-level projects in the NTPs) must be integrated into the land-use plans before any construction work can begin. This gives municipalities significant influence on which projects can proceed and at what pace. Indeed, local-government control via land-use is often the cause of implementation delays and a source of project modification. To avoid these issues central government has begun to use planning provisions that allow it to develop combined land-use and transport plans for national-infrastructure projects ("state-determined" plans). The state-determined plans in effect mean central government dictate

Figure 2.6. **Investment efficiency of projects selected in Norway's National Transport Plan 2014-23**

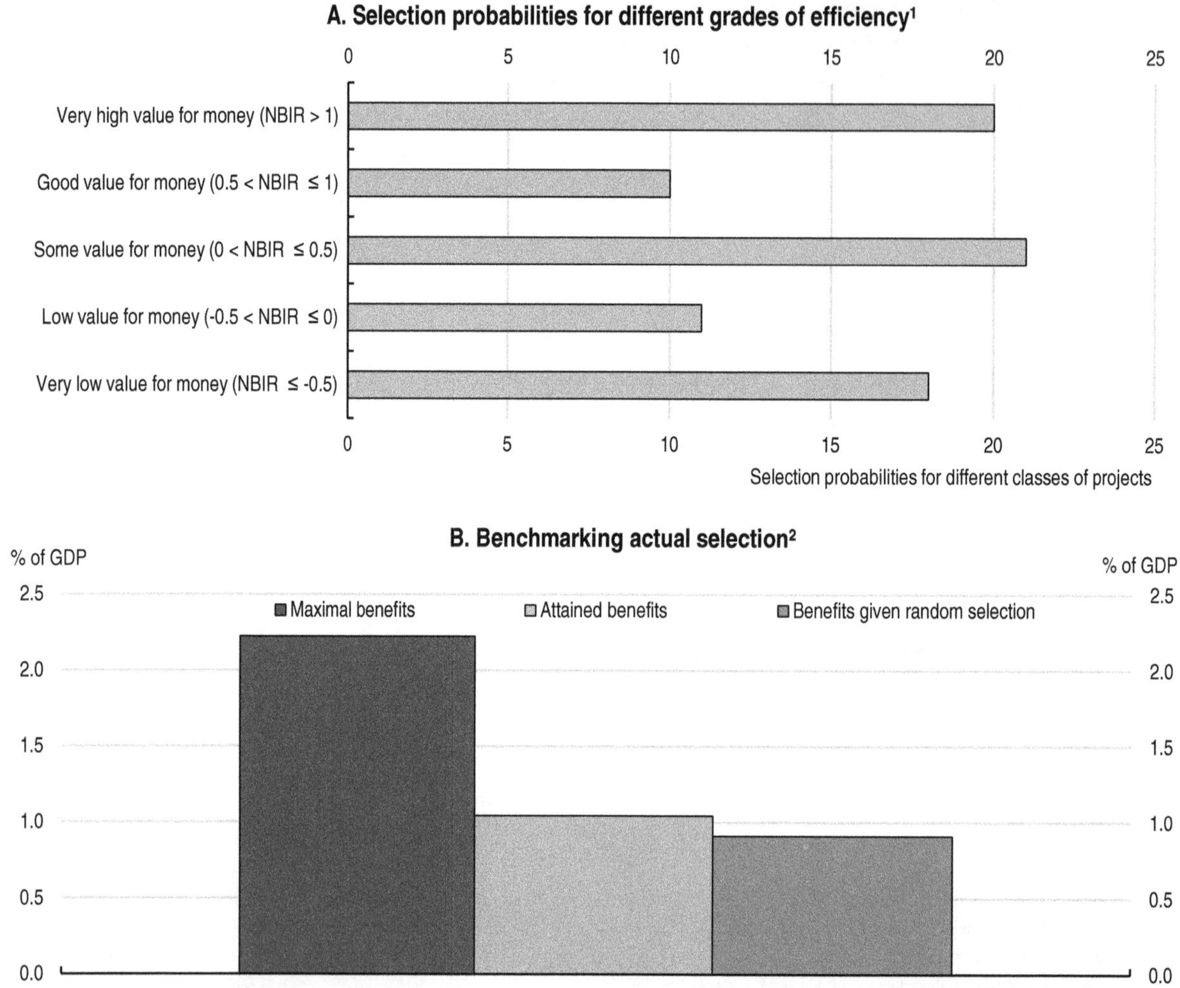

1. Panel A: NBIR, Net-benefit to Investment Cost Ratio. The probabilities show the proportion of projects selected by government in each of the classes of NBIR. For instance, the government chose 20% of the candidate projects that had NBIRs greater than one.
2. Panel B: "Attained benefit" is the total net benefit of the projects selected by the government. "Maximum benefit" is the maximum net benefit possible from the candidate projects for the same spending as in the attained budget. "Benefit under random selection" is the statistically expected benefit under random selection. The data are expressed as a % of nominal annual GDP in 2012, the year in which the selection was made. The results shown here are those for the government selected projects in Eliasson et al. (2015).

Source: Eliasson et al. (2015).

StatLink http://dx.doi.org/10.1787/888933639398

elements of regional or local land-use planning (for instance, so as to create a new transport route). According to the central government, local governments affected by state-determined plans have generally responded positively, and planning time has been reduced.

State-determined plans cannot be imposed in all contexts and conflicts between local plans and national policy will remain an issue. The conflicts not only often take a lot of time to resolve but also absorb administrative and policy-making resources as they involve negotiations between municipalities, counties and central ministries (if the parties fail to agree then the Ministry of Local Government and Modernisation intervenes). According to data provided by the Ministry of Local Government and Modernisation, in 2014 objections were expressed against 20% of local land-use plans, with the majority resolved through negotiations and only a small minority required Ministerial intervention.

Measures already taken include steps for more evidence-based project selection

There is welcome concern in policy-making circles regarding the challenges in transport-infrastructure planning and selection outlined above. Indeed, there have already been positive developments. The latest National Transport Plan's shift to a 12-year plan period (instead of 10 years, see discussion above) is significant in that the plan for a six-year gap could imply that the next transport plan will be drawn up half way through a government's term of office (Norway has a fixed 4-year electoral cycle at national level). This would break with the tradition of transport plans being finalised in the run up to general elections, which many believe has contributed to an undesirable degree of politicisation in transport-infrastructure investment. However, the rolling of the next plan is not yet decided and it is possible that traditional timing will prevail.

In addition, efforts are underway to make project selection more strongly evidence-based. The new Instructions for Official Studies of Central Government Measures and the QA scheme reflect greater emphasis on evidence-based decision-making and value for money, as does the greater prominence given the cost-benefit analysis in the latest transport plan (Box 2.3). Measures include requirements to log changes in the scope and cost of projects, with large changes requiring discussion by government. While these steps almost certainly will have some positive impact on infrastructure decisions, they are unlikely to resolve the problems entirely. Therefore, this strengthening of procedures should be accompanied by other steps that raise awareness and concern for economic efficiency, and the desirability of speedy implementation, by policymakers at all levels of government (Sager, 2016).

Further steps should include stronger top-down influence in the planning process

Norway's transport-infrastructure selection, especially in the road sector, has strong "bottom-up" processes involving the regional offices of the NPRA with input from local governments. This is not unusual. Bottom-up processes feature strongly in infrastructure selection in most OECD economies, meanwhile strong top-down steerage tends to be less common as discussed in the OECD *International Transport Forum*'s analysis of best practice in strategic planning (OECD/ITF, 2017a). There are, however, important merits to strong top-down steerage. It can bring good interdependencies both within and across sectors (e.g. transport and energy) and better incorporate emerging technologies into infrastructure planning needs (e.g. autonomous vehicles). Stronger top-down steerage in Norway may be particularly beneficial as it could act as a counterweight to the substantial bottom-up influence arising from groups in favour of supporting communities in rural and remote areas.

A range of technical changes to processes should also be considered to strengthen the role of economic analysis in project selection. "Soft" measures, for instance could include requiring a written explanation by government for the projects selected in the National Transport Plan. Hard measures could, for instance, comprise a new end-stage filter that requires a minimum net-benefit to cost ratio for projects to proceed further. In Denmark initial investment cost estimates are increased to allow for cost inflation in the planning phase ("buffers"). This may be a route for policy in Norway but this depends on whether this type of mechanism can transposed to the Norwegian planning process. At the same time, improvements to CBA should continue so as to strengthen its credibility. In addition, some claim (for instance Odeck et al., 2015) that obligations in financing infrastructure are not sufficient to incentivise socially beneficial or cost-effective choices. Especially in road infrastructure, stakeholder participation in financing, notably as regards local and regional government is already fairly comprehensive. Nevertheless there may be room for alterations to central government financing of projects that ensure local and regional governments (and, by consequence their electorates) are more strongly guided by the prospect of participation in financing.

Project implementation, delivery and *ex post* assessment

In Norway, the decision on delivery mode is separated from project selection under the NTP process. To date, most transport infrastructure delivery has used "traditional" public procurement processes whereby the agencies tender out approved projects to construction companies. Reforms in the 1990s more strongly separated procurement and state-run construction. In 2003 a state-owned construction company was established that has to compete on an equal basis with private companies. Today this company primarily focuses on operation and maintenance contracts, and not on construction projects. In general, Norway's procurement process is now regarded as efficient, with comparatively small cost and time overruns – though this may also reflect that costs are often pushed up at earlier stages in the investment process.

Greater use of public-private partnerships is planned

There are plans to make greater use of public-private partnerships in the transport sector as an alternative to traditional procurement. Notably the latest NTP proposes using PPPs for three of the planned new motorway sections. In 2015 the government established a new framework for public-private partnership (PPP). The framework is developed primarily for the road sector but is of a general nature and therefore applicable to other sectors. Projects considered for PPPs tend to be large, and therefore attract debate. As is often the case in other countries, involving the private sector in what has traditionally been a government activity does not always command universal political support.

A key strength of Norway's approach is that PPPs receive neutral treatment from a public-sector budgeting perspective. The PPPs have the "build-operate-transfer" structure that is widely used elsewhere. However, budgetary allocations and appropriations for PPPs follow the same basis as projects executed through traditional procurement methods; they are not based on the disbursement of payments to the sponsor company. This results in the fiscal cost of PPPs being front-loaded in the budgeting system, differing little from other procurement methods from this perspective. This approach ensures that projects are selected on their merits (whether economic or political), rather than on their financing and delivery modality. Nevertheless, the criteria applied for selecting PPPs as a delivery modality could benefit from being more formalised and better communicated.

Ex post *evaluations could play a more public role*

Requirements for *ex post* evaluations are set by the Ministry of Transport and Communication, and are conducted by the relevant agency. For instance, the road-transport agency, NPRA, conducts three to five evaluations each year, and the criteria for evaluation include that the project has been operational for at least 5 years and has a cost in excess of NOK 200 million (Nicolaisen and Driscoll, 2016). The assessments focus on testing the accuracy of the *ex ante* CBAs and, as such, cover what the CBA analysis is able to capture.

Ex post evaluation by the government agencies could play a more significant role in providing insights into the performance and outcomes of transport infrastructure planning and decision making, and in informing the public. The evaluations could be broadened, notably with *ex post* assessment of wider social and environmental impacts, impacts from land-use change, or impacts on regional development. Broadening the evaluation framework would strengthen scope, accuracy and credibility. There are already blueprints on how to do this, for instance the Concept Research Programme at the Norwegian University of Science and Technology (Mennier and Welde, 2017 for a discussion).

Additional *ex post* evaluation that is more arms-length from policy should be considered. In self-evaluation there is a risk that some dimensions of project performance are not probed deeply. This could be addressed by complementing the existing internal and university-based evaluation with evaluation by an independent authority (perhaps along the lines of the European Court of Auditors). This could help strengthen the scope and visibility of *ex post* evaluation, expanding it beyond project-by-project CBAs to address broader questions regarding outcomes, performance, value-for-money, processes and portfolios of projects.

Public awareness of economic efficiency could be strengthened

Elected politicians are most likely to respond to demands from their constituents. Public awareness of, and demand for, efficient public investment is therefore an important influence on project selection. Norway's communication with the public on transport infrastructure is admirably transparent and encourages public participation. However, there may be ways of strengthening public awareness of value-for-money issues that would feed positively through to decision making at the political level. Engaging civil society and the media are key channels for strengthening generating public awareness. An initiative by the Government Agency for Financial Management to provide courses on cost-benefit analysis for journalists exemplifies the type of measure that can be taken.

Summing up the strengths and weaknesses

Table 2.4. **Strengths and weaknesses in transport-infrastructure investment**

Strengths	Weaknesses
Planning and co-ordination	
Infrastructure planning and project development has effective consultation and coordination with sub-national governments and other stakeholders at an early stage.	The multi-level planning process can be slow and ponderous, and provide opportunities for introducing changes that negatively affect projects' scope and cost.
The development of the National Transport Plan involves effective cooperation across transport agencies.	Discontinuity between infrastructure planning (mostly national level) and municipal-level land-use planning often delays implementation.
Project appraisal	
Norway has well-structured project appraisal and quality assurance processes, grounded in economic analysis.	Despite the rigorous CBA methodology and other quality assurance mechanisms, projects with weak scores in economic efficiency are frequently presented to politicians.
There is a clear and well-documented process and set of requirements for project preparation.	Costs are often lowballed in initial stages and later significantly escalated, particularly between the two stages of the quality assurance process that applies to large projects.
Cost-benefit analyses are rigorous and based on comprehensive guidelines.	While ex post evaluations are regularly conducted for infrastructure projects their visibility and impact could be greater.
Project selection and prioritisation	
Political decision making on project selection is explicit and transparent.	Multiple motives lie behind the final-stage political decision making and economic efficiency often does not have significant influence.
Project delivery	
Public procurement process is generally regarded as efficient; cost and time overruns on finalised projects are generally small. The establishment of new road and rail management companies will further strengthen the system.	The small cost and time overruns at the delivery stage partly reflect gold plating and other forms of cost inflation at earlier stages.
PPPs focus on long-term efficiency and not on making short-run fiscal savings.	The framework for the administration and oversight of PPPs is insufficiently formalised.

Policy recommendations

Recommendations on how to improve transport-infrastructure investment in Norway

Roles and responsibilities: strengthen top-down influence in the planning process

- In metropolitan areas strengthen co-ordination across municipalities and counties.

Project appraisal and selection: strengthen the influence of economic-efficiency considerations in project selection

- Consider hard rules that raise economic efficiency of selected projects, for instance via:
  - A new end-stage filter that requires a minimum net-benefit to cost ratio for projects to proceed further.
- Strengthen the role of economic analysis through "soft" measures:
  - Require a written explanation by government for the selection of projects in the National Transport Plan, especially those with weak CBA results
  - More strongly flag CBA results at the stage of political negotiation
  - Monitor the impact of the recent introduction of the cost-target system that aims to limit cost inflation in the planning phase
  - Repeat more often cost-benefit analysis at the second stage of the Quality Assurance process
  - Continue refining CBA techniques and coverage with a view to strengthening accuracy, credibility and scope, especially as regards economic benefits that are difficult to monetise.
- Re-examine infrastructure financing arrangements with a view to ensuring stakeholders with influence, such as local authorities and communities, also face an appropriate funding responsibility.
- Devote more resources to drawing from transport-planning experiences in other countries.

Implementation, delivery and *ex post* assessment: reduce delays, broaden *ex post* assessment

- Make greater use of "state-determined" planning in which central-government formulates integrated land use and transport plans for major national projects.
- Widen the scope of the *ex post* evaluations conducted by the government transport agencies.
- Strengthen independent *ex post* evaluations that complement the self-evaluations conducted by the transport agencies, for instance by establishing an independent evaluation body, or by tasking an existing body.

Bibliography

Andersen, B., K. Samset and M. Welde (2016), "Low estimates – high stakes: Underestimation of costs at the front-end of projects", *International Journal of Managing Projects in Business*, 9(1), 2016.

DFØ (2016), *Guidance notes on the Instructions for Official Studies – Instructions for Official Studies of Central Government Measures*, Norwegian Government Agency for Financial Management (DFØ), Oslo, March 2016.

Eliasson, P., M. Bőjesson, J. Odeck and M. Welde (2015), "Does Benefit-Cost Efficiency Influence Transport Investment Decisions?", *Journal of Transport Economics and Policy*, Vol. 49, Part 3, July 2015.

Meunier D. and M. Welde (2017) "Ex-post evaluations in Norway and France", *Transport Research Procedia*, Volume 26, 2017.

Nicolaisen, M.S. and P.A. Driscoll (2016), "An International Review of Ex-Post Project Evaluation Schemes in the Transport Sector", *Journal of Environmental Assessment Policy and Management*, Vol. 18, No. 1, March 2016.

NTP (2017), *National Transport Plan 2018-2029, Meld. St. 33 (2016-2017)*, Report to the Storting (White Paper).

NPRA (2013), *Key Figures*. Norwegian Public Roads Administration.

NPRA (2016), *About the Norwegian Public Roads Administration*, Norwegian Public Roads Administration.

Odeck J., M. Welde and G.H. Volden (2015), "The Impact of External Quality Assurance of Costs Estimates on Cost Overruns: Empirical Evidence from the Norwegian Road Sector", *European Journal of Transport and Infrastructure Research*, 15(3), 2015.

OECD (2013), *Value for Money in Government: Norway*, OECD Publishing, Paris.

OECD (2016), OECD *Economic Surveys: Norway, 2016*, OECD Publishing, Paris

OECD (2017), *Getting Infrastructure Right: A framework for better governance*, OECD Publishing, Paris.

OECD/ITF (2017a), *Strategic Infrastructure Planning: International Best Practice*, OECD Publishing, Paris.

OECD/ITF (2017b), *Quantifying the Socio-economic Benefits of Transport*, OECD Publishing, Paris.

Sager, T.O. (2016), "Why don't cost benefits results count for more? The case of Norwegian road investment priorities", *Urban, Planning and Transport Research*, Vol. 4, No. 1, Taylor & Francis Group.

Samset, K. and G.H. Volden, (2013), *Investing for impact. Lessons with the Norwegian state project model and the first investment projects that have been subjected to external quality assurance*, Concept Report No. 36, Norwegian University of Science and Technology.

Welde M. and J. Odeck (2017): "Cost escalations, in the front-end of projects – empirical evidence from Norwegian road projects", *Transport Reviews*, Volume 37, 2017.

ORGANISATION FOR ECONOMIC CO-OPERATION AND DEVELOPMENT

The OECD is a unique forum where governments work together to address the economic, social and environmental challenges of globalisation. The OECD is also at the forefront of efforts to understand and to help governments respond to new developments and concerns, such as corporate governance, the information economy and the challenges of an ageing population. The Organisation provides a setting where governments can compare policy experiences, seek answers to common problems, identify good practice and work to co-ordinate domestic and international policies.

The OECD member countries are: Australia, Austria, Belgium, Canada, Chile, the Czech Republic, Denmark, Estonia, Finland, France, Germany, Greece, Hungary, Iceland, Ireland, Israel, Italy, Japan, Korea, Latvia, Luxembourg, Mexico, the Netherlands, New Zealand, Norway, Poland, Portugal, the Slovak Republic, Slovenia, Spain, Sweden, Switzerland, Turkey, the United Kingdom and the United States. The European Union takes part in the work of the OECD.

OECD Publishing disseminates widely the results of the Organisation's statistics gathering and research on economic, social and environmental issues, as well as the conventions, guidelines and standards agreed by its members.

OECD PUBLISHING, 2, rue André-Pascal, 75775 PARIS CEDEX 16
(10 2018 01 1 P) ISBN 978-92-64-28640-5 – 2018

www.ingramcontent.com/pod-product-compliance
Lightning Source LLC
Chambersburg PA
CBHW061221240926
51846CB00006B/1308